History of The Council of Bishops of The United Methodist Church 1939–1979

Roy H. Short

ABINGDON
Nashville

HISTORY OF THE COUNCIL OF BISHOPS
OF THE UNITED METHODIST CHURCH 1939–1979

Copyright © 1980 by Abingdon

All rights reserved.
No part of this book may be reproduced in any manner whatsoever without written permission of the publisher except brief quotations embodied in critical articles or reviews. For information address Abingdon. Nashville, Tennessee.

Library of Congress Cataloging in Publication Data

SHORT, ROY HUNTER, Bp., 1902-
  History of the Council of Bishops of the United Methodist Church, 1939-1979.
  Includes index.
  1. United Methodist Church (United States). Council of Bishops
—History. I. Title.
BX8382.2.S46   287'.73   80-16423
          ISBN 0-687-17190-3

MANUFACTURED BY THE PARTHENON PRESS AT
NASHVILLE, TENNESSEE, UNITED STATES OF AMERICA

To Louise

who has been a good companion
in the episcopal experiences
of thirty years, and who
helped write this book

Contents

Introduction 11

I. Again One People, 1939–1944 13

II. Crusading for a Better World, 1944–1948 50

III. In Defense of the Church and Its
     Leadership, 1948–1952 70

IV. Toward Full Rights for All People,
    1952–1956 88

V. Toward a Church Without Barriers,
   1956–1960 107

VI. A Church in a Changing Day, 1960–1964 130

VII. New Structures for Mission, 1964–1968 161

VIII. Launching a New Church in a Time of
      Turbulence, 1968–1972 185

IX. A Restructured Council in a Restructured
    Church, 1972–1976 220

X. New Problems, Responsibilities, and
    Opportunities, 1976–1979 249

XI. Council Sidelights 265

XII. After Forty Years 278

Appendixes 283
  A. Regular and Called Meetings of the Council..283
  B. Officers of the Council of Bishops 289
  C. A Listing of Some Major Actions
     of the Council of Bishops 291

Index of Names 297
General Index 309

History of the Council of Bishops
of
The United Methodist Church
1939–1979

Introduction

This book is written at the request of the Council of Bishops of The United Methodist Church. It is a part of the celebration of the fortieth anniversary of the council.

The council was established in 1939 at the reunification of three branches of American Methodism—the Methodist Episcopal Church; the Methodist Episcopal Church, South; and the Methodist Protestant Church—forming The Methodist Church. The council has been continued as an integral part of the structure of The United Methodist Church, which came into being in 1968 as the result of the union of The Methodist Church with the Evangelical United Brethren Church.

This book is not merely about individual bishops in our tradition, it focuses particularly on the *Council* of Bishops. A Council of Bishops has been and is provided for constitutionally by the *Discipline* of our denomination (Para. 52). It is charged with "the general oversight and promotion of temporal and spiritual interests" of the church. Many important responsibilities of bishops are fulfilled only in and as a council. There is an implicit understanding of our *collegiality* as general superintendents. The same constitution that provides for episcopacy and a Council of Bishops in our connection carefully safeguards it by a restrictive rule (Para. 17).

HISTORY OF THE COUNCIL OF BISHOPS

The plan of this book is simple. It does not pretend to be exhaustive, but it does attempt to outline the activities of the council during these forty years, and to set forth the major concerns and issues to which it has devoted its attention from time to time.

It proceeds chronologically. A brief account is given successively of selected meetings. For a time these were held annually, but for most of its history the council has met semiannually. Special meetings have also been called along the way. Since the council invariably met several times at the times and places of the General Conferences, brief mention of these General Conferences is made, but the council's role in them is not dealt with in depth. Likewise, passing reference is made to the sessions of the Jurisdictional and Central Conferences, at which bishops retired and their successors were elected and consecrated. Otherwise these conferences are not themselves discussed.

In addition, the book seeks to present brief, pen portraits of those council members who have already finished their course. The book concludes with a brief summary and evaluation of the council up to April 1979.

What is written here is based upon the Minutes of the body and personal recollections growing out of membership in the council for three-fourths of the period covered.

—Roy H. Short
1979

I

Again One People
1939–1944

At approximately nine o'clock on Wednesday evening, May 10, 1939, in Kansas City, Missouri, the Methodist Episcopal Church; the Methodist Episcopal Church, South; and the Methodist Protestant Church witnessed the healing of a century of division with the unanimous adoption of the Declaration of Union by the Uniting Conference. Thus "The Methodist Church" came into being. The vote was a standing one. The bishop presiding asked the bishops to vote also, which they did, although technically they had no vote.

The Methodist Episcopal Church came into the union with twenty-one effective bishops, twelve retired bishops, two missionary bishops, and seven Central Conference bishops. All the Methodist Episcopal bishops were present except Bishop Juan E. Gattinoni of Latin America, and Bishops Thomas Nicholson, Charles B. Mitchell, Eben S. Johnson, and Charles E. Locke, retired, who were unable to attend because of age or illness.

The Methodist Episcopal Church, South came into the union with twelve active bishops and eight retired bishops. The active bishops were all present. Of the retired bishops, Bishop Collins Denny was not present since he did not wish to be regarded as a bishop of the new church. Three other retired bishops of the Church, South, Bishops

Warren A. Candler, Horace M. DuBose, and William N. Ainsworth, were unable to attend for health reasons. Of the twelve active bishops, seven had been elected at the last Southern General Conference only a year before. These were Bishops Ivan Lee Holt, William W. Peele, Clare Purcell, Charles C. Selecman, John L. Decell, William C. Martin, and William T. Watkins.

The Methodist Protestant Church had no bishops, but under the authorization of the Plan of Union, the Methodist Protestant delegates met separately at Kansas City and elected John C. Broomfield and James H. Straughn to the episcopacy.

The Plan of Union provided that the Uniting Conference should assign the bishops to the various jurisdictions and to the episcopal areas. The responsibility for making assignment recommendations was lodged with a special committee. At first there was some thought of assigning the bishops to parts of the country other than where they had been elected, but after considerable tension and some maneuvering this suggestion was discarded.

The first assignment of the bishops was as follows:
Northeastern Jurisdiction
    Boston area: Bishop G. Bromley Oxnam
    New York area: Bishop Francis J. McConnell
    Philadelphia area: Bishop Ernest G. Richardson
    Pittsburgh area: Bishop Adna W. Leonard
    Syracuse area: Bishop Charles W. Flint
    Washington area: Bishop Edwin H. Hughes
Southeastern Jurisdiction
    Atlanta area: Bishop William T. Watkins
    Birmingham area: Bishop John L. Decell
    Charlotte area: Bishop Clare Purcell
    Jackson area: Bishop Hoyt M. Dobbs
    Louisville area: Bishop Urban V. W. Darlington
    Nashville area: Bishop Paul B. Kern
    Richmond area: Bishop William W. Peele
North Central Jurisdiction
    Chicago area: Bishop Ernest L. Waldorf

AGAIN ONE PEOPLE

    Cincinnati area: Bishop H. Lester Smith
    Des Moines area: Bishop J. Ralph Magee
    Detroit area: Bishop Edgar Blake
    Indianapolis area: Bishop Titus Lowe
    St. Paul area: Bishop Ralph S. Cushman
South Central Jurisdiction
    Dallas area: Bishop Ivan Lee Holt
    Houston area: Bishop A. Frank Smith
    Kansas City area: Bishop Charles L. Mead
    Oklahoma City area: Bishop Charles C. Selecman
    Omaha area: Bishop William C. Martin
    St. Louis area: Bishop John C. Broomfield
Central Jurisdiction
    Columbus area: Bishop Robert E. Jones
    New Orleans area: Bishop Alexander P. Shaw
Western Jurisdiction
    Denver area: Bishop Wilbur E. Hammaker
    Los Angeles area: Bishop James C. Baker
    Portland area: Bishop Wallace E. Brown
Special Service
    Outside the U.S.: Bishop Arthur J. Moore
    Within the U.S.: Bishop James H. Straughn
Overseas
    Geneva area: Bishop John L. Nuelson
    Stockholm area: Bishop Raymond J. Wade
    Delhi area: Bishop Brenton T. Badley
Missionary Bishops
    Singapore area: Bishop Edwin F. Lee
    Elizabethville area: Bishop John M. Springer

No mention was made in the committee's report of the Central Conference bishops, since their assignment had already been determined by the nature of the Central Conference legislation.

Of the bishops assigned at Kansas City, Bishop Brown died within a year, and Bishops Hughes, Blake, Nuelson, and Mead retired at the first Jurisdictional Conferences in 1940.

Throughout the Uniting Conference, the respective

episcopal colleges of the former churches continued to operate. From time to time Bishop H. Lester Smith, secretary of the Board of Bishops of the Methodist Episcopal Church, and Bishop Paul Kern, secretary of the College of Bishops of the Methodist Episcopal Church, South, would report to the Uniting Conference on matters referred to the colleges or originating with them.

At the Uniting Conference all the bishops of the church were seated on the platform, not in deference to their office but as a symbol of the unity of the church.

The bishops presided in the various sessions and conducted the devotional services. Bishop John M. Moore gave the Episcopal Address and Bishop Edwin H. Hughes the closing address. On the closing night Bishop John M. Moore of the Church, South, Bishop James H. Straughn of the Methodist Protestant Church, and Bishop Edwin H. Hughes of the Methodist Episcopal Church joined hands in a dramatic symbolizing of the new union.

The bishops participated in this historic conference as follows:

Bishop Herbert Welch led in the opening communion service, with Bishops Brown, Hammaker, Hay, Peele, and Selecman assisting. Doctors E. A. Sexsmith and S. W. Rosenberger of the Methodist Protestant Church also participated.

The devotional services were led by Bishops Holt, Peele, H. Lester Smith, Purcell, Mead, Decell, Jones, Brown, Baker, Jashwant R. Chitambar, and Hammaker. The messages were brought by Bishops Waldorf, Oxnam, William C. Martin, Flint, A. Frank Smith, McConnell, Broomfield, Selecman, Blake, Watkins, and Magee.

Bishops presiding were Bishops Hughes, John M. Moore, Straughn, Mead, Kern, Darlington, Richardson, Arthur J. Moore, Waldorf, A. Frank Smith, H. Lester Smith, Holt, McConnell, Broomfield, Blake, Selecman, and Lowe.

There was particular awareness at the Uniting Conference of certain persons who had done much to pave the way for union, but who had gone on to the better world before union finally came. These included Bishop Earl Cranston and Bishop William F. McDowell of the Methodist Episcopal Church; Dr. William Norman Ward and Dr. Thomas Hamilton Lewis of the Methodist Protestant Church; and Bishop Eugene R. Hendrix and Bishop Edwin D. Mouzon of the Church, South. They were commonly referred to as "the six heroes of union." The desk of Bishop Hendrix was transported to the auditorium and was used by the secretary throughout the conference.

The bishops at the time of the Uniting Conference are now (1979) deceased except for Bishop William C. Martin and Bishop J. Waskom Pickett.

Present bishops who sat in the Uniting Conference as delegates are Bishops Nolan B. Harmon, Fred G. Holloway, Richard C. Raines, and Roy H. Short. Bishops Hobart B. Amstutz and Charles W. Brashares were alternates.

On several occasions the bishops as a group were requested to sing what was familiarly called "the bishops' hymn," which was a melody making use of the verse, "Beloved, we are the sons of God." Bishop Leonard or Bishop Lowe would lead the group, with Bishop Mead at the piano. The bishops' hymn was a tradition in the Methodist Episcopal Church. Bishop Lowe, at his Annual Conferences, would acknowledge the death of a preacher by having the preachers gather around the casket and sing this hymn at the close of the service. This is still a tradition in Indiana.

The bishops coming out of the Church, South and those coming out of the Methodist Episcopal Church were somewhat different concerning the conventions they observed. The bishops of the Methodist Episcopal Church had long been in the habit of calling each other by their first names, while the Southern bishops were more formal, generally using the term "Bishop." Not all the members of the new council ever got around to applying first names to at least some of the bishops, but eventually using first names became common practice.

The new Council of Bishops was composed of the Board

HISTORY OF THE COUNCIL OF BISHOPS

of Bishops of the Methodist Episcopal Church; the College of Bishops of the Methodist Episcopal Church, South; and the two bishops elected by the Methodist Protestant delegates at Kansas City. The council met periodically on call during the Uniting Conference.

The Board of Bishops had followed for some years the procedure of having the various bishops following the order of their election preside over each session. This was symbolic of the fact that the episcopacy was still regarded as a general superintendency, with no one bishop having some status that others did not have. There was a secretary with some continuity in office. The College of Bishops of the Church, South had followed the old procedure of having the senior bishop preside, with a secretary who continued for a period. The Methodist Protestants had no bishops but had a president elected by the General Conference.

Organization of the Council of Bishops

The minutes of the first meeting state that Bishops John M. Moore and Edwin H. Hughes were "in charge." They had been the chairmen of the Commissions on Union in the two larger churches. They alternated in the chair, and Bishop H. Lester Smith served as secretary.

On May 1, 1939, a committee was named to suggest a plan of organization for the council. Bishop Ernest G. Richardson served as chairman of the committee. The committee proposed later that the council organize with a president, vice-president, and secretary. These with two additional bishops would compose an executive committee. The committee further recommended that the council meet annually during the first half of December. On motion of Bishop Edwin H. Hughes the recommendations of the committee were approved, and a time was set for organization.

Later the recommendation was reconsidered, and it was voted that the two senior active bishops, Bishops Edwin H.

Hughes and Urban V. W. Darlington act as cochairmen for the first year of the new church. This was at the suggestion of Bishop Adna Leonard. The basis of this action may have been an oversight associated with the consecration of the two Methodist Protestant bishops. Bishop Darlington, the senior bishop of his branch of Methodism, was given no part in this service, and his friends felt that he was due rightful recognition as the senior active bishop of the Southern Church.

The council elected Bishop H. Lester Smith as secretary and Bishops Francis J. McConnell and Paul B. Kern as the additional members of the executive committee. Later at the meeting of the council in December of 1939, it was voted that the officers continue in office to the December, 1940, meeting; thus they held office for one year and a half.

Bishop Darlington moved that following a suggestion made by Bishop Kern, a churchwide Forward Movement be launched involving meetings in every episcopal area. The motion was approved, and a Forward Movement Committee was named, composed of Bishops Kern, Selecman, Arthur Moore, Leonard, Lowe, Oxnam, and Broomfield. Dr. J. Manning Potts of the Virginia Conference was named director of the Forward Movement.

Great rallies were held everywhere across the new church. All the bishops were involved, and the assignments were across jurisdictional lines. Thus the entire church was introduced to the total episcopal body, and the bishops, in turn, to parts of the new church that hitherto they had not served.

An interesting incident occurred at one of these rallies. Bishop Ralph Magee was sent from Des Moines to speak at the rally in Atlanta. He was a matter-of-fact type of man. As he began speaking, he said, "I am glad to be here. I have never been in Atlanta before, but my father was here. He was here with Sherman." To his utter surprise, the audience broke into laughter and into loud applause.

The council approved an official order for listing the

jurisdictions: Northeastern, Southeastern, Central, North Central, South Central, and Western.

Bishop Matthew W. Clair, retired, was authorized to hold certain Central Jurisdiction conferences; and retired Bishop J. W. Robinson was authorized to do the same thing in India. This was at the request of the colleges involved.

At the request of Bishop Leonard, Bishop Peele was associated with him in holding the West Virginia Conference. Bishop Peele had the Southern work in West Virginia previously.

Bishop Arthur Moore was designated to hold nine overseas conferences in Belgium, Poland, Czechoslovakia, the Congo, and three in China; and to attend the Japan Mission Council and the Korea Central Council.

Council meeting: Chicago, December 6-9, 1939

The Council of Bishops met in its first session after the Uniting Conference at the Stevens Hotel in Chicago, December 6-9, 1939. The cochairmen, Bishop Edwin Hughes and Bishop Darlington, alternated in presiding.

The council was particularly happy to have Bishop Thomas Nicholson present since he had been quite ill. It proved to be the last time he would meet with his colleagues. On the last afternoon he said farewell to them, and the council broke into singing, "Blest Be the Tie That Binds." Subsequent minutes report various communications from him, but he never met with his episcopal brethren again.

While the council was in session, word was received that Bishop Eban S. Johnson, who had served faithfully for some years in Africa, had just passed away.

It was at this meeting that the council adopted the first set of rules of procedure which it was to follow for the next sixteen years. They had been proposed by a committee chaired by Bishop Richardson. They were brief, covering only two pages. They provided for (1) the officers; (2) an annual meeting; (3) an executive committee; (4) an order of business which included opening with a communion service, the privilege for each bishop to give a five-minute report, and the transaction of necessary business; (5) Rules of Order, which included limiting speeches to five minutes; and (6) provision for an annual rotation of the presidency. A specific provision was made that "the Jurisdictional Colleges may not make public pronouncements for The Methodist Church nor for the Council of Bishops."

There were two standing committees, one on Law and Administration and one on Reference. Each bishop was appointed to one of these committees annually. All business of the council was considered by the council sitting as a whole. Motions to limit debate or to call for the previous question were considered not in good taste. Election of bishops to agencies or committees were by ballot, without nomination.

On motion of Bishop Waldorf, a committee was named to prepare a statement on the world situation. It appears that this is the first of the messages that the council has issued across the years. Bishops Oxnam, Arthur Moore, Broomfield, McConnell, Kern, and Lowe were named as the committee.

In addition to his other duties, Bishop Straughn was assigned to take over the Portland area, replacing Bishop Brown, deceased.

First General Conference, The Methodist Church Atlantic City, April 24–May 1, 1940, and Council meeting, April 18, to Conference

The first General Conference of The Methodist Church assembled in Atlantic City, April 24 to May 6, 1940, against the backdrop of World War II. As the delegates walked along the boardwalk to the auditorium, they were conscious of the terrible conflict raging on the opposite shores of the Atlantic, which was soon destined to engulf the United States.

The opening communion service of the 1940 General Conference was led by Bishop Leonard.

HISTORY OF THE COUNCIL OF BISHOPS

The devotional services were in the charge of Bishops Springer, Watkins, Hammaker, Chitambar, Jones, Ralph A. Ward, Lee, Cushman, and Purcell. The messages were brought by Bishops Dobbs, Baker, Shaw, Decell, Pickett, Peele, Lee, Cushman, and Purcell.

The presiding officers of the General Conference were Bishops Nuelsen, Darlington, Baker, Hughes, Straughn, McConnell, Mead, Arthur Moore, Leonard, Kern, Waldorf, Richardson, A. Frank Smith, Jones, Blake, Holt, and H. Lester Smith.

The Council of Bishops met periodically during the General Conference of 1940. Bishops Hughes and Darlington alternated in presiding.

The council named a small agenda committee to bring forward items for consideration. The agenda committee disappeared after 1940, this responsibility being left in the hands of the secretary.

The election of the first bishops of the new church lay immediately ahead, and the council took action recommending to the General Conference that at least a sixty-percent majority be necessary for election.

The council further recommended that the credentials of the newly elected bishops be signed by the bishops of the jurisdiction, in addition to a bishop assigned from another region to represent the council. In time it became customary for all the bishops to be asked to sign, though this was never officially ordered.

It was voted that the term "message" should be used with reference to the address of the bishops of a jurisdiction to the Jurisdictional Conference.

Apparently the plan for the officers to continue for a year and a half was abandoned, and on May 6, 1940, the officers for the new year were elected. Bishop A. Frank Smith was elected president and Bishop Richardson vice-president.

Bishop H. Lester Smith, who had served as secretary in the new church and on the Board of Bishops of the Methodist Episcopal Church for twelve years, asked to be

AGAIN ONE PEOPLE

relieved; Bishop Oxnam was elected secretary. Bishops Peele and Leonard were elected to the executive committee.

Bishop Oxnam was to serve as secretary of the council for the next sixteen years. He wrote shorthand which added to his efficiency as secretary. He not only made up the agenda for each meeting, but he largely determined it himself. The other bishops, including the president, saw it when it was laid on the tables at the opening session. While the president occupied the chair, it was Bishop Oxnam who steered the meetings. He had an incisive mind that could grasp a problem quickly and set it in proper perspective. To some extent he was not merely a secretary but also an executive secretary. The bishops respected him and fell into the habit of letting him carry the council's business.

Official files of the records of either the Board of Bishops of the Methodist Episcopal Church or the College of Bishops of the Church, South are not available prior to Bishop Oxnam's day. There was no official depository for these, and if any such records remain, they are probably among the personal papers of whatever bishop happened to be secretary at a particular time. Bishop Oxnam saw that this situation was corrected.

It was voted that the Council of Bishops procure stationery printed with the names of all its members, but this instruction was never followed.

Between the Uniting Conference in 1939 and the first General Conference in 1940, three of the bishops died. One of these was Bishop Wallace Brown, who had been assigned to the Portland area. He had been elected in 1924 and had served the Foochow, Helena, and Chattanooga areas.

Bishop Eben S. Johnson also passed away. He had been a pastor and district superintendent in Iowa prior to his election in 1916. He had also been secretary of the General Conference. He served his entire episcopacy in Africa.

The third bishop to die was Bishop Charles Locke, elected in 1920. He was a preacher of rare skill and served as bishop first in the Philippines and then in Minnesota.

The passing of Bishops Lauress J. Birney, William F.

HISTORY OF THE COUNCIL OF BISHOPS

Oldham, Wilbur F. Thirkield, Charles W. Burns, and William F. McDowell of the Methodist Episcopal Church, who died between the last General Conference of that church and the Uniting Conference in 1939, was noted at the 1940 General Conference. They were, of course, never members of the new Council of Bishops of "The Methodist Church."

Bishops Blake, Hughes, Mead, Nuelson, and John Gowdy appeared at this General Conference for the last time as active bishops. Each of them had seen only one year of service in an area of the new church. Upon the retirement of Bishop Blake, Bishop Wade came from the Stockholm area to the Detroit area. Upon the retirement of Bishop Edwin H. Hughes, efforts were made in the General Conference to change the law to make it possible for a bishop from another jurisdiction to be assigned to Washington, preferably Bishop Arthur J. Moore. This effort failed, however, and at the following Northeastern Jurisdictional Conference Bishop Leonard was moved from the Pittsburgh area to Washington; and Bishop Straughn, who had been in special service, was assigned to the Pittsburgh area.

With the retirement of Bishop Mead, the Kansas City area was merged with the Omaha area over which Bishop William C. Martin presided. With the retirement of Bishop Nuelson, Bishop Moore assumed responsibility for the Geneva area in connection with his responsibilities in the Atlanta area.

The retired bishops had not been assigned to jurisdictions by the Uniting Conference, and the 1940 General Conference took care of this oversight.

The 1940 General Conference fixed the salary of an active bishop at $6,000, with an office allowance of $1,500 and a rental allowance of $500 to $1,800, depending upon place of residence. The pension of a retired bishop was fixed at $2,700 and that of a bishop's widow at $1,500. Travel expenses of the bishop were by voucher. Most of their travel was by train, and all of them held some passes on railroads, particularly in their own territory. Expense for travel by air was not allowed even as late as 1948–1952, unless authorized by specific action of the Council of Bishops.

The Jurisdictional Conferences of 1940 added three new members to the Council of Bishops. The Central Jurisdiction elected William A. C. Hughes and Lorenzo H. King. Bishop Hughes had been for some while a staff member of the Board of Missions. Bishop King was pastor of St. Marks Church in New York City and a brilliant preacher.

The Western Jurisdiction elected Bishop Bruce R. Baxter to fill the vacancy caused by the death of Bishop Brown.

In 1941 the Central Conference of Southern Asia elected Bishops Shot K. Mondol and Clement D. Rockey; the Latin America Central Conference elected Bishop Enrique C. Balloch; and the China Central Conference elected Bishops Z. T. Kaung, W. Y. Chen, and Carleton Lacy. Thus the Council of Bishops found itself with nine new members as the first quadrennium of the new church began.

It is interesting to note that of the first nine bishops elected in the new church, three died shortly, and three were to know imprisonment, suffering, and finally death as a result of treatment suffered during the Communist take-over of China. Bishop Balloch had a relatively short period of active service. Of the nine only Bishop Mondol and Bishop Rockey were to serve terms of episcopal service of some length.

In the beginning, Central Conference bishops were accorded only limited participation in the council, inasmuch as they were not general superintendents but rather were limited by election to a particular area. No Central Conference bishop was privileged to preside in the General Conference. At first Central Conference bishops were allowed travel expenses only to the meetings of the council at the time of General Conference, or perhaps to one additional meeting during the quadrennium. This situation changed as time moved on, so that the same prerogatives essentially applied to all bishops.

At the General Conference of 1940 the first Judicial Council of The Methodist Church was elected. The provision for a Judicial Council was new so far as the Methodist Episcopal Church and the Methodist Protestant Church were concerned; the Methodist Episcopal Church, South, where the idea originated, had seen the council in operation for only one year.

The creation of the Judicial Council had far-reaching ramifications for the bishops, insofar as it took over judicial functions at times held by the episcopacy in two of the uniting churches; and insofar as legal decisions made by each bishop in the course of the business of the conference now automatically became subject to review by the Judicial Council.

Council meeting: Chicago, July 22-26, 1940

The first meeting of the council after the General Conference of 1940 was held July 22-26 at the LaSalle Hotel in Chicago, with Bishop A. Frank Smith presiding. Bishop Waldorf was the host.

Bishops King and Baxter were present for the first time and were introduced. The death of Bishop W. A. C. Hughes, elected only a few weeks before, was reported.

There were nineteen items of business on the agenda, most of them routine in nature.

A letter received from Bishop John M. Springer indicated that the Africa Central Conference, which then included Liberia, was too large for him to travel, and he requested that a bishop of the Central Jurisdiction take over Liberia. The council replied that it had no such authorization and that furthermore travel was almost impossible because of the war.

The Methodist Episcopal Church, South, after the organization of the autonomous church in Brazil, had a provision for a bishop to be assigned for official visitation in Latin America as a means of keeping contact with the new autonomous church. The bishop thus assigned had no prerogatives beyond friendly visitation. The provision for such assignment was carried over into the new church and was under the responsibility of the South Central Jurisdiction.

While the Methodist Episcopal Church, South had work only in Brazil and Mexico, the Methodist Episcopal Church had work in Mexico, Peru, Argentina, Chile, Uruguay, Bolivia, Panama, and Costa Rica. Retired Bishop George Miller, who had long been associated with the work of the Methodist Episcopal Church in South America, in a letter addressed to the council, raised the question of having a bishop from only a Southern background appointed to a position where so much of the work involved had long been Methodist Episcopal. Presumably the real question Bishop Miller had in mind was that of the necessity for such appointment on a continent where there was a regular Central Conference of The Methodist Church. The Council replied that nothing could be done about the matter. Bishop Ivan Lee Holt held this visitation assignment from 1938 to 1944. Then in turn Bishop W. Angie Smith and Bishop Aubrey Walton held the assignment. When The United Methodist Church was formed in 1968, this provision was dropped.

Another problem dealt with was that at first there were two Atlanta areas, one of the Central Jurisdiction and one of the Southeastern Jurisdiction. The matter was resolved by changing the name of the Central Jurisdiction area to the Atlantic Coast area.

The college membership of Bishop J. W. Robinson, who had served in India but who had been elected as a general superintendent, was lodged in the North Central Jurisdiction.

Bishop John Gowdy had reached retirement age, but it was judged that he should continue effective until such time as the China Central Conference could meet.

The 1940 meeting of the council perfected the first plan of episcopal visitation. In most cases the resident bishop was assigned to hold the conferences in his area, but great care was taken to see that a few bishops were appointed to hold conference sessions outside their own area, and, if possible, across jurisdictional lines. The purpose of making the schedule itself and the special assignments was to insure that the episcopacy would continue a general superintendency. As the years have passed, the council has given less attention to this emphasis, and today filing the plan of episcopal visitation is little more than a listing of the time and place of the respective Annual Conference sessions.

Council meeting: Atlantic City, December 3-5, 1940

The council met December 3-5, 1940, at the Dennis Hotel in Atlantic City with Bishop A. Frank Smith presiding.

At the opening session the newly elected bishops were recognized in a special service, the order for which was prepared by Bishop Leonard.

The council dealt with thirty miscellaneous agenda items.

The war was very much in the thinking of the group, and many of the discussions and actions reflected this. One of the most important things the council did regarding the war was to set up the Committee on the War Emergency and Overseas Relief. Bishop Hughes was named as chairman, and Bishops Oxnam, Arthur Moore, Frank Smith, Flint, Waldorf, and Leonard were the other members of the committee. The various boards of the church were authorized to name representatives to the committee. The council recommended a churchwide appeal for work in military camps, help to British Methodist missions, and relief in wartorn areas. From this vital beginning came the future work of the Commission on Camp Activities and the Methodist Committee on Overseas Relief.

Bishop James Cannon, Jr., sponsored a resolution that was adopted asking that the government seek ways and means of protecting the military against easy access to liquor.

A policy was approved that persons desiring to speak to the council be heard only after the vote of the executive committee, or in emergencies after the approval of the president and secretary. This policy was followed throughout Bishop Oxnam's time as secretary.

Bishop Selecman was elected by the council as president of the Board of Evangelism. This unique provision for the election of a board chairman was actually good strategy, for it tended to relate the bishops closely to the board. The Board of Evangelism legislation also provided that the president report regularly to the council. The board became, therefore, the one board of the church which by Disciplinary provision was guaranteed a place on each agenda of the council.

Lengthy letters were received from Bishops Melle, Lee, and Gowdy, all of them presenting problems in administration with which they were dealing, growing out of the war.

The news was received from Germany that Bishop Melle had been reelected bishop by fifty-two out of fifty-three votes.

Council meeting: Chicago, March 5, 1941

A short meeting of the council was held at the Stevens Hotel in Chicago on March 5, 1941, with Bishop A. Frank Smith presiding. The chief item to which attention was given was the worsening situation in China. A lengthy communication was considered from Bishop Ward stating that the State Department was recommending that missionaries be evacuated. He affirmed that there were mixed reactions to this recommendation. He said that no missionary wanted to leave and that they were evacuating "only those who ought to go."

The only formal action taken at this meeting was endorsement of a Day of Compassion with a special offering.

Bishop Baker reported on a recent visit to Japan and Korea, made at the request of the council.

A motion was adopted that the council look with disfavor upon recognition dinners at its sessions.

Council meeting: Nashville, May 7-9, 1941

The council met in Nashville in the Bishop's Room at the old Publishing House, May 7-9, with Bishop A. Frank Smith presiding.

Bishop Kern, the host bishop, announced that in accord with the wish of the council expressed at its previous meeting there would be no social affairs.

There were fifteen agenda items listed and ten legal questions submitted for consideration. Large attention was given to the Committee on War Emergency and Overseas Relief and its work. The need for a bishop's seal was pointed out, and Bishop Watkins was appointed a committee of one to work on the matter and report at a later meeting.

One of the legal questions raised was the question of the status of a Central Conference bishop who fails to be reelected. The Committee on Law and Administration recommended that "a Central Conference bishop who fails to be reelected ceased to sustain the relationship of a bishop of The Methodist Church. His name should not continue on the list of bishops." The recommendation was debated at length and then withdrawn. This represented the introduction of a problem that was to remain with the church for years to come, involving the status not only of Central Conference bishops where term episcopacy prevailed and who failed to be reelected, but also the status of bishops who reached retirement age as set by the Central Conference and therefore were ineligible for reelection.

The council considered at length a communication from Bishop Lee regarding problems he was facing because of the war.

Council meeting: Sea Island, Georgia, December 9-12, 1941

The council met at the Cloisters, Sea Island, Georgia, on December 9-12, 1941, with Bishop A. Frank Smith presiding. The bishops arrived for the fatal Sunday of Pearl Harbor and assembled at ten P.M. to hear President Roosevelt as he addressed the nation. Following the president's remarks, Bishop McConnell conducted a short service of meditation and prayer, and a telegram was sent to

President Roosevelt. Of those present at Sea Island on that solemn Sunday evening only Bishop William C. Martin is still living at this time of writing (1979).

There were eleven agenda items and nine legal questions submitted for consideration.

Bishop Oxnam raised the question of racial discrimination in the defense program, and Bishop Jones reinforced his concern.

A communication was received from Bishop Enrique Balloch, recently elected in Latin America, in which he said: "What I least expected has happened and I really don't know why. Nothing was further from my mind." This was characteristic of his genuine humility of spirit.

A letter written by Bishop Chen to Bishop Gowdy reported his being under incessant air attack, and a letter from Bishop Lee told of further troubles in Southeast Asia. Note was taken of the election of Bishop Shot K. Mondol and of the fact that "he is our only Indian bishop," since Bishop Chitambar died some months before.

Bishop Ainsworth, whose home was in Georgia, was able to be present for his first and only time. Bishop Blake was also able to be present, having recovered from a serious automobile accident on his way to the General Conference at Atlantic City.

The council at this session named Drew University as the official depository for the Minutes.

Bishop Richardson was elected as the new president of the council.

A wartime message to the church was prepared by Bishop Flint and adopted by the council. It appeared in the Congressional Record of February 13, 1942, at the request of Bishop James Cannon, Jr.

With the nation at war the council soon turned its attention to the need for chaplains and for support of their work with the armed forces. Thus the Commission on Chaplains was born as an agency directly related to the council.

HISTORY OF THE COUNCIL OF BISHOPS
Council meeting: Cleveland, December 7-9, 1942

The council met at Epworth-Euclid Church in Cleveland, December 7-9, 1942, with Bishop Richardson presiding.

The nation had been at war for a year, and there was a pronounced feeling that a message should be addressed to the church. A strong message was prepared, revised, and released. Among other things it said:

We are under no disillusion regarding the unchristian character of war as a method of settling international disputes, but we are in the midst of it because there has arisen in the world a pagan philosophy driven by unchristian motives and bent upon establishing its will upon mankind. We pledge ourselves to the destruction of this brutal and unwarranted aggression and to the preservation for all mankind of the sacred liberties of free men.

At the same time the council began to look forward to planning for peace, though the nation was still deep in the war effort. It appointed delegates to the Delaware Conference on the Christian Basis for a World Order, scheduled for March 8-11, 1943.

Bishop Gowdy reported on a letter from Bishop Chen in which he said, "Never before has there been a greater opportunity to preach the Gospel to the young of China. In every government and private university there is Christian fellowship."

The question came up again of Central Conference bishops who were not reelected, and the judgment was conveyed to the book editor of The Methodist Publishing House that the printing of the names of such bishops should be discontinued. The specific case in point was that of Bishop Elphick.

Bishop Watkins reported on the matter of an episcopal seal. His suggestion was approved. All seals were to be uniform with the words "The Methodist Church," with the name of the individual bishop in the outer circle, the figure of a circuit rider in the center, and the dates 1738 and 1939. Heretofore each bishop had had his own seal, carrying in the outer circle a Scripture quotation of his selection.

Bishop Peele was elected the new president of the council.

The Council of Bishops began to give attention to looking beyond the war and achieving a lasting and just peace. It stated early its judgment that there was "grave danger that the war may be won but that the moral objectives for which it has been waged may be lost." It voted to spend a weekend in Washington conferring with high government officials regarding this concern. Led by Bishop Oxnam, it listed a number of questions in which it was interested. Thirty-two of the bishops resident in the United States met in Washington, February 22-28, 1943, with Bishop Peele presiding. Interviews were had with such dignitaries as President Franklin D. Roosevelt; Vice-President Henry Wallace; Secretaries Henry Stimson, Harold Ickes, Franklin Knox, Jesse Jones, Frances Perkins, and Claude Wishard; Justice William O. Douglas; and John L. Lewis.

Council meeting: Chicago, July 13, 1943

The council met at the LaSalle Hotel in Chicago on July 13, 1943, with Bishop William W. Peele presiding.

It was at this meeting that the council mourned the death of Bishop Adna W. Leonard in a plane crash in Iceland while on a mission for the Commission on Chaplains. Bishop Edwin Holt Hughes was called from retirement to care for the Washington area for the remainder of the quadrennium.

A large number of legal questions were on the agenda of this meeting, following the old pattern of devoting much council attention to matters of this character.

It is interesting to note that the council had requested an additional twenty-five dollars per month for the office of the secretary. Dr. Costen J. Harrell, later bishop, who was on the Council on World Service, addressed a letter to the council saying this could not be allowed.

The chief thing coming out of this session of the council

was the beginning of the Crusade for a New World Order. This was the brainchild of Bishop Oxnam, and the council gave it its full support, as did the 1944 General Conference. The Crusade was an effort to register the opinion of Methodists on the question of the participation of the United States in such international cooperation as might be necessary to establish world order and law. It involved a flow of letters to the President of the United States and to Congress; a series of mass meetings under the guidance of the council where the cause of a just peace would be lifted up; cooperating with the Federal Council of Churches in centering attention upon what were termed the "Six Pillars of Peace"; and a Day of Compassion to be observed in each congregation during Lent, 1944; as well as the use of three small study books.

A commission of twelve bishops was named to carry forward the crusade.

Council meeting: Princeton, New Jersey, December 15-17, 1943

The council met at the Princeton Inn, Princeton, New Jersey, December 15-17, 1943, with Bishop William W. Peele presiding.

A memorial service was held with Bishop Flint in charge. The memorial services of the council have regularly included deceased bishops, wives, and widows only, but this memorial service took notice of the death of U. V. W. Darlington, Jr., who only a short while before had been killed in battle in Europe.

It was at this meeting of the council that the plan of overseas visitation by the bishops had its inception. The plan was again originated by Bishop Oxnam. Back of it was the realization that the time had come when almost no active bishop remained who had seen a period of administration outside the United States. It was noted that every bishop needed to have some knowledge of the entire church, and therefore the plan provided for each active bishop to visit overseas once each quadrennium. The plan was later approved by the General Conference of 1944 and has been in operation ever since, to the great advantage of all concerned.

The council devoted a period of time to the consideration of the rural church. Bishop Baker had arranged the program in which Bishop Magee presided. Invited speakers were Dr. Floyd W. Reeves, Dr. Francis D. Ferrell, Dr. David Lindstrom, and Dr. Murray Lieffer. A period of questions and discussion followed their presentations, and the council resolved to plan for definite action in this field.

At this session the council also took note of a need for emphasis upon evangelism and endorsed the idea of a Crusade for Evangelism in 1945. Following the action of the General Conference this became a part of the quadrennial program for 1944-1948. It is worthy to note that following this action in 1944 the need for a stress upon evangelism appears again and again in subsequent considerations and actions of the council.

Note was taken of an honor recently conferred upon Bishop Decell. In company with President M. C. Smith of Millsaps College, he was driving along Route 51, near Tugaloo, Mississippi, when a Negro boy called to them. They responded and found that a rail on the Illinois Central Railroad had been dislodged. Bishop Decell knew that an express train was due shortly. He ran down the track and flagged the train. The Illinois Central presented a medal to him, as well as one to President Smith and one to the Negro boy.

The council engaged at this session in the first of many subsequent discussions concerning procedures to be followed when a bishop dies. The first decision was that the secretary notify all members of the council and that arrangements be made for at least six bishops to be present at the service.

At one of its devotional periods the council joined in singing "A Soldier's Hymn," written by Bishop Lowe.

Bishop Kern pointed out the need to plan for the

expansion of the church in newly developing urban areas, and first steps were taken to address the attention of the council to this problem.

In Memoriam—1940–1944

Fourteen bishops died during the 1940–1944 quadrennium. Many of them were of advanced years and had not been able to participate in the meetings of the council. The bishops included:

> William N. Ainsworth
> Edgar Blake
> Warren A. Candler
> Jashwant R. Chitambar
> Matthew W. Clair, Sr.
> Collins Denny
> Horace M. DuBose
> Sam R. Hay
> W. A. C. Hughes
> Adna W. Leonard
> Charles L. Mead
> Charles B. Mitchell
> Thomas Nicholson
> Ernest L. Waldorf

William Newman Ainsworth
(1872–1942)

William N. Ainsworth had been elected by the Methodist Episcopal Church, South in 1918. He had for years been a leader in the church in Georgia, where he was born February 10, 1872, in Camilla.

He was tall, bald, and straight as an arrow. He was a Southern orator of the old school, who delighted to paint word pictures with his preaching.

An interesting incident occurred when Bishop Ainsworth was first bishop in the Orient. He was preaching in Japan, following his usual ornate, oratorical style. He rolled his sentences for a minute or two and then paused. The Japanese interpreter said briefly in Japanese, "He is describing a sunset." The bishop looked surprised at so brief a translation of his eloquence, but took up his sermon again, continuing to roll his sentences. He paused for a second time, and the interpreter said, "He is still describing a sunset." The bishop was still more surprised and said, "Brother, are you telling them what I said?"

As a bishop he served the work of the Church, South in the Orient, in west Texas and New Mexico, in Holston and in Georgia. He was always marked by great dignity and finish. His home was at Macon, Georgia, where he continued to live regardless of what conferences were assigned to him.

He died at Asheville, North Carolina, July 7, 1942, and was buried in Riverside Cemetery, Macon, Georgia.

Edgar Blake
(1869–1943)

Edgar Blake, born in Gorham, Maine, December 8, 1869, was elected to the episcopacy in 1920 by the Methodist Episcopal Church.

He was a short man, full of energy and fire. Bishop McConnell said that in the very first meeting Bishop Blake attended of the Board of Bishops he took the floor to tell the older bishops what to do. This procedure was somewhat unusual for that day when it was held that new bishops should keep silent for the first quadrennium until they learned something of the task before them.

Bishop Blake was a liberal and found himself not infrequently in the center of controversies. He served the Paris area, the Indianapolis area, and the Detroit area.

In retirement he lived in Coral Gables, Florida, and died there May 26, 1943. He is buried in Evanston, Illinois.

HISTORY OF THE COUNCIL OF BISHOPS

Warren Akin Candler
(1857–1941)

Warren A. Candler was elected to the episcopacy by the Methodist Episcopal Church, South in 1898.

Born August 23, 1857, in Villa Rica, he was a native Georgian and a member of the North Georgia Conference when elected. He had served as pastor, as president of Emory College at Oxford, Georgia, and had been made a presiding elder when only twenty-three years of age.

He was short and heavy and as broad as he was tall. He used to say that he never played golf because when he was near enough to the ball to hit it he couldn't see it, and when he was far enough away to see it he couldn't reach it! Close friends knew him lovingly as "Shorty." He had bulging eyes and a most expressive face.

Bishop Candler was primarily a preacher. He used to preach holding his Testament in his hand, glancing occasionally at its pages. His oratory frequently moved great audiences deeply. He had a rare sense of humor, and his sermons were sprinkled with witticisms, many of which became proverbial among those who knew him.

On one occasion when preaching at the Louisville Conference, Bishop Candler was talking about Ananias and Sapphira. He said, "Some folks say God killed Ananias and Sapphira for lying. God don't kill people for lying. If he did, where would I be?" When the laughter subsided, he added, "Standing up here, all by myself, with a house full of corpses and nobody to help me carry them out."

In 1930 in the Church, South, prompted by the experiences of Bishop James Cannon, Jr., in the stock market, the Committee on Episcopacy decided to interrogate all the bishops concerning their financial holdings. When it came Bishop Candler's turn to take the stand, he said that the only stock he ever owned was an old Jersey cow and she went dry.

The bishop had a deep voice, almost sepulchral in its tones. He was a man of many moods, and his emotions ran deep. He ranged at times the full distance between the depths of depression and the heights of exaltation.

When in the chair of an Annual Conference, he ran things with an iron hand, and he acquired a reputation for being arbitrary in making the appointments. For more than thirty years he was the dominating figure in the Church, South. He had bitter memories of the Civil War and of Reconstruction days, when as a child he saw the South laid waste. He remained an unreconstructed Southerner to the last. He was ultraconservative theologically, but he had little patience with conservative Methodists of the "second-blessing" school, though these supported him at the time of his election.

His brother, Asa G. Candler, was the founder of the Coca Cola empire, and the bishop enlisted his support in making possible the establishment of Emory University, following the loss of Vanderbilt University in 1914.

Bishop Candler took leadership in defeating Methodist union when it was first considered in 1924. He was retired at the age of seventy-seven in 1934 when the Church, South for the first time adopted an automatic retirement age for bishops. By the time the question of unification came up again in 1938, he was too old, too tired, and too broken to raise effective objection. He chose simply to go along with a current he had no power to stop. While a member of the new Council of Bishops for several years, he was never able to attend one of its meetings or the Uniting Conference or the 1940 General Conference.

The friend who wrote his biography entitled it *Giant Against the Sky,* and such he was against the Southern Methodist sky for long, long years. He died in Atlanta, September 25, 1941, and is buried in Oxford, Georgia, a place always dear to him.

Jaswant Rao Chitambar
(1879–1940)

Jaswant R. Chitambar was the first native-born Indian to be elected a bishop. Elected in 1931, he was the second national elected to the episcopacy in the Methodist Episcopal Church. The other was Chih Ping Wang elected in China the year before but who resigned from the episcopacy a few years later.

Born at Allahabad, Uttar Pradesh, India, on September 5, 1879, Bishop Chitambar was of high caste Hindu background. His father, a Brahmin of Hanarashtra, had converted to Christianity but was forced to leave his home state because of persecution. Bishop Chitambar earned high educational degrees from colleges both in India and the United States, and before his election to the episcopacy he was principal of Lucknow Christian College.

Bishop Chitambar was a striking figure. He had a notable sense of humor, including the ability to laugh at himself. Very often, when visiting the United States, he wore a large and distinctive turban. Once he was approached by a man on the street and asked where he was from. When he replied, "India," the man said, "Well, I thought you were from somewhere."

Mrs. Chitambar likewise came of high-caste Hindu background whose family had been persecuted because of their conversion to Christianity. She was a saintly and strong-willed woman, and an avid temperance worker. Her unvarying practice was to begin every letter with the words: "That in All Things He May Have the Pre-eminence."

Bishop Chitambar gave distinguished leadership in the episcopal office. Shortly after the General Conference of 1940 he was taken ill and died the following September in Jubbulpore, a day before his birthday celebration. He is buried in Jubbulpore.

Matthew Wesley Clair, Sr.
(1865–1943)

Matthew Wesley Clair, Sr., was elected by the Methodist Episcopal Church to the episcopacy in 1920. He and Bishop Robert E. Jones were the first black bishops elected by the Methodist Episcopal Church to serve as general superintendents. Before 1920 several other black ministers had been elected as missionary bishops to Liberia. Bishop Clair's first assignment was also to Liberia where he served eight years; afterward he served the Covington, Kentucky, area for eight years.

Born at Union, West Virginia, October 21, 1865, Bishop Clair was a fervent, warm personality. He was decidedly black and used to smile and refer to several tiny, white spots on his skin as his "blackheads." He was a moving preacher and made effective use of the ministry of song.

He died June 28, 1943, in Covington, Kentucky, and is buried in Washington, D.C.

Collins Denny
(1854–1943)

Collins Denny made formal request to the General Conference of 1940 that his name not be listed among the bishops of The Methodist Church. He refused for the rest of his life to receive the pension to which he was properly entitled. Notice was taken of his passing, however, by the General Conference of 1944.

Bishop Denny was a Virginian, born in Winchester, May 28, 1854, and a Southerner to the core. He was ever the perfect gentleman, firmly committed to the amenities so much cherished in the culture out of which he came. He was elected bishop by the 1910 General Conference of the Methodist Episcopal Church, South following a professorship of some years at Vanderbilt University.

In the episcopacy he remained the teacher, and often when in the chair he would pause to give some reflection on history or church polity or to correct a mistake in English, which someone speaking on the floor of the conference had made. He had a legal mind and was the best parliamentarian in the Church, South in his day. He specialized in church law and revised Bishop Holland N. McTyeire's *Manual of the Discipline.*

Bishop Denny was a master preacher who centered his sermons on unfolding Scripture. His pulpit style was quiet and eloquent in its simplicity, and his command of words deeply moving. Normally he preached for about an hour, but so effective was his preaching that his hearers scarcely noted the passing of time.

The bishop was a pronounced conservative, and he never moved beyond the old school patterns of thought. Instead, he was their strong defender. He was an adamant foe of unification, and at the last General Conference of the Church, South in Birmingham in 1938, he stood almost alone in his efforts to defeat it. Even the many who disagreed with him there admired the gallant efforts of the aged, honored, old warrior, fighting his last battle which he, himself, knew full well could not be won. He used to say that he did not leave the Methodist Episcopal Church, South, but that the Methodist Episcopal Church, South went off and left him.

His remark recalls another remark made at the time by Bishop Randall A. Carter of the then Colored Methodist Episcopal Church. This church, originally sponsored by the Church, South and close to it for a long period of time, was not taken in on the negotiations for Methodist union. Bishop Carter did not like the idea. He said, "When your mother goes off and marries another man, she ought at least to tell you about it."

Bishop Denny died in Richmond, Virginia, May 12, 1943, and is buried in Riverside Cemetery, Richmond.

Horace Mellard DuBose
(1858–1941)

Horace M. DuBose, born in Choctaw County, Alabama, was elected to the episcopacy by the Methodist Episcopal Church, South in 1918. He served the California and then the Nashville areas, retiring in 1934 under the newly adopted retirement rule.

He was a short man, and like several of the other bishops,

measured as much around as he did in height. He was a self-educated man, the author of several valuable books, one of which was his *History of the Methodist Episcopal Church, South*, bringing up to 1914 Bishop McTyeire's *History of Methodism*. Bishop DuBose's book covered a seriously neglected gap in the annals of the church.

He was a master of language and never used a familiar word if he could find an unfamiliar one. He lived in the scholar's world and much of the time gave the impression of being a man "in a fog."

An interesting story is told about him. Bishop DuBose was at Lake Junaluska in the summer of 1929 and was in a group which was discussing who might be elected bishop at the coming General Conference of the Church, South. Someone said, "What do you think of the chances of young Dr. Kern?" Dr. Kern was a short man and slight of build. Bishop DuBose immediately interjected, "Oh, no, a bishop must be tall, broad-shouldered, impressive." Then realizing the corner into which he had painted himself, for he was a short man, he added, "or rotund."

Bishop DuBose had difficulty with administrative tasks but seemed scarcely aware of this. To a considerable extent he was a naïve man, no match for shrewd and clever brethren either among his colleagues or in the Annual Conferences.

He was ecumenical in spirit, ahead of his time, and was a strong advocate of Methodist union long before that position was common in the Church, South. His great disappointment was that while he lived to the time of Methodist union, his health would not permit him to be an on-the-scene witness at Kansas City.

He became something of the last leaf upon the tree for the generation in Methodism to which he belonged. His last days in Nashville, despite its being "a capital" of the Southern Church, were marked by considerable loneliness. He died there January 15, 1941, and is buried in Woodlawn Park Cemetery of that city.

HISTORY OF THE COUNCIL OF BISHOPS

Samuel Ross Hay
(1865–1944)

Sam R. Hay, born at Decaturville, Tennessee, October 15, 1865, claimed Texas as his home state. He was elected to the episcopacy by the Methodist Episcopal Church, South in 1922.

He served as a bishop in China, California, Alabama, and Florida. While he was a gifted preacher, there was always a certain roughness about him, which in his period of time was not expected to mark the episcopacy. He was a storyteller, and a few of his stories came too near to not being in good taste. He had a rare sense of humor and used to explain his own election by observing that at last the rougher element in the church rose up and demanded to be recognized.

It is said that before Bishop Hay was elected one serious-minded brother said to him, "Sam, you can't be elected bishop unless you give up some of your stories." He replied, "I've got one story that's so good that I wouldn't give it up to be bishop."

On one Sunday night he dropped in on Dr. Bascom Watts, later Bishop Watts. Dr. Watts insisted that he preach. He demurred at first, but on Watt's insistence he agreed. When it came time to take the pulpit, he read the letter to Philemon. Then he said, "Paul wrote that. It can't be improved upon. Rise and receive the benediction." And thereupon he dismissed the congregation.

There was a strange friendship between him and Bishop Darlington, from whom he differed almost completely in manner, in viewpoint, and in his concept of the episcopacy. He was close to Bishop William F. McMurray also, but he had far more in common with him.

Bishop Hay was firm in his administration of his conferences, and while he acquired some reputation for tending to be dictatorial, at the same time he was generally thought of as being fully fair.

He retired at the last General Conference of the Church,

South in 1938. He lived too short a time thereafter to participate to any extent in the newly formed Council of Bishops. He died in Houston, Texas, February 4, 1944, and is buried there.

William Alfred Carroll Hughes
(1877–1940)

W. A. C. Hughes had the honor of being the first bishop elected by the new Central Jurisdiction in 1940. He was ill at the time of his election and was almost too sick to go through the service of consecration, but probably the seriousness of his condition was not fully realized.

Born in Westminster, Maryland, June 19, 1877, Bishop Hughes had a distinguished career, especially as Board of Missions executive, and became one of the best-known leaders of his race in his day.

He died a few weeks after his consecration as bishop, July 12, 1940, in Baltimore, Maryland, where he is buried.

Adna Wright Leonard
(1874–1943)

Adna W. Leonard was one of the unforgettable bishops of the church. He was elected to the episcopacy by the Methodist Episcopal Church in 1916 and served the San Francisco, Pittsburgh, and Washington areas. His father, Dr. A. B. Leonard, was for long years general secretary of the Board of Missions and one of the greatest missionary statesmen Methodism has ever had.

Born November 2, 1874, in Cincinnati, Ohio, Bishop Leonard was a stern and serious man, apparently with not much sense of humor. He always kept his dignity and reserve and regularly urged his preachers to be careful of their dress, their conduct, and their observance of the amenities. He set high standards for himself and for his conferences. There were those who thought him autocratic, but he did his work efficiently and well. He was unafraid of controversy and stood by his convictions at whatever cost.

During World War II he took leadership in the Commission on Chaplains. He perished in a plane crash in Iceland, May 3, 1943, on a visit to the troops, a trip authorized by President Roosevelt. Thus he sealed his long record of devotion to his God, his church, and his fellowmen.

His body was buried in Reykjavik, Iceland, and later returned for final burial in Springfield, Ohio.

Bishop Leonard had for years been a recognized leader among his Methodist Episcopal colleagues. In the relatively short time he was a part of the Council of Bishops of the new Methodist Church, he proved himself one of its most diligent and effective members.

Charles Larew Mead
(1868-1941)

Charles L. Mead, born July 20, 1868, in Vienna, New Jersey, was elected to the episcopacy by the Methodist Episcopal Church in 1920. He was a member of the Colorado Conference, and upon his election he was assigned to the Denver area. Previous to his pastorate at Trinity Church, Denver, he had been the pastor of large churches in Newark, Hoboken, Baltimore, and New York City. He served the Denver area from 1920 to 1932 and the Kansas City area from 1932 to 1940. He saw only one year of service as an active bishop in the new Methodist Church, as he retired at the end of the first year after union.

Bishop Mead was primarily a popular preacher, and in the episcopacy he remained definitely the same pastoral type that he had represented throughout his ministry. He took great plaesure in serving as pianist for meetings of the bishops.

Bishop Mead lived only a year after retirement and died May 17, 1941. He is buried in Denver, Colorado, where he served as bishop for twelve years.

AGAIN ONE PEOPLE

Charles Bayard Mitchell
(1857–1942)

Charles B. Mitchell had been elected in the Methodist Episcopal Church in 1916. He was born August 27, 1857, in Pittsburgh, Pennsylvania. For years he was transferred, serving large churches scattered from New Jersey to Minnesota. At the time of his election he had been a member of eight conferences.

He served as episcopal leader in the St. Paul area from 1916 to 1924, and the Philippines from 1924 to 1928, when he retired. He was well up in years and had been retired for some time when the Methodist union came. He therefore never became a familiar figure in the Council of Bishops of the new church.

Bishop Mitchell and Bishop Charles E. Locke were strong friends. When Bishop Mitchell's wife developed health problems in the Philippines, Bishop Locke, who had been serving the St. Paul area, exchanged areas with him in order that Bishop Mitchell might remain in the active relationship. The two remained fast friends throughout their lives and were buried side by side in Forest Lawn Cemetery. Bishop Mitchell died February 23, 1942, in Pasadena.

Thomas Nicholson
(1862–1944)

Thomas Nicholson was elected to the episcopacy by the Methodist Episcopal Church in 1916.

Born January 27, 1862, in Woodburn, Ontario, Canada, Bishop Nicholson was long associated with educational work, both in Canada and the midwestern United States. He held the principalship of the Academy of Cornell College, Iowa, from 1894 to 1903, and was president of Dakota Wesleyan University, 1903 to 1908. From 1908 to 1916 he was secretary of the General Board of Education.

After his election to the episcopacy, Bishop Nicholson served the Chicago area from 1916 to 1924, and the Detroit area from 1924 to 1932. He was forced to retire in 1932 because of ill health.

Bishop Nicholson was an ardent foe of the liquor traffic and took strong leadership against the wet forces in the presidential campaign of 1928.

His wife, Evelyn, was a recognized leader in women's work at the national and international levels, and was for nineteen years president of the Women's Foreign Missionary Society.

Bishop Nicholson was able to participate in only one session of the Council of Bishops. For some years he was confined to his home in Iowa. He lost the ability to speak, suffered from cataracts, and had serious locomotive difficulties. Despite being thus confined, he continued his interest in all that was taking place in the church and in national and world affairs. His regular letters to the council bespoke his great disappointment in not being able to participate in the meetings and of his continuing love of his brethren. He died March 7, 1944, in Mt. Vernon, Iowa, and is buried there.

Ernest Lynn Waldorf
(1876–1943)

Ernest L. Waldorf was elected to the episcopacy by the Methodist Episcopal Church in 1920 after serving several of the most prominent pulpits of the church. He served the Wichita, Kansas, area from 1920 to 1924, the Kansas City area from 1924 to 1932, and the Chicago area from 1932 to his death in 1943.

Born May 14, 1876, in South Valley, Ostego, New York, Bishop Waldorf was a large man and some people thought somewhat Jewish in appearance. He had a jovial disposition and a good sense of humor. He was always the master of the situation and planned carefully and sometimes cleverly for what he wished to occur.

As a presiding officer, Bishop Waldorf did not hesitate to suggest motions or to observe that he thought a particular brother would like to make a certain motion, which he would then proceed to state. Usually the brother would agree. Bishop Waldorf had strong business ability, and he had much to do with planning and perfecting the financial system that was followed in the church for years.

As a bishop, Bishop Waldorf was the Methodist Episcopal counterpart of Bishop William F. McMurray of the Church, South, who died shortly before Methodist union. It is interesting to note that these two unique characters, having so much in common personality-wise and in manner of administration, should both have served in Missouri for an overlapping period between 1924 and 1930.

Many knew Bishop Waldorf as the father of Lynn Waldorf, a famous football coach at Northwestern University.

Bishop Waldorf died July 27, 1943, and is buried in Morningside Cemetery, Syracuse, near his close friend, Bishop Wallace E. Brown.

II

Crusading for a Better World
1944–1948

The council met periodically during the General Conference of 1944, April 26–May 6, at Kansas City, on call of the chairman, Bishop H. Lester Smith. Bishops Wen Yuan Chen and G. Carleton Lacy were present for the first time.

The council approved in principle an emphasis for the quadrennium upon evangelism, church school attendance, and stewardship.

Bishop Peele reported that the Negro delegates were not adequately provided for in the matter of restaurant facilities and that certain discriminations had been reported. The council appointed Bishops Broomfield, Wade, and Peele to see that the situation was corrected.

As the General Conference assembled, the United States had been at war for more than two-and-a-half years. Most of the conferences of Methodism as a world church were in nations that were also involved in the war on one side or the other. Only a relatively few conferences outside the United States were located in countries that were neutral. Overtones of the war situation were felt, therefore, on every hand.

The Episcopal Address was given by Bishop Arthur J. Moore. Most of the bishops resident in the United States were present. Bishop Edwin Holt Hughes, long an outstanding General Conference figure, was absent for the first time because of illness. Most of the bishops resident overseas were unable to attend because of the war. A service of remembrance for the fourteen bishops who had died in the previous quadrennium was held.

The communion service, with which the 1944 General Conference opened, was in the charge of Bishops Welch and Hammaker.

Devotional services were led by Bishops Baxter, L. H. King, Lacy, Broomfield, Wade, Lee, Decell, Shaw, and Balloch, who also brought the devotional messages.

Bishops presiding at the sessions of the General Conference were H. Lester Smith, Straughn, Selecman, Lowe, McConnell, Jones, Peele, Purcel, Hammaker, William C. Martin, Richardson, Magee, A. Frank Smith, Baker, Arthur J. Moore, Wade, Flint, Cushman, and Decell.

The Jurisdictional and Central Conferences of 1944 saw the retirement of Bishop Brenton Thoburn Badley, who had served for twenty years as bishop in India; Bishop Urban V. W. Darlington, who had served for twenty-one years in the Church, South and five years in the united church; Bishop Hoyt M. Dobbs, who had served for seventeen years in the Church, South and five years in the new church; Bishop Robert E. Jones, who had served for nineteen years in the Methodist Episcopal Church and five in The Methodist Church; Bishop Francis J. McConnell, who had served for twenty-seven years in the Methodist Episcopal Church and five years in the new church; Bishop Ernest G. Richardson, who had served for eighteen years in the Methodist Episcopal Church and five years in the united church; and Bishop John M. Springer, who had been a missionary bishop in Africa for eight years. These retiring brethren had given a total of one hundred sixty years of active service in the episcopacy.

When the council met in the fall meeting of 1944, the following newly elected bishops were present:

Central Jurisdiction: Robert N. Brooks
         Edward W. Kelly
         Willis J. King

HISTORY OF THE COUNCIL OF BISHOPS

Northeastern Jurisdiction: Fred P. Corson
                             Lewis O. Hartman
                             Earl W. Ledden

Elected by the Northeastern Jurisdiction for service in Africa, under a special authorization of the General Conference for such an election: Newell S. Booth

Southeastern Jurisdiction: Costen J. Harrell
                             Paul N. Garber
South Central Jurisdiction: Paul E. Martin
                             W. Angie Smith
North Central Jurisdiction: Charles W. Brashares
                             Schuyler E. Garth

During the quadrennium of 1944–1948 elected by Central Conferences:

Southern Asia: John A. Subhan
Philippines: D. D. Alejandro
Northern Europe: Theodor Arvidson
Latin America: Arthur F. Wesley
Germany: Johann W. E. Sommer

All, except Bishop Sommer, were elected to fill vacancies created by retirement or transfer for service elsewhere of former general superintendents or missionary bishops. Bishop Sommer was elected to take the place of Bishop F. H. Otto Melle, who had recently died.

Council meeting: Chicago, July 24-27, 1944

The Council of Bishops met at the LaSalle Hotel, Chicago, July 24-27, 1944, with Bishop H. Lester Smith presiding. Bishop G. Bromley Oxnam continued as secretary, a position he was to hold until 1956, a total of sixteen years.

The death of Bishop William F. Anderson was announced. The funeral services were scheduled at Christ Church, New York, at the same time the council was in session.

A Commission on the Relation of Races in The Methodist Church was named consisting of one bishop, one minister, and one lay person from each jurisdiction, plus Central Conference representatives. The committee as named included six women, Blacks, Hispanics, Asians, and citizens of India. This commission anticipated by a quarter of a century the emphasis upon minorities in the church, which came with the 1972 General Conference.

A Commission on Central Conferences was named representing a first step in many Central Conference developments to follow in later years.

The beginning of the quadrennium 1944–1948 saw the launching of the Crusade for Christ and His Church program with a great conference in St. Louis, Missouri. The program was authorized by the 1944 General Conference. Leadership in the program was given by Bishop J. Ralph Magee, chairman, Dr. J. Manning Potts, executive secretary, and others. The goal of $25,000,000 was oversubscribed making it possible for the church to repair much war damage and to launch significant new programs. The Crusade also provided for certain annual program emphases, including evangelism, stewardship, and church school attendance.

The Crusade for Christ and His Church had as an integral part The Crusade Scholarship Program. The program continues to the present and has been responsible for the advanced training of thousands of promising young men and women from all over the world.

Council meeting: Buck Hill Falls, December 6, 1944

The council had a one-day meeting at the Inn in Buck Hill Falls, Pennsylvania, on December 6, 1944, with Bishop H. Lester Smith presiding.

The chief item of attention was a resolution relative to the Dunbarton Oaks proposals for the "continuing collaboration of the United Nations and in due course other nations"—which summoned the entire church, as a part of the Crusade for a New World Order, to study, support, and improve upon where necessary.

Council meeting: Chicago, April 23-27, 1945

The council met at the Stevens Hotel in Chicago, April 23-27, 1945, with Bishop H. Lester Smith presiding.

Bishop Arthur Wesley, recently elected by the Central Conference of Latin America and assigned to the Santiago area, was present for the first time.

The council took note of the death of President Roosevelt on April 12, 1945, and stood in silent tribute, after which prayer was offered by Bishop John M. Moore. A message was sent to President Truman, who had recently taken office.

Bishop Charles W. Brashares introduced a paper dealing with the need to enlist young people for Christian service. Another paper, presented by Bishop Fred P. Corson, called for Vocational Guidance Conferences on the campuses of church-related colleges and at Wesley Foundations. Bishops Brashares, Corson, Garth, and Paul Martin were appointed a Committee on Recruitment for the Ministry. The ultimate issue of this interest of the council was the establishment by the General Conference of 1948 of the Commission on Christian Vocations.

Council meeting: Buck Hill Falls, December 3-6, 1945

The council met at Buck Hill Falls, December 3-6, 1945, with Bishop Charles C. Selecman presiding.

There was rather extended discussion of the relation of Bishop Melle to the Nazi government in Germany, growing out of statements in the Methodist press, particularly *Zion's Herald*. There were those who felt that the bishop had been misunderstood. There was common consent that the matter did not require any decision by the council.

Bishop Kern presented a statement on peacetime military training, which was adopted after certain amendments. It definitely opposed universal military training in peacetime. The statement was sent to the President, the Secretary of the Navy, the Secretary of War, the Chairman of the Military Affairs Committee, and the Chairman of the Naval Affairs Committee of the House and of the Senate.

Council meeting: Atlantic City, February 20-25, 1946

The council met at the Hotel Dennis in Atlantic City, February 20-25, 1946, with Bishop Selecman presiding.

CRUSADING FOR A BETTER WORLD

A lengthy communication was received from Bishop Melle in reply to the assertions concerning him discussed at the last meeting. He affirmed that he had never been a member of the Nazi party and that some of his statements which had been the subject of discussion had been made prior to the war and under totally different circumstances.

Considerable discussion was given to the plight of the church in Germany. Bishop Oxnam had recently visited Germany and reported on the situation.

The council constituted a Committee on Veterans' Affairs, the purpose of which was to help Methodist veterans adjust to a return to civilian life. A convocation of a thousand returned veterans was envisioned. Bishop W. Angie Smith took leadership in the committee. The convocation was held in Columbus, Ohio. The committee was not continued thereafter.

It was at this meeting that the visit of Bishop Schuyler Edward Garth to China was authorized, a visit in which he and Mrs. Garth lost their lives in a plane crash, January 28, 1947.

At this meeting the council took leadership in the establishment of a Department of Research in The Methodist Church.

It was also at this meeting that the council authorized a statement to the church that it was appointing a committee to consider Protestant and Roman Catholic relationships. This was years in advance of Vatican II.

The council now adopted the policy of having two meetings a year, one in the spring and one in the fall.

Council meeting: Buck Hill Falls, December 10, 1946

At the one-day meeting at Buck Hill Falls, December 10, 1946, Bishop Raymond J. Wade presented a comprehensive report on the situation in Germany. By appointment of the council, he had made an extended visit to the Central Conference there.

HISTORY OF THE COUNCIL OF BISHOPS

Council meeting: Riverside, California, May 1-6, 1947

The council met at Mission Inn, Riverside, California, May 1-6, 1947, with Bishop Titus Lowe presiding.

Considerable attention was given to the Commission on Chaplains and its concerns and activities. Bishops Peele, Oxnam, Purcell, and Flint were named to the General Commission on Chaplains.

The council had before it a considerable number of legal questions. One of these was the question of retired bishops having no vote in the council. It was the expressed judgment of the council that they should be able to vote.

Bishop Magee reported on the excellent progress of the Crusade for Christ and His Church program.

Council meeting: Atlantic City, December 2-6, 1947

The council met at the Dennis Hotel, Atlantic City, December 2-6, 1947, with Bishop Kern presiding.

The council approved a proposed new quadrennial program, the Advance for Christ and His Church, and also a Youth Emphasis.

Council meeting: Atlantic City, April 15-21, 1948

The council met at the Dennis Hotel, Atlantic City, April 15-21, 1948, giving its attention to the Episcopal Address and planning for the coming General Conference.

In Memoriam—1944-1948

During the quadrennium, 1944 to 1948, ten of the bishops had died:
>William F. Anderson
>Bruce R. Baxter
>James Cannon, Jr.
>John L. Decell
>Schuyler E. Garth

CRUSADING FOR A BETTER WORLD

Lorenzo H. King
F. H. Otto Melle
John L. Nuelson
Ernest G. Richardson
John W. Robinson

William Franklin Anderson
(1860–1944)

William F. Anderson had been elected by the Methodist Episcopal Church in 1908 to the episcopacy. He was the senior bishop of that church at the time of union. Bishops Edwin Holt Hughes and John L. Nuelson had been elected at the same General Conference but on later ballots.

Bishop Anderson served the Chattanooga, Cincinnati, and Boston areas, and for a period supervised the work in much of Europe.

Born in Morgantown, West Virginia, April 22, 1960, Bishop Anderson was an impressive figure—tall, straight, and dignified in apperance. Even when far along in years he maintained his erect carriage.

He had a lifelong interest in education and at the time of his election was secretary of the Board of Education. As a bishop he was president of the Board of Education for twelve years. After his retirement in 1932 he taught at Carleton College and at Florida Southern College.

During World War I he was particularly active in wartime work programs and was decorated for his services by the French government. He belonged in the same category of "patriot" bishops to which Bishops Matthew Simpson and Edward R. Ames before him belonged. He shared with them a national affection that impressed some as being perhaps too unquestioning. A dramatic preacher, during World War I he had a favorite sermon that he preached on many occasions. At the close he would draw a small American flag from his pocket, and waving it would bring his audience to cheers as he would quote the then much-loved poem of Henry Van Dyke with its moving lines:

So its home again and home again, America for me!
My heart is turning home again, and there I long to be,
In the land of youth and freedom beyond the ocean bars
Where the air is full of sunlight and the flag is full of stars.

Bishop Anderson took great pride in his son, William K. Anderson, who was also for many years an acknowledged leader in the church. He served from 1940 to his death in 1947 as executive secretary of the General Commission on Courses of Study.

Bishop Anderson died July 22, 1944, and is buried in Kensico, New York.

Bruce Richard Baxter
(1892–1947)

Bruce R. Baxter was born August 18, 1892, at Rock Run, Ohio, and was graduated from Oberlin College and Boston University School of Theology. After holding professorships at Mount Union College in Ohio and the University of Southern California, he became president of Willamette University in Eugene, Oregon.

In 1940 he was elected bishop and assigned to Portland, Oregon. He was a happy, jovial, informal type of person who wanted everybody to call him by his first name. He was a delightful preacher whose sermons were sprinkled with wit and humor, and he represented a new departure in administration. He died suddenly in Portland, June 20, 1947, at Annual Conference. He is buried at Forest Lawn, Los Angeles.

Though Bishop Baxter's time in the episcopacy was brief, he will be recalled for long years to come as a radiant, democratic, free spirit who quickly captured the hearts of all he met.

James Cannon, Jr.
(1864–1944)

James Cannon, Jr., was born in Salisbury, Maryland, November 13, 1864. He had served long years in the

Virginia Conference as pastor and as college president before his election to the episcopacy. He had also been very active in general church affairs and was often on the floor of the General Conference. He was elected by the Methodist Episcopal Church, South to the episcopacy in 1918, and there was strong opposition to his election, not only among some of the delegates to the General Conference but also to some extent among the bishops.

The General Conference had ordered the election of six bishops. The last person elected was Dr. Franklin N. Parker of Emory University. To the disappointment of many, Dr. Parker declined the election. Dr. Cannon was a runner-up with a substantial vote. The bishops met in conference and decided that Bishop John C. Kilgo, who was to be in the chair, would rule that the General Conference had ordered the election of six bishops, and six had indeed been elected. Therefore the matter should be closed. Bishop Kilgo did so rule, but the position of the bishops was reversed by the General Conference, and Dr. Cannon was elected.

Bishop Cannon seemed to relish debate. Conflict and opposition did not disturb him. All his day he had the reputation of being a cold man, almost totally without emotions so far as could be observed.

He was neither popular nor very effective as an administrator. Changes were made in his episcopal assignment during his first quadrennium, and he served different years in Mexico, West Texas, New Mexico, and Alabama. At least one of these conferences is said to have asked for his removal.

In 1922 Bishop Cannon was assigned the work in Brazil where he followed Bishop John M. Moore, who had a remarkably effective quadrennium from 1918 to 1922. He kept the Brazil assignment for eight years, but was never popular there, chiefly because he chose not to live in Brazil but to serve it by occasional visits from the United States. There was some reaction, also, to what was thought of as his autocratic method of operation. When the autonomous church was set up in Brazil in 1930, he was practically ignored when other bishops took the lead in the organizing conference. He felt deeply wounded at this.

From 1930 to 1934 Bishop Cannon had the work in Cuba and in Africa. Again he followed, as in Brazil, the plan of absentee administration.

Throughout his episcopal career Bishop Cannon gave much of his time and attention to the "dry cause" and to the Anti-Saloon League. He was one of the top leaders of the Temperance Movement and was recognized as an astute and powerful politician. He took particular leadership in the 1928 presidential election campaign, seeking the defeat of the Democrat nominee, Al Smith, an outspoken wet. Bishop Cannon was generally credited with being the major factor in the defeat of the Democratic ticket that year in four of the states of the old South. Because of his political efforts, particularly in this campaign, Bishop Cannon made strong enemies, both among wets and among party loyalists. On the other hand, he became the popular idol of many drys. H. L. Mencken once described him as "the most powerful ecclesiastic ever heard of in America."

Charges were preferred against Bishop Cannon twice in 1930, first at the General Conference of 1930 on the grounds of conduct unbecoming to a bishop by participating in questionable stock market shares; and again later in the year by four ministers. All the charges were disposed of, leaving the bishop in office and subject to appointment.

Between 1928 and 1934 Bishop Cannon went through hearings before two Senate committees and a trial on charges of violation of the Corrupt-Practices Act. In this trial he was found not guilty.

At the General Conference of 1934 the Committee on Episcopacy recommended the retirement of Bishop Cannon by a vote of 43 to 28. The matter was carried to the General Conference floor, and under a roll call vote he was continued in effective service by a vote of 269 to 170. Many delegates rallied to his support because they felt that much of the opposition to him and the charges against him stemmed from resentment to his dry stand.

He was assigned to the work on the Pacific Coast and served there until he reached the automatic retirement age in 1938. He died September 6, 1944, in Chicago, where he had gone to attend a meeting. His body was taken "home" to Virginia, where he is buried in Hollywood Cemetery, Richmond.

In 1949 Virginius Dabney of Richmond, Virginia, published a life of Bishop Cannon entitled *The Dry Messiah*. It is a bitter book in which the author admits the brilliance, ability, and shrewdness of the bishop, but relates unsparingly many alleged details of his private life. In 1955, with the help of Bishop Cannon's son, James Cannon III, who was dean of Duke Divinity School, Richard L. Watson edited and published a biography entitled *Bishop Cannon's Own Story*. It pictures the bishop in an entirely different light.

Bishop Cannon was a lonely figure among the bishops. When he came into the College of Bishops of the Church, South, there were those of the older bishops who did not welcome his coming. He had no close friends among the bishops. Perhaps the one most kindly disposed toward him was Bishop DuBose, who for a long time defended him but eventually dared to suggest that he resign. There was marked tension between Bishop Cannon and Bishop Mouzon. Bishop Cannon was more popular in the Methodist Episcopal Church than he was in his own Church, South. This was probably due to admiration of his dry leadership.

When union came in 1939, he found himself with new colleagues from the Northern Church and from the Methodist Protestant Church. He was, however, now a retired bishop. He was still marked by an inclination to take the floor frequently and to assume leadership. It is said that the Disciplinary provision that retired bishops cannot vote in the council is traced back to a reaction to Bishop Cannon's floor activity and that of several other retired brethren.

Bishop Cannon was to the end an austere, cold, humorless bishop, often gruff in his manner and sometimes sharp in what he had to say. In his late years he suffered from an arthritic condition that made it necessary for him to use crutches. He was a pathetic figure in his later years, having great difficulty in moving about, but undaunted in his determination to keep going.

John Lloyd Decell
(1887–1946)

John L. Decell, elected to the episcopacy by the Methodist Episcopal Church, South in 1938, was a favorite son of Mississippi, where he was born August 12, 1887, near Brookhaven. He had been a conference leader in Mississippi and had served in several districts and in large churches. He served as a bishop for only eight years.

From 1938 to 1944 his episcopal assignment was the Birmingham area, and from 1944 to his death in 1946 the Jackson area. He was active in the achievement of Methodist union prior to 1939 and was the secretary of the Committee on Church Union.

Bishop Decell was dignified in manner and neat in appearance. On most occasions he still chose to wear the cutaway formal coat, the use of which had been common among more formal ministers in the years of his earlier ministry. He was the pastoral type, gentle in spirit and outgoing in nature. Moving deliberately and calmly at all times, he was adept at contributing to resolving tense situations and calming those who were troubled or distressed. There were those who thought of him as being clever in working out whatever he had in mind.

Bishop Decell was a devout man by nature and often tended to feel that he had the divine endorsement for his conclusions. Appointment-making was a job that he enjoyed but which at the same time he found taxing. At times he suffered from the pressures which were put upon him, particularly by his friends. A perhaps apocryphal story is told of how on one occasion Bishop Decell called in a brother who had been disappointed in his appointment. The bishop said, "My brother, I want you to know that this appointment has been sanctified by long hours of thought and prayer." The man replied, "Bishop, that's the strangest Methodist theology I ever heard of." The Bishop replied, "What do you mean, brother?" and the man answered, "According to Methodist theology a thing has to be justified before it can be sanctified."

Generally speaking, Bishop Decell was a moderate conservative who had the respect of both those who felt that a new day must come for the church, and those who were inclined to cling to older views and former ways.

Bishop Decell died January 10, 1946, in Jackson, Mississippi, and is buried in Greenwood Cemetery there.

Schuyler Edward Garth
(1898–1947)

Schuyler E. Garth, born September 1, 1898, in Saffordsville, Kansas, was elected to the episcopacy by the North Central Jurisdictional Conference in 1944. He had served as a popular pastor in Miami, St. Petersburg, Pittsburgh, and Youngstown, and was known as a fine preacher.

He was assigned to the Wisconsin area. His episcopal service was only two years in duration as he and his wife were killed in a plane crash, January 28, 1947, near Hankow while on an episcopal visit to China.

The plan of episcopal overseas visitation was adopted by the General Conference of 1944. Since that time the bishops of the church have traveled thousands of miles on such missions. Some of them have incurred illnesses that have proved costly, but thus far only the Garths have made such journeys at the cost of their lives. Bishop Adna Leonard also was killed in a plane crash, but it was on a mission of another type.

Lorenzo Houston King
(1878–1946)

Lorenzo H. King, after a brilliant career as pastor, teacher, and editor, was elected to the episcopacy by the

Central Jurisdiction in 1940. He was the first bishop to be elected across jurisdictional lines, for his membership at the time of his election was in the Northeastern Jurisdiction.

Born January 2, 1878, in Macon, Mississippi, both his parents had been slaves. He was on every occasion an ardent advocate of the rights of the Negro.

He was able to give only six years to the episcopacy, as he died December 17, 1946, in a New York City hospital. During these six years he served the Central Jurisdictional Conferences in South Carolina, Alabama, Georgia, and Florida.

He was a leader in Negro education and served effectively on the Board of Trustees of Gammon Seminary and Claflin, Clark, and Bethune-Cookman Colleges.

F. H. Otto Melle
(1875–1947)

F. H. Otto Melle was elected to the episcopacy by the Germany Central Conference in 1936. Born in Liebengruen (now East Germany), August 16, 1875, he was a leading pastor in Germany and had been president of the seminary at Frankfort. In earlier years he did missionary work in Yugoslavia and Hungary.

Bishop Melle was a large man physically. Intellectually he was a man with a trained and able mind. Spiritually he was a decided Pietist. To his way of thinking the social gospel was to be identified with social service activities—such as hospitals, homes for the aged, and caring for the poor and the neglected.

When Hitler first came to power, Bishop Melle saw in him new hope for the German people. While he may have differed privately on occasion with Hitler's policies, publicly he not only was uncritical but at times defended him. At the Oxford Conference in 1937, he entered a protest against sending a message of assurance to the confessing church in Germany. He seemed to retreat more and more into thinking of religion as purely a private and personal matter, and of the role of the church as being confined to worship and Christian fellowship.

Bishop Melle attended the General Conference in Atlantic City in 1940. He was treated wih courtesy but also with reserve by many, as most delegates were sympathetic with the Allies. After the entrance of the United States into the war, Bishop Melle's relations with his American brethren naturally became strained. As the war progressed and adjoining lands were occupied by Germans, Bishop Melle took the position that the conquests of the German armies were the conquests of the church also. He annexed the Methodist churches in conquered territory to the nearest German conferences.

The war years were a great strain upon him, as were also the subsequent years of occupation by the Russians. Bishop Garber visited him in 1945 and found that when the Russians took over Berlin, twelve Russian soldiers occupied the episcopal residence. The Melles were placed in the basement, Mrs. Melle forced to cook for the soldiers, and Bishop Melle to carry water from a mile away.

Broken in health because of great strain over a long period of time, Bishop Melle died in Berlin, March 26, 1947.

John Louis Nuelson
(1867–1946)

John L. Nuelson, born January 19, 1867, in Zurich, Switzerland, had lived much of his life in Europe. His father, though an American citizen, served churches in Europe for thirty-eight years.

John Nuelson was elected to the episcopacy by the Methodist Episcopal Church in 1908. At the time of his election he was a professor at Nash Seminary in Ohio and only forty years of age. His election came primarily as a result of a rather strong insistence upon the part of the German constituency of the church that they should be represented in the Board of Bishops. This election was thus an early manifestation of the conviction registered often in late years that minority groups in the church should furnish a part of the episcopal panel.

Once elected, however, Bishop Nuelson was assigned, not to presiding over German Conferences, but to a regular area of the church in the United States. From 1908 to 1912 he served the Omaha area. In 1912 he was assigned all the work in Europe, with residence in Zurich. He was associated with the work in Europe for the rest of his active episcopacy. In 1920 the European work was divided into three areas: the Stockholm area, the Paris area, and the Zurich area, to which Bishop Nuelson was assigned.

Bishop Nuelson was an impressive man. He looked the scholar that he was. His library, which can still be seen in the Methodist Publishing House in Zurich, bears silent testimony to the wide range of his interests and the eagerness of his mind for acquiring knowledge. He wrote constantly and was the author of a number of books and of a multitude of articles. He was an indefatigable traveler, and much of his study and writing was done on the road.

The outbreak of World War I created serious problems for Bishop Nuelson. He loved the German Methodists and the German people and hastened to defend them in the early years of the war. When the United States entered the war, matters were further complicated for him. The charge of being "pro-German" was then a serious charge to the thinking of many Americans during the highly emotional days of 1917 and 1918. Nuelson was attacked in some of the American church papers. Even some of his episcopal brethren were not too understanding of the situation in which he found himself. During the last period of the war he was forbidden to travel and was immobilized in Switzerland for long months. A further complication for him was the fact that the conferences of his area were divided between countries on the side of Germany and countries on the side of the Allies.

When the war was over, Bishop Nuelson took strong leadership in an enthusiastic program of relief, rehabilitation, and expansion which involved all the European work. Before too long, however, he found himself living with the failure of the Centenary Campaign to realize anything like the funds promised, an income drop as a result of the depression in the United States, and the economic collapse of Germany.

Bishop Nuelson watched Hitler's coming into power with much misgiving and had no good word for him. What he saw happening to the church in Germany brought distress to his heart. Eventually it became clear to him that the only way for Methodism to go on in Germany was with the measure of self-determination afforded by a Central Conference and under the leadership of a German bishop. Thus he faded out of the picture, and the Germany Central Conference came into being in 1936.

During the war years, he administered as best he could what remained of the Zurich area until his retirement after the Uniting Conference of 1939. In the end, he was a sad but not a bitter man. He died in Bethesda Hospital, Cincinnati, Ohio, June 26, 1946, and is buried in Cincinnati.

Few bishops have been called upon to carry a heavier load than he carried for almost a quarter of a century.

Ernest Gladstone Richardson
(1874–1947)

Ernest G. Richardson was elected to the episcopacy by the Methodist Episcopal Church in 1920.

Born February 24, 1874, in St. Vincent, British West Indies, he had been a pastor and a district superintendent in the New York East Conference for better than twenty years.

In his episcopal capacity he served the Atlanta area from 1920 to 1928 and the Philadelphia area from 1928 to 1944, when he retired. He was active in the achievement of Methodist union and took leadership in planning for the Uniting Conference.

Bishop Richardson was a tall, thin man, with large expressive eyes and white hair. He moved calmly and deliberately and always was in full command of himself. He was a church-lawyer type, a master of the *Discipline,* and one of the most effective presiding officers in the church.

After retirement he was called to care for the Wisconsin area following the death of Bishop Garth. This assignment proved of short duration, for he, too, died within a short time on September 5, 1947, in Philadelphia, Pennsylvania.

John Wesley Robinson
(1866–1947)

J. W. Robinson was elected a missionary bishop for India by the 1912 General Conference of the Methodist Episcopal Church. In 1920 he was elected a general superintendent.

He served the Bombay and Delhi areas, and for a period also supervised the work in Malaya, Sarawak, Dutch East Indies, and the Philippines, due to the death of the bishop in that area.

Born January 6, 1866, in Moulton, Iowa, after graduation from Garrett Seminary and ordination as elder in the Des Moines Conference, he decided on missionary service in India. He gave his entire life to that land.

He was a very versatile man and had skills in many fields, including a thorough knowledge of printing, architecture, and building, all of which he used to great advantage in India. He likewise had great skills in administration and preaching. He was the master of the simple and memorable sermon. Bishop Robinson was more than once called upon to serve as editor of *The Indian Witness* and did it superbly. His total contribution was very impressive.

After retirement he filled an episcopal vacancy created by the death of Bishop Chitambar. Again retiring, he was called back to serve a period as superintendent of the Delhi district.

Bishop Robinson was the father of Mrs. J. Waskom Pickett. Mrs. Pickett, therefore, had both a father and a husband in the episcopacy. There was a similar situation in the Church, South years ago in the case of Mrs. John J. Tigert, whose father was Bishop Holland N. McTyeire.

CRUSADING FOR A BETTER WORLD

After his third retirement, Bishop Robinson never returned to the United States. He died May 30, 1947, in Naini Tal, a hill station in Uttar Pradesh, India, and is buried at Kaladungi Cemetery, Naini Tal, near the graves of his predecessor, Bishop Edwin W. Parker, and early Methodist pioneers.

He was a much-beloved bishop in India, familiarly known as Bishop J. W., to distinguish him from a former episcopal colleague, Bishop J. E. Robinson, who had also served in India. They were not related. A man of great dignity, Bishop J. W. was a very kind and thoughtful person, and a great man to know as a personal friend.

III

In Defense of the Church and Its Leadership
1948-1952

The General Conference of 1948 met in Boston, at Mechanics Hall, April 28 to May 8, 1948. All the bishops were present except Bishops Badley, Balloch, Darlington, Dobbs, Elphick, Gattinoni, Lacy, Leete, and Miller. This was the last General Conference at which the bishops from China and the Chinese delegates were able to be present. Delegates from Germany and other European countries were able to attend and did. Most of the bishops who were absent were detained because of illness or the infirmities of age. The names of the eight bishops deceased during the previous quadrennium, 1944-1948, were read as the conference stood in silence.

The Episcopal Address was prepared and read by Bishop Oxnam. It dealt vigorously with issues then particularly pertinent in the life of the church and of the world.

The communion service opening the General Conference sessions was led by Bishop Welch.

Devotional messages were brought by Bishops McConnell, Ledden, Kelly, Garber, Brashares, Paul Martin, Mondol, Chen, and Hughes.

Bishops presiding at the sessions were Bishops Kern, Hartman, Baker, Arthur Moore, W. Angie Smith, Shaw, Brashares, Selecman, Straughn, Corson, Paul Martin,

IN DEFENSE OF THE CHURCH AND ITS LEADERSHIP

Harrell, Oxnam, A. Frank Smith, Lowe, H. Lester Smith, Wade, Brooks, William C. Martin, Magee, Holt, and Peele.

The Council of Bishops met as necessary during the General Conference. Bishop James C. Baker was the presiding officer.

At the 1948 Jurisdictional Conferences the following bishops retired:

Northeastern Jurisdiction:	Lewis O. Hartman
	James H. Straughn
North Central Jurisdiction:	Titus Lowe
	H. Lester Smith
	Raymond J. Wade
South Central Jurisdiction:	Charles C. Selecman
Western Jurisdiction:	Wilbur F. Hammaker

Bishop Edwin F. Lee, missionary bishop who had seen service in the Southeast Asia area, also retired.

The 1948 Jurisdictional Conferences saw the election of thirteen new bishops:

Northeastern Jurisdiction:	John Wesley Lord
	Lloyd C. Wicke
North Central Jurisdiction:	H. Clifford Northcott
	Richard C. Raines
	Marshall R. Reed
	Hazen G. Werner
Central Jurisdiction:	John W. E. Bowen
South Central Jurisdiction:	Dana Dawson
Southeastern Jurisdiction:	Marvin A. Franklin
	Roy H. Short
Western Jurisdiction:	Gerald M. Kennedy
	Glenn R. Phillips
	Donald H. Tippett

Bishops Werner, Reed, and Wicke were assigned to the areas from which they were elected, a procedure no longer countenanced by the *Discipline*. All the 1948 elections were the results of deaths or retirement, except in the case of the Southeastern Jurisdiction where the election of an additional bishop was allowed by membership growth; and in the Western Jurisdiction where the election of an additional bishop was allowed under the basic formula for the number of bishops in a jurisdiction. The new areas created in 1948, therefore, were the San Francisco area and the Jacksonville area. No bishop remaining on the active list was changed that year.

During the quadrennium beginning in 1948, Sante U. Barbieri was elected by the Latin America Central Conference; Raymond L. Archer by the Central Conference of Southeast Asia; and José A. Valencia by the Philippines Central Conference.

At the end of the first nine years after union, only sixteen bishops who became bishops of the united church and were assigned to areas in the United States remained in active service. Thus by the end of nine years the council, so far as active members were concerned, was fifty percent new. This was a foreshadowing of future turnover in the active membership of the council.

The original thirty-five active bishops assigned by the Uniting Conference gave a total of 332 years of service, or an average of slightly less than ten years each in the new church. The last of them to remain in active service was Bishop William C. Martin who retired in 1964.

Council meeting: Cincinnati, November 30–December 2, 1948

The first regular meeting of the council for the new quadrennium was held at the Netherland Plaza Hotel, Cincinnati, Ohio, November 30 to December 2, 1948, with Bishop Baker presiding.

The first two days were given to the orientation of the newly elected bishops. The program had been prepared by Bishop Baker. All the bishops present who had seen previous service were assigned parts, and they dealt with many different problems of the office. The orientation idea of Bishop Baker has been followed ever since. At first the orientation sessions were at regular sessions of the council, but beginning in 1964 retreats were held for the new bishops with a limited number of seasoned bishops presenting the program topics. Since 1972 the standing Committee on Pastoral Concerns has been in charge of the orientation experience.

At this meeting the council took notice that the Committee on Un-American Activities of the House of Representatives had issued a report entitled "100 Things You Ought to Know about Communism and Religion," in which the impression was created that the churches had become infiltrated by Communists and that responsible leaders of the churches were following the party line. A resolution was prepared and approved by a committee, of which Bishop Magee was the chairman, which strongly condemned the report. It affirmed that no evidence had been presented for the charges. It also expressed its resentment that false statements were made concerning individuals who had never been interviewed or allowed to refute allegations. It noted that only Protestant organizations were attacked in the report. The council strongly denied that the church was infiltrated by Communism and pointed to paragraphs in the previous Episcopal Address specifically repudiating Communism. The resolution called upon the press and radio to correct the false impression that had been created.

The council took note of the honor that had come to Bishop Oxnam in his being elected one of the presidents of the World Council of Churches at Amsterdam the previous summer.

Council meeting: Buck Hill Falls, December 6-8, 1948

The council met on call at Buck Hill Falls during the meeting of the Board of Missions, December 6-8, 1948.

Bishop Costen J. Harrell presented the Advance for Christ and His Church program. The chief feature of this program was the "Advance Special," which has since remained a part of the economy of the church. The plan envisioned both general Advance Specials and conference-initiated Specials. A week of dedication was called for in which the entire church was asked to give to certain mission projects selected annually. Bishop Harrell was the father of the idea.

At this meeting there was considered, apparently for the first time, the question of preparing a manual for district superintendents. A committee was appointed composed of Bishops Harrell, Magee, and Corson to consider the matter. The question of such a manual has arisen periodically in the council. Beginning in 1972 an annual training conference for new district superintendents has been developed under the auspices of the Committee on Pastoral Concerns of the council.

It was announced that after conference with the Council on World Service travel by air would now be allowed. Automobile mileage was approved at seven cents per mile.

Council meeting: Atlantic City, April 26-30, 1949

The council met at the Hotel Dennis in Atlantic City, April 26-30, 1949, with Bishop Baker presiding.

One of the chief items of consideration was the situation of the church in China. Bishop Carleton Lacy was present and addressed the council at some length and answered questions. In the course of his remarks he read a letter from Bishop Kaung in which the bishop said:

The church must have a vision of a new order of social justice. . . . A church had no right to exist if it does not take up this great task and go on until it is accomplished here and now. . . . The Church in China is weak, weak in its message, weak in its life, weak in its work, weak in its sacrifice. . . . We are all right here and have freedom of faith. . . . A church that is nominal, great in words but small in action with much preaching and little doing, will itself die a natural death.

A statement was adopted authorizing the executive committee to mobilize the church for active opposition to the establishment of diplomatic relationships with the Vatican.

IN DEFENSE OF THE CHURCH AND ITS LEADERSHIP

Plans were perfected for a teaching and preaching mission of the Advance for Christ and His Church, to be held September 29 to November 2, 1949. The general theme was to be "Our Faith." At least two meetings were envisioned in each episcopal area. Addresses were scheduled by two guest bishops, one pastor, one layman, and one laywoman at each meeting. The bishops were thus deployed over the church. The meetings were later reported as having large audiences and being very effective.

A full evening was given to the hearing of reports on overseas visitations, and a pattern was thus established which the council was to follow for some years to come.

Council meeting: New York City, November 30–December 3, 1949

The council met at the Commodore Hotel, New York City, with Bishop Holt presiding.

The entire time was given to a consideration of the subject "The Church and Communism." Nationally known figures addressed the council, including Sherwood Eddy, John C. Bennett, Reinhold Niebuhr, Norman Thomas, Louis Fischer, and Pitirim A. Sorokin.

At the close of the meeting Bishop A. Frank Smith pointed out that an Episcopal Address came only once in four years. At least an annual message was needed from the bishops. This was probably the first lifting up of the idea of periodic messages to the church, a proposal that was handled in various ways in the years ahead.

Council meeting: Cleveland, April 17-21, 1950

The council met at the Hotel Cleveland, Cleveland, Ohio, with Bishop Holt presiding.

A lengthy letter was received from Bishop Ward in China breaking the silence of a year. In it he described how the country had been "liberated" but asserted that "it is too early for comfortable assurance as to what will happen next in

China under the new Democracy." He stated that "there is clear official declaration for freedom of religion but an equally clear emphasis on freedom for anti-religion." Reporting that under the new regime all schools and hospitals would be taken over by the State, he said that there was no objection to the entry of mission money from America. He reported many Christians as holding strongly to their faith and that there were still sixty-four American Methodist missionaries in the Shanghai area. Bishop Ward affirmed that the missionaries would remain until they were forced out or until their Chinese colleagues judged it best for them to leave.

The bishops found much of the church disturbed over charges of Communist infiltration in Methodism. The charge became first-page news in many papers.

Organizations of Methodist conservatives were formed, such as the Circuit Riders, based in Cincinnati, and the Committee for the Preservation of Methodism, based in Houston. Independent papers, such as Bob Shuler's *Methodist Challenge,* joined in the charges of Communist infiltration. The Methodist Federation for Social Action came under particular attack. The fact that it was an independent body, over which the church had no control, did not seem to register with many people.

The battle became particularly hot in Illinois, in Ohio, and in Texas. Bishop Frank Smith, who had been the idol of many strong conservative Texas businessmen, found himself under the necessity to defend the church against reckless charges that were being made on every hand.

In February, 1950, *Reader's Digest* published an article by one of its editors, Stanley High, entitled "Methodism's Pink Fringe." High had been in his younger days a nationally known and honored youth leader in Methodism, and was a Methodist minister's son. The article directly attacked positions taken by the Methodist Federation for Social Action, but indirectly attacked the church also. It pointed out that the offices of the federation were in the Methodist

IN DEFENSE OF THE CHURCH AND ITS LEADERSHIP

Building in New York City and that the executive secretary was a member of a Methodist Annual Conference and whose character and administration had to be approved by that conference.

The article created a furor throughout the church. Bishops, district superintendents, and pastors were called upon on every hand for an explanation. Individuals and congregations in increasing numbers threatened to withdraw support. Bishop Oxnam wrote a reply to the article, but *Reader's Digest* refused to publish it.

The bishops recommended to the federation membership that the word "Methodist" be dropped from its title. This the federation refused to do. The council also took exception to certain statements that had recently been published in the federation's "Bulletin."

Some of the bishops who had been members of the federation for years, including Bishop Welch who had been one of the founders, now withdrew from membership, either because they could not agree with some positions the federation had taken, or because they could not accept the federation's executive leadership. Others continued their membership, such as Bishop Hartman and Bishop Love.

Bishops Kern and Ledden were appointed to prepare a statement on John T. Flynn's book *The Road Ahead*. The council adopted a statement that the book was full of errors and misrepresentations.

Bishops Reed, Magee, and Brashares were appointed a Committee on a Methodist Foundation. This item was to appear on agendas for some time to come.

Bishop Kern was elected to prepare the Episcopal Address to the 1952 General Conference.

The council endorsed Senator Brien McMahon's proposal that ten billion dollars be diverted annually from war budgets and devoted to world prosperity and peace. In addition to this action there would be concurrence on restraint in the development of thermonuclear weapons and a drastic reduction in expenditures for armaments.

HISTORY OF THE COUNCIL OF BISHOPS

Council meeting: New York City, December 4-7, 1950

The council met at the McAlpin Hotel in New York City, December 4-7, 1950, with Bishop Magee presiding.

The 1948 General Conference had asked the Council of Bishops to nominate a committee to study the desirability of forming a Commission on Social Action and Industrial Relations. Composed of one minister and one layman from each jurisdiction, the committee was to report to the Council of Bishops within two years and the council was authorized to take such action as it deemed wise. The committee recommended unanimously that the church should establish such a commission. The ultimate issue of the matter was the establishment of what is now the Board of Social Concerns.

Dr. John O. Gross suggested a program of two-day visitations to all the campuses of the church by the bishops, each bishop to visit campuses other than those of his own area. The suggestion was approved, and all the active bishops joined in the visitation.

Council meeting: Grand Canyon, April 23-27, 1951

The Council of Bishops met at Bright Angel Lodge, Grand Canyon, Arizona, April 23-27, 1951, with Bishop Magee presiding.

Word was received that Bishop Chen had been forced to start on a "program of reeducation" and that no one would be allowed to see him during this period. Word was also received that at the request of friends in North China Bishop Kaung had returned there.

The council heard an encouraging report on the Japan International Christian University, a project in which it had been much interested since its inception.

A communication was received from the Dover district of the Delaware Conference expressing deep concern over racial segregation in Methodism. The communication was

IN DEFENSE OF THE CHURCH AND ITS LEADERSHIP

in fine spirit and presented its argument effectively. The council received it with appreciation. It was an early presentation of a subject to which the church is still addressing itself.

Council meeting: Atlantic City, January 10-14, 1952

The Council of Bishops met at the Hotel Dennis, Atlantic City, January 10-14, 1952, with Bishop Arthur J. Moore presiding.

Much of the time was spent considering the Episcopal Address and arranging for the coming General Conference.

The Committee on a Methodist Bookshelf made its report. The committee was composed of Bishop Reed, Chairman, and Bishops Bowen, Garber, Kennedy, Lord, and William C. Martin. The committee recommended a set of ten to twelve books, of about two hundred pages each, to sell for two dollars per volume. It was suggested that the volumes include both reprints of earlier works and newly written books. Among proposed subjects were the life of Christ; the life of Paul; history of Methodism; techniques of the spiritual life; the message of Methodism; Methodist personalities; Christian social problems. The idea of the Bookshelf was approved by the council but never was realized.

In Memoriam—1948-1952

During the 1948-1952 quadrennium seven bishops entered the life eternal:
>Brenton T. Badley
>John C. Broomfield
>Edwin Holt Hughes
>G. Carleton Lacy
>Edwin F. Lee
>John M. Moore
>H. Lester Smith

HISTORY OF THE COUNCIL OF BISHOPS

Brenton Thoburn Badley
(1876–1949)

Brenton T. Badley was born in Gonda, Uttar Pradesh, India, May 29, 1876, the son of missionary parents who had gone to India in 1872. He became a missionary himself in 1900.

At the 1924 General Conference he was elected a bishop. From 1924 to 1936 he was bishop of the Bombay area, covering also Gujerat, Hyderabad, and Southern India. From 1936 to 1940 he covered the Delhi area, comprising the North India and Indus River Conferences as well as Delhi.

Bishop Badley was a master of both the Hindi and Urdu languages, especially Urdu, in which he was completely eloquent. Although he impressed one as very dignified in his episcopal office, he had a marvelous human and lighter side to him and a great sense of humor. He was a master at telling stories and kept his audience in rapt attention with stories of Indian history and mythology. His knowledge and interest in the Himalaya mountains, through which he had trekked extensively, was remarkable. On this subject he was an authority.

Bishop Badley was strongly committed to evangelism and was a very effective churchman. He was the author of twelve books.

After the death of Mrs. Badley he lived for a time with his daughter, Mrs. Samuel Burgoyne (Mary Esther) and her husband, a British missionary, in Mirzapur, where he died February 1, 1949.

John Calvin Broomfield
(1872–1950)

John C. Broomfield was elected to the episcopacy by the delegates from the Methodist Protestant Church at the Uniting Conference in Kansas City in 1939. He was at the time the president of the Methodist Protestant Church. He was assigned to the St. Louis area, where he served for five years.

Bishop Broomfield was born in Eyemouth, Scotland, July 4, 1872. As a youth he was a cabin boy on a sailing vessel. After his career as sailor he came to the United States. In 1891 he entered the ministry of the Methodist Protestant Church and in time came to fill some of its strongest pulpits.

He was a short man, full of energy and enthusiasm, with a sparkle in his eyes. He was an effective and vigorous preacher who held his audiences captive as he preached. He was particularly effective in evangelism and continued in great demand for special services not only during his active years but also throughout the six years of his retirement. He was a literal embodiment of the warmth of the gospel.

He died January 8, 1950, and is buried in Fairmont, West Virginia.

Edwin Holt Hughes
(1866–1950)

Edwin Holt Hughes, born December 7, 1866, in Moundsville, West Virginia, was elected to the episcopacy by the Methodist Episcopal Church in 1908 and served the San Francisco, Chicago, Boston, and Washington areas. There have been few bishops in Methodism more widely known or more greatly loved than Bishop Hughes.

He was primarily a preacher, and the pulpit was his throne. He was dramatic in his preaching, able by his deep humanness to move audiences to both laughter and tears. His sermons were unforgettable.

During the days when Methodist union was under consideration, he became the evangelist of union; particularly in the South he made thousands of friends for union. He delivered the closing address at the Uniting Conference, and no more appropriate choice could have been made, either from the viewpoint of ability or of past contribution.

Bishop Hughes was delightful company. He had a rare sense of humor which sometimes got away with him, and on occasion got him into trouble as a result of some unplanned, laughable remark. There was a certain boyishness about him down to the very end. He delighted particularly in teasing his more staid brethren. Often when a colleague was scheduled to speak, he would approach him and say slyly, "I am going to hear you if it kills me."

The bishop was a strong leader in the council, as he had been in the Board of Bishops before union. In retirement he continued to take the floor without apology. His remarks were incisive, and his colleagues recognized that he possessed wisdom and skill from which all of them could profit.

At the memorial service at the meeting of the council following the death of Bishop Hughes, the tribute to him was brought by Bishop McConnell. It will never be forgot by those who heard it. They had been close friends for many years. Bishop McConnell rambled back across the years, recounting experiences they had shared together. Finally he said, "I had to miss the meeting of the council last time. I wanted to see Ed. There were some things I wanted to talk to him about." Then looking over his glasses in typical McConnell style, he added, "But that can wait." And with those impressive words he took his seat.

Bishop Hughes died February 12, 1950, and is buried on the campus of DePauw University, Greencastle, Indiana, where he had served so ably as president before his election to the episcopacy.

George Carleton Lacy
(1888–1951)

Born December 28, 1888, in Foochow, China, G. Carleton Lacy was elected to the episcopacy by the China Central Conference. He was a member of a well-known and large missionary family embracing several generations of missionaries.

He served as pastor, district superintendent, and school principal for many years. He was the author of several books and wrote extensively for the church press. His son continues as a professor at Duke University.

IN DEFENSE OF THE CHURCH AND ITS LEADERSHIP

When the Communist government took over the country and other missionaries were forced to leave China, Bishop Lacy was refused an exit permit. He was kept under surveillance and house arrest until his death of a heart attack December 11, 1951.

He was buried in Foochow next to his parents in the mission cemetery. By Communist orders no one was allowed to attend his funeral except his devoted cook.

Edwin Ferdinand Lee
(1884–1948)

Edwin F. Lee was elected to the episcopacy by the Methodist Episcopal Church in 1928 and assigned as a missionary bishop.

Born July 10, 1884, in Eldorado, Iowa, he was a member of the Upper Iowa Conference, but decided to invest his life in missionary service. He was sent to Batavia, Java, but also served in Malaya, the Philippines, and Singapore.

From 1919 to 1924 he was associate secretary of the Board of Foreign Missions in New York. After his election to the episcopacy he was assigned to care for the work in the Philippines and Malaya until his retirement in 1948. He was one of the great missionary statesman bishops.

During World War II Bishop and Mrs. Lee were evacuated from Singapore along with some fifty other missionaries just hours before the Japanese armies took over the city. When he could no longer administer his area, the Council of Bishops assigned him to special responsibilities with the Commission on Chaplains.

After the war he was able to return to Malaya and the Philippines, where he took up the task of rehabilitation. He died September 14, 1948, and is buried in Fayette, Iowa.

John Monroe Moore
(1867–1948)

The Methodist Episcopal Church, South elected John M. Moore to the episcopacy in 1918. Born January 27, 1867, in

Morgantown, Kentucky, his pastoral ministry was spent in Missouri and Texas. He was unusually well educated for his day, attending Yale, Leipzig, and Heidelberg Universities. He received a Ph.D. degree from Yale. He was ordained local deacon by Bishop Charles Fowler of the Northern Church while a student at Yale.

As a young preacher he served three of the strongest churches of Southern Methodism in a row: Travis Park, San Antonio; First Church, Dallas; and St. John's, St. Louis. At his first year at Travis Park Church he was not eligible to serve the sacrament since he had not yet been ordained an elder.

In 1910 he became Home Mission secretary of the Church, South and served in that position until elected bishop.

His episcopal assignments included Brazil, Texas, Oklahoma and New Mexico, Georgia and Florida, Missouri and Arkansas. As a bishop he introduced what he called the open cabinet, which was something new at that time in the Church, South. He made himself available for interviews during the Annual Conference. He would announce that any preacher at any time during the session could know exactly how he was listed in the appointments. He was almost unmovable, however, if a preacher did not like the appointment planned for him.

Bishop Moore was a little giant. He was only five feet, five inches tall, but was a man of iron will. He had no toleration for what he used to call "flabbiness," and he could express his indignation in scorching words and often did. He did not hesitate to take issue with his episcopal colleagues. He was one of those who challenged and helped to break down the seniority system which had persisted among the Southern bishops for many years. Nevertheless, when the day came when he had seniority, he felt quite strongly that some due attention should be paid to it. He was an exceedingly courageous man and did not hesitate to do what he thought was right at whatever cost.

Bishop Moore was not a popular preacher. His sermons

were carefully thought out and had solid meat in them, but they did not have the warmth of popular preaching in them. The bishop had no use for what he regarded as "emotional preaching."

The beginning days of Methodist union represented an era of good feeling. There was a strong desire in each part of the new church to recognize the other part. The trustees of Des Plaines Campground in Illinois, sharing this feeling, decided to invite a Southern Methodist to hold the camp meeting. Not knowing the South, they asked someone from that section who would be a good camp-meeting preacher, and the reply was, "Bishop Moore." The respondent had in mind Bishop Arthur Moore, who was a fervent preacher and had been in his early days a professional evangelist. Not knowing there were two Bishop Moores, the trustees wrote Bishop John Moore, and he accepted the invitation. Bishop John Moore was quiet, measured, didactic, and unemotional in his preaching. After a few nights the trustees met in conference and said, "Who was it that thought this bishop was a camp-meeting preacher?"

Bishop Moore was primarily a church statesman. He took leadership in whatever committee or commissions of which he was a part. He always did his homework and went to every meeting fully prepared, having anticipated what might come up. He had a habit of writing down his possible contribution on a bit of paper kept in his pocket. When the discussion would reach an impasse, he would reach in his pocket and bring out his paper. Again and again it would be accepted as the solution to the problem.

He was always sure of himself and was fully independent in his life-style. A frugal man, despite his constant traveling, he always took an upper berth because it was less expensive. For many years he stayed at the same hotel when in Nashville. The time came when the hotel began to decline, and finally its reputation became none too good. Someone upbraided him and said, "Bishop, you ought to quit staying at that hotel as it isn't a first-class hotel any longer." He replied calmly, "When I write John M. Moore upon the register of a hotel, it becomes a first-class hotel."

Bishop Moore was a liberal for his day and was ecumenically ahead of his time. His absorbing interest for many years was in Methodist union, and he was one of its chief architects. Some of the features of the structure of which he was once so sure have now become considerably eroded and even radically altered with the passing of only forty years. Perhaps the high watermark of life for him was the Uniting Conference in which he played so prominent and significant a role.

He lived to see nine years of membership in the Council of Bishops and died August 1, 1948, in Dallas, Texas, where he is buried.

Harry Lester Smith
(1876–1951)

In 1920 the Methodist Episcopal Church elected H. Lester Smith to the episcopacy. He served the Bangalore, India, area, as well as the Helena, Chattanooga, and Cincinnati areas. For some years he was secretary of the Board of Bishops of the Methodist Episcopal Church. For its first year after the Uniting Conference, he was also secretary of the Council of Bishops.

Bishop Smith was born April 15, 1876, in Indiana, Pennsylvania. He was a rigorous, manly type of person and was a fine athlete. He had a happy, rollicking disposition with a fine sense of humor. His company was always pleasant—he enjoyed companionship and always had time for a good chat. He took his administrative tasks in stride and never let them overwhelm him.

Bishop Smith never forgot the years in India and seldom preached a sermon thereafter without making some reference to them.

On one occasion when he was to preach for Dr. John Gross, Dr. Gross said to his little boy, "You listen carefully and if the bishop doesn't mention India I will give you a dollar." The lad got a front row seat and listened intently. After the bishop had preached for half an hour with no word of his favorite topic, the boy thought he had the dollar made. But as the bishop reached his climax, he said, "When I was in India . . ." The boy slouched in his seat, feeling the bishop had let him down. Without realizing what he was doing, he blurted out, "Doggone!"

Bishop Smith retired in 1948 and died of a heart attack suffered on a Sunday morning, October 7, 1951. He was buried in Spring Grove Cemetery, Cincinnati, Ohio.

IV

Toward Full Rights for All People
1952–1956

The 1952 General Conference met in San Francisco, April 23 to May 6.

The communion service with which the conference opened was in charge of Bishop Herbert Welch. Grateful tribute was paid to those of the body who had passed on during the last quadrennium, 1948–1952, including seven bishops of the church.

The Episcopal Address was prepared and read by Bishop Paul B. Kern. It was well written and eloquent, and it took the bishop more than two hours to read. Along toward the end he had included the verse from the Gospels, "Rise, let us be going." As he read this, the conference broke into laughter, which took the bishop by surprise.

In its consideration of the Episcopal Address at its meeting prior to the General Conference, the council followed the procedure of calling the roll of bishops alphabetically and letting each bishop make suggestions for any change. The procedure was lengthy and cumbersome and most trying on the author, who had spent long months in its preparation. Bishop Kern was greatly disappointed when what he regarded as an important part of his proposed section, dealing with the question of the Central Jurisdiction in the life and functioning of the church, was eliminated. This elimination was largely upon the joint

TOWARD FULL RIGHTS FOR ALL PEOPLE

recommendation of the Central Jurisdiction bishops and all the Southeastern bishops, except Bishop Kern himself and two other colleagues. The elimination, in Bishop Kern's judgment, watered down the original proposal. One wonders to what extent things would have been different had Bishop Kern's view fully registered in that earlier day in the life of the church.

Devotional messages were brought by Bishops Lord, Kennedy, Kelly, Franklin, W. Angie Smith, Short, Subhan, Wicke, Brashares, Shaw, and Tippett.

The bishops presiding at the General Conference were Bishops Corson, Tippett, Arthur Moore, William C. Martin, Baker, Paul Martin, Shaw, Cushman, Oxnam, Purcell, A. Frank Smith, Garber, Raines, Magee, Harrell, Phillips, W. Angie Smith, Reed, Kern, Kennedy, and Holt.

Council meeting: General Conference, San Francisco, April 23–May 6

The council met periodically on call of the president, Bishop Arthur J. Moore, during the General Conference. It rejoiced in the fact that Bishop Moore's life had recently been spared when a plane in which he was a passenger crashed in a field in Kansas.

During the General Conference Bishop Fred P. Corson, the newly elected president, assumed his duties.

The council in these sessions gave considerable attention to a survey report which had been ordered by the previous General Conference and had been made by a commercial firm. The council found itself out of agreement with many of the recommendations of the report. The same was true of the general agencies. The 1952 General Conference modified the report to a large extent.

The General Conference approved a Youth Emphasis as a program for the new quadrennium. The council welcomed this and appointed Bishop John Wesley Lord to lead the emphasis, with Bishops Bowen, Voight, Paul Martin, Kennedy, and Short to assist him.

HISTORY OF THE COUNCIL OF BISHOPS

Bishop Ralph Ward turned the attention of the council to the twenty million Chinese living in Free China and elsewhere in the free world and suggested that a concern for them would be in order. He stated that the church in Communist China continued, though under great handicaps. Bishop Ward's plea was heard, and thus was born a new interest in Formosa, Hong Kong, and elsewhere with concentrations of Chinese. Thousands of Chinese Methodists had fled the mainland of China, and these became the nucleus of new congregations and afforded leadership for new enterprises.

The council assigned Bishop Ward to Hong Kong to supervise the Free China work. He served until his death, whereupon Bishop Arthur J. Moore, Bishop Richard Raines, Bishop Angie Smith, and Bishop Fred Corson each served for a one-year period. From 1964 to 1968 Bishop Hazen Werner supervised the work; from 1968 to 1972 retired Bishop Otto Nall took up residence in Hong Kong and served until the autonomous church came into being.

At the Jurisdictional Conferences of 1952 the following bishops retired:

North Central: Bishop J. Ralph Magee
                 Bishop Ralph S. Cushman

They had been elected together in 1936 and were often referred to as "the two Ralphs."

South Central: Bishop Charles C. Selecman
Southeast: Bishop Paul B. Kern
Western: Bishop James C. Baker
Central: Bishop Edward W. Kelly
           Bishop Alexander P. Shaw
Northeast: Bishop Charles W. Flint

Nine new bishops were elected at the 1952 Jurisdictional Conferences and took their places in the council at its fall meeting:

Central: Bishop Matthew W. Clair, Jr.
           Bishop Edgar A. Love
Northeastern: Bishop Frederick B. Newell
Southeastern: Bishop John W. Branscomb

TOWARD FULL RIGHTS FOR ALL PEOPLE

South Central: Bishop Henry B. Watts
North Central: Bishop D. Stanley Coors
Bishop F. Gerald Ensley
Bishop Edwin E. Voight
Western: Bishop A. Raymond Grant

Bishops Branscomb, Clair, Coors, Grant, and Watts all died while in active service. Bishop Ensley died only a few months after retirement. Bishop Newell died in 1979. No other class of bishops since union saw as many bishops die in active service as did the class of 1952.

Bishop Branscomb and Bishop Newell had the distinction of being assigned to the areas from which they were elected and where each was highly popular.

Of the entire 1952 group only Bishops Ensley, Coors, Love, and Clair occupied the chair at a General Conference.

Shortly after the new quadrennium began, Friedrich Wunderlich, Odd A. Hagen, Julio M. Sabanes, and Ferdinand Sigg were elected by Central Conferences.

Council meeting: Atlantic City, November 17-21, 1952

The Council of Bishops met at Atlantic City, November 17-21, 1952, with Bishop Corson presiding.

A service of orientation for the newly elected bishops in which all the bishops participated occupied a full day.

One evening was given to a dinner celebrating the ninetieth birthday of Bishop Herbert Welch. Bishop Baker and Bishop McConnell spoke, and Bishop Welch made happy response.

In making his response Bishop Welch said, "I think tonight I can tell you something that I have kept secret for many years." Then he went on to say, "When I was being considered for the presidency of Ohio Wesleyan, the committee wrote to my good friend, Frank McConnell, to ask, 'What do you think of young Dr. Welch?' He wrote back, so they let me know, 'If you want refined inefficiency, here is your man.' " The surprised look upon the face of Bishop McConnell was beyond description.

Bishop Welch was to live and be active for yet another sixteen years.

Council meeting: Omaha, Nebraska, April 28–May 1, 1953

The council met at the Hotel Fontinelle, Omaha, Nebraska, April 28 to May 1, 1953, with Bishop Corson presiding. Bishop Watts was the host bishop.

A change was made in the former pattern of dividing annually the entire council between the Committee on Reference and the Committee on Law and Administration. Each committee was reduced to one bishop for each jurisdiction and functioned for the quadrennium.

Out of a concern for a strong educational institution in the national capital, the council had shown interest for some time in the further development of American University, which had been founded by Bishop John Fletcher Hurst. The 1952 General Conference had allocated $100,000 annually to the operation of the institution. Bishop Oxnam reported that proper steps had been taken to vest the institution in the church and to provide that all trustees be approved by the Board of Education. He reported also that steps had been taken to move Westminister Seminary to the campus and that plans for a School of International Service had been developed. The council appointed a committee to consider possible proposals regarding the university for presentation to the next General Conference.

This session of the council issued a call for a Convocation on Urban Life on motion of Bishop Glenn R. Phillips.

The council adopted a statement read by Bishop Costen J. Harrell defending the leadership of the church. The background of the paper was the accusation made against Bishop Oxnam when he had recently effectively defended himself before the House Committee on Un-American Activities.

Bishop Oxnam was one of a group of outstanding religious leaders who were the targets of the loose and wild charges that marked the Senator Joseph McCarthy era in American history. It is interesting to note that the statement adopted by the council in defense of Bishop Oxnam and others was written by Bishop Harrell, who was himself a social conservative but who knew full well that Bishop Oxnam's social liberalism in no sense even remotely bordered on Communism.

Council meeting: Epworth-by-the-Sea, Georgia, December 8-11, 1953

The council met at Epworth-by-the-Sea, December 8-11, with Bishop William C. Martin presiding.

This was the first time for the council to meet at a place other than at a hotel. Epworth-by-the-Sea is a facility owned by the South Georgia and North Georgia Conferences. It is located near Frederica, where John Wesley exercised his ministry in America in 1736. The council visited some of the sites connected with Wesley, including an ancient oak tree under which he is reported to have preached.

Bishop Arthur Moore was the host for this meeting of the council, and he and Methodists of Georgia were lavish in the entertainment which they provided. Included was a visit to an old plantation house, with supper in the yard by the light of flares. There was oyster-shucking and corn chowder antebellum style, and entertainment by a group of local Negro singers who gave a program of songs long traditional among the black people of that coastal section and largely unknown elsewhere.

Bishop Alexander P. Shaw was named to take over the Texas Conferences of the New Orleans area following the death of Bishop Robert N. Brooks; and Bishop Willis King took over the Mississippi Conferences in addition to his assignment in Liberia.

Most of the business of this session was of a routine character. The fact that all were living together on a relatively small assembly grounds afforded an unusual opportunity for episcopal family fellowship.

HISTORY OF THE COUNCIL OF BISHOPS

Council meeting: New York, April 26-30, 1954

The council met at the Beekman Towers, New York City, April 26-30, 1954, with Bishop William C. Martin presiding.

This meeting was primarily occupied with visits to the United Nations and addresses by members of that body. It was addressed by Secretary General Dag Hammarskjold, as well as by Benjamin Cohen, Andres Cordier, Ralph Bunche, and John P. Humphrey.

The council released a statement to the church in which it pointed to the dual importance of the World Council of Churches and of the United Nations.

Council meeting: Chicago, November 18-21, 1954

The council met at the Palmer House, Chicago, with Bishop Brashares presiding.

It took note of the Supreme Court decision of May 17, 1954, outlawing segregation in the public schools. It received with appreciation a letter from a group of Methodist students meeting at Junaluska applauding the decision and expressing concern regarding the response of the church. The council adopted a statement that the "historic decision of the Supreme Court abolishing segregation in the public school system is in keeping with the attitude of The Methodist Church." It recognized that time would be necessary for the implementation of the decision and held that the church had a responsibility for leadership in this period.

In the course of the discussion the Southeastern bishops affirmed their acceptance of the court's decision as being in harmony with the pronouncements of The Methodist Church. Likewise they affirmed that their purpose was to lead their people to a Christian attitude and an orderly adjustment to the changes involved. However, they stated that a statement by the council at this time would make their task more difficult. The judgment of the council as a whole, however, was that a statement was imperative.

TOWARD FULL RIGHTS FOR ALL PEOPLE

The council considered a paper by Bishop Oxnam concerning a possible movement to undergird Christian education through greater emphasis upon the church school and upon higher education, and through the establishment of a School of International Service at Washington. After lengthy discussion the paper was approved and passed to the coordinating council for consideration as a possible program for the next quadrennium. Bishops Oxnam, Harrell, Paul Martin, and Short were named as a committee to confer with the coordinating council on the matter.

Council meeting: Seattle, April 19-21, 1955

The Council of Bishops met at the Olympia Hotel, Seattle, April 19-21, with Bishop Brashares presiding.

Bishop Grant introduced a proposal for the establishment of a university in Alaska. The council took the position that support should be given through Advance Specials without conference or church quotas.

The council took action at this meeting requesting that the decisions of the Judicial Council be in standard format, preferably in bound volumes.

Bishop Oxnam moved that Bishop Lord be requested to prepare a ritual for a funeral service for a deceased bishop and to report at the next session. Later Bishop Lord reported that it would be inadvisable in his judgment to prepare a separate order. There the matter ended.

The council voted to request the General Conference to amend the *Discipline* so that all effective bishops would serve both on the Board of Missions and on the Board of Education.

Bishop Oxnam asked to be relieved as secretary, but the council asked him to continue through the General Conference period.

The bishops of the Central Jurisdiction invited the bishops of the South Central and Southeastern Jurisdictions to meet with them to discuss issues related to integration. The invitation was gladly accepted.

HISTORY OF THE COUNCIL OF BISHOPS

In Memoriam—1952-1956

Robert N. Brooks
U. V. W. Darlington
Hoyt M. Dobbs
Lewis O. Hartman
Frederick T. Keeney
Paul B. Kern
Francis J. McConnell
J. W. Ernst Sommer

As one contemplates the eight bishops whose careers came to an end during the 1952-1956 quadrennium, one is forced to say, "What a group!" They were indeed some of the strongest episcopal leaders Methodism has had in the last century. Moreover, they represented a study in both contrasts and similarities—Keeney, a rather typical Northerner, and Dobbs, typical of the older deep South; Hartman, the Northern liberal, and Kern, the new liberal of the South; Brooks, the strong leader of the black membership in the United States, and Sommer, a strong leader in Central Conference work overseas; Darlington, the conservative and the evangelist, and McConnell, the liberal and the social gospel advocate.

The oneness of the Methodist episcopacy, despite personal differences, was dramatized by the fact that at Bishop McConnell's burial at Lucasville, Ohio, Bishop Darlington came from his home in Huntington, which was not far away. It was the only occasion involving the episcopacy where Bishop Darlington appeared after his retirement. Other bishops present were Bishop Newell of New York, who was in charge of the services, Bishop Ensley, the bishop's nephew, and Bishop Lowe, who was a longtime associate.

Robert Nathaniel Brooks
(1888-1953)

Robert N. Brooks was elected by the Central Jurisdiction in 1944 and served his entire episcopacy in the New Orleans area. Prior to his election Bishop Brooks had been the editor of *The Central Christian Advocate* for twelve years; prior to that he had been professor of church history at Gammon Seminary for twelve years.

Born May 8, 1888, in Hollis, North Carolina, Bishop Brooks was impressive in his appearance. He was tall, always immaculate in dress, dignified and deliberate in his movements. He was the perfect gentleman, but he could be firm when he chose to be. There were those who sometimes thought him too firm in administration.

He was ever the defender of his people and spoke out without apology against anything that he felt savored of racism. He had the high confidence and respect of his episcopal brethren.

Bishop Brooks died August 2, 1953, in Waveland, Mississippi.

Urban Valentine William Darlington
(1870–1954)

U. V. W. Darlington was the last of the old-style Southern bishops. Born August 3, 1870, in Graefenburg, Shelby County, Kentucky, he had been elected to the episcopacy by the Methodist Episcopal Church, South in 1918.

He was tall, straight, bald, with great searching eyes that were most eloquent in their power of expression. He was primarily an evangelist, and he loved to call people to the altar. A highly gifted preacher, he usually preached with his open Testament in his hand, and he had no equal in his ability to read the Scriptures. His inflection, pauses, and facial expression made the Bible come alive. In his preaching he either soared to the heights and carried the congregation with him, or failed noticeably. He had a rich tenor voice and often would break into song in the course of a message. His favorite song seemed to be "Pass Me Not, O Gentle Savior." Singing it, his tenor would reach a climax, particularly as he came to the haunting words of the chorus, "Saviour, Saviour, hear my humble cry."

As an administrator, Bishop Darlington followed the methods of the older bishops in the Church, South. His appointments were not made until the conference was in session, and they were kept secret to the time they were read. Sometimes he kept his cabinets in confusion, and they did not know what his final decisions would be until the last. On one occasion one of his superintendents observed to Bishop Kern that it seemed to him in the cabinet that sometimes Bishop Darlington did not know where he was going. Bishop Kern, who knew his method, replied quietly, "He always knows where he is going, no matter how confused an impression he may make."

Bishop Darlington was not enthusiastic about Methodist union. He accepted it as inevitable and went along with it quietly. He was the only one of the older Southern bishops who saw a period of active service in the new Methodist Church. He had been serving the Louisville area and continued to serve it for five more years. He ignored the expectations of the General Conference for the bishop to live in his area. Not only did he not live in his area, but he did not even live in the Southeastern Jurisdiction. Huntington, West Virginia, his home, was in the Northeastern Jurisdiction.

Bishop Darlington was a moody and deeply emotional man. Following his retirement in 1944, he never again attended a meeting of the Council of Bishops, or of the General Conference, or of the Southeastern Jurisdictional Conference, although at times his health would have permitted such attendance. He found it difficult to adjust to change and in his late days used to say, sadly, "The church I loved is dead."

Bishop Darlington had some unusual habits. One of them was that he would never say "goodbye." Instead he would end every visit with the words, "I will see you again." Those who loved him expect his words to be realized for them and for him "when the morning breaks eternal, bright, and fair."

He died October 1, 1954, and is buried at Frankfort, Kentucky.

TOWARD FULL RIGHTS FOR ALL PEOPLE

Hoyt McWhorter Dobbs
(1878–1954)

Hoyt M. Dobbs was elected in 1922 to the episcopacy by the General Conference of the Methodist Episcopal Church, South. He served first in Brazil and subsequently in Alabama, Florida, Louisiana and Arkansas, and Mississippi.

He was from Alabama, born November 16, 1878, in Antioch, Cherokee County. He served in the pastorate in Alabama most effectively. For a period he was also a professor at Southern Methodist University.

Bishop Dobbs was a tall, thin, bald-headed man who normally wore a cutaway. Perhaps he was the most formal of the bishops of his time.

He was always soft spoken. Every word was carefully measured and every action deliberately taken. Polite to a fault, he called all the preachers "Doctor." His father was a leader in the North Alabama Conference. When Bishop Dobbs was appointed to hold the conference, he found his father in the cabinet. Invariably in the cabinet he addressed him as "Dr. Dobbs," and in his dealings with him as presiding elder gave no visible indication of the fact that they were father and son.

When Bishop Paul Martin was a young preacher, he had Bishop Dobbs as a teacher. When Bishop Martin was elected bishop, he met Bishop Dobbs who addressed him as "Bishop Martin." Bishop Martin said, "Please call me Paul as you always have." Bishop Dobbs replied, "Yes, Bishop Martin."

Bishop Dobbs did not enjoy good health, and the late years of his active episcopacy were taxing for him. He had the high respect of all who knew him and will always be remembered by them as an ideal Christian gentleman.

He died December 10, 1954, in Shreveport, Louisiana, and is buried there.

Lewis Oliver Hartman
(1876–1955)

The Northeastern Jurisdiction of The Methodist Church elected Lewis O. Hartman to the episcopacy in 1944. He had served for twenty-four years as the distinguished editor of *Zion's Herald,* a widely circulated and important Methodist paper based in Boston. Dr. Hartman was an outstanding leader of New England Methodism. His first and only assignment was to the Boston area, from which he came, though he was born in LaGrange, Indiana, May 3, 1876. Because of the age at which he was elected, he was able to give only one quadrennium of active service. He lived seven years after retirement, dying June 30, 1955, in Newton, Massachusetts, where he is buried.

Bishop Hartman was a thin, wiry man who was quick in all his movements. He had penetrating eyes, a quiet manner, and a smile that his critics often found disarming. He was a pronounced social liberal, forever expressing his convictions in editorials and on the conference floor. He took leadership in opposing Methodist union because of his inability to accept with good conscience the plan of union at the point of its provision for setting up the Negro work in a separate jurisdiction.

He was active in the Methodist Federation for Social Action and was its president for three years of his episcopacy. He was particularly interested in granting the fullest freedom to the church overseas from United States domination. No one made greater contribution to the development of the legislation providing for Central Conferences than did he, and no bishop since Methodist union in 1939 has represented the reformer type in the ministry more completely than did Bishop Hartman.

Bishop Hartman was served by a wonderful secretary throughout his career as editor as well as during his quadrennium as an active bishop. She was Miss Ida M. Moody. Miss Moody was a typical representative of New England womanhood at its best and an honors graduate of Boston University. She was very meticulous, demonstrating thorough mastery of good English. It was said of her that during all her years of proofreading for *Zion's Herald* there were no grammatical or typographical errors. She was not above correcting the grammar of the several bishops she served. While taking dictation, she might say: "Would that perhaps be better expressed this way . . . ?"

This book is about bishops and the Council of Bishops. Behind many of them, however, were such colleagues as Miss Moody—overworked, underpaid, and devoted to their work as a ministry.

Frederick Thomas Keeney
(1863–1952)

Frederick T. Keeney was elected to the episcopacy by the Methodist Episcopal Church in 1920 after a distinguished career as a pastor in New York state, where he was born February 9, 1863, in Fabius. He had given outstanding leadership also as executive secretary of the Methodist Centenary for the Methodist Episcopal Church. His episcopal assignments were the Foochow, China; Omaha; and Atlanta areas.

Bishop Keeney had the gift of organization. He was an acknowledged leader in the period when there was strong emphasis upon what was then termed "church efficiency." He took leadership in the development of the Million Unit Fellowship, which was something that was popular for a while, on the order of the original Methodist class system, revised and applied to the modern day of his time.

Bishop Keeney retired in 1940 and made his home with his daughter in Miami. In his late years he became an invalid and was confined to his room. He was kind, patient, and bore his infirmities with a brave spirit. His strong interest in what was happening in the life of the church continued to the end. He realized things were changing and that the problems of the church and world were different from those in the days of his active ministry.

The writer, after his own election to the episcopacy in 1948, visited Bishop Keeney in his home in Miami. As the time came to separate, his last words were, "I am willing for those of you who are younger to face the new problems that have to be faced in the new day."

Bishop Keeney died September 24, 1952, and is buried in Oakwood Cemetery, Syracuse, New York.

Paul Bentley Kern
(1882–1953)

Paul B. Kern, born June 16, 1882, in Alexandria, Virginia, was elected to the episcopacy by the Methodist Episcopal Church, South in 1930, at the same time as Bishop Arthur Moore.

The two had served as pastors of Travis Park in San Antonio, and their paths had crossed in other ways as well. Generally speaking, the coming of Bishop Arthur Moore into the College of Bishops was welcomed by the conservative bishops such as Bishop Ainsworth, who was largely his father in the gospel, Bishop Candler, and Bishop Darlington. The coming of Bishop Kern into the college was welcomed by the more liberal bishops, such as Bishop Mouzon and Bishop John M. Moore. Bishop Arthur Moore and Bishop Kern remained fast friends throughout their careers, though frequently they found themselves on opposite sides of a question.

Bishop Kern was small of stature and often called attention to the fact that he was exactly the same height as John Wesley. His episcopal service was rendered in China, in Cuba, and in the Tennessee, Holston, and Florida Conferences. He retired in 1952.

Bishop Kern lived ahead of his day. He was the leading liberal among the bishops of the Church, South at the time of Methodist union. His father, Dr. John A. Kern, had been one of the scholars of the Church, South and had taught at both Randolph-Macon and Vanderbilt Universities. His book, *The Ministry to the Congregation,* was long a standard in its field. Bishop Kern inherited his father's scholarly bent and taught for a period at Southern Methodist University. He was the author of books that enjoyed a wide circulation. One of the best of these was his *Methodism Has a Message.*

Throughout his career Bishop Kern was tremendously

interested in education. He was the chief proponent of the plan for the merger of the Sunday-School Board, the Epworth League Board, and the Board of Education, adopted by the 1930 General Conference of the Church, South. It is quite fitting that the building at Nashville, which houses the Board of Higher Education and the church school section of the Board of Discipleship, should be called the Kern Building.

Bishop Kern was quiet in manner but firm in his convictions and possessed of an iron will. He was never afraid of difficulties. He did not welcome controversy, but he did not shrink from it. While he was a liberal in thought, in his administration he maintained much of the firmness of the older bishops. There were those who felt that while his office door was always open, it was not to easy to engage fully in free dialogue with him and that in the end he was keeping his conclusions to himself. In his appointment-making he followed largely the old style. He was ever a master strategist, giving careful attention to every detail of all that he undertook.

On one occasion he asked one of his preachers, who was a unique character, to come to his office for an interview. The brother came and after "good morning" was spoken, he said to the bishop: "Bishop, before you begin whatever you have to say to me, there is one thing I would like to say to you. You are a much smarter man than I am. Whatever I reply, whether it is 'yes,' 'no,' or 'maybe so,' you will know how to hang on to it and do whatever you intend to do anyhow. So I am not going to reply." The bishop smiled and proceeded to make his statement. When he finished, to his surprise, the brother rose and said, "Thank you," and walked out of the office.

Bishop Kern had a high sense of honor. He manifested clearly a sense of contempt for anything shady or little in the ministry or in the laity. No man among us ever had greater disdain for cheap ecclesiastical politics than he did.

The delivering of the Episcopal Address at San Francisco in 1952 was physically and emotionally exhausting for him.

His plans for teaching, lecturing, and writing during his retirement had to be laid aside. He lived only a short time after release from active assignment. He died December 16, 1953, at Vanderbilt Hospital in Nashville, and is buried at the Mt. Olivet Cemetery in that city.

Francis John McConnell
(1871–1953)

Francis J. McConnell was one of the strongest and most widely known bishops of Methodism. He was elected by the 1912 General Conference of the Methodist Episcopal Church from the presidency of DePauw University at the age of only forty. He often referred to the fact that his election did not come until the twenty-first ballot. He served in time the Denver, Pittsburgh, and New York areas. The Denver area at the time of his service included the work in Mexico.

Bishop McConnell was a genuine scholar. He had an incisive mind and an almost unlimited store of knowledge upon which he drew constantly in preaching, in writing, in debate, in discussion, and in casual conversation. He was said to be one of the few men of his day who had no difficulty in grasping what Albert Einstein was talking about. He was the author of many books that had wide circulation. In addition, he wrote constantly for the church and secular press. He was in constant demand for lectures, not only in the United States but throughout the world. In 1930 he delivered the Yale University Lectures on preaching, one of the few Methodist bishops who had this honor.

Bishop McConnell was a strong champion of the social gospel. In the leadership that he gave to this emphasis he became the father of countless disciples throughout Methodism and in the Christian world as a whole. At the same time, he created enemies, especially among some lay persons who did not want Christianity to interfere with business. For thirty years he was a leader in the Methodist Federation for Social Action.

As an administrator, Bishop McConnell was a master. He

took his administrative responsibilities in stride and always kept in calm command of the situation. Because of this, the Board of Bishops of the Methodist Episcopal Church often called upon him to handle delicate matters where his particular ability was needed to deal with problems and tension.

As a presiding officer he was unusually effective. He used to say that the chief duty of one in the chair is to get the motion before the house straight, then insist upon keeping the body to the consideration of the motion, and then not care at all how the motion finally was decided. At the same time, such were his powers of concentration that he would preside at Annual Conference and simultaneously work on a problem of calculus.

Bishop McConnell was a man of fair size who always moved deliberately. As he spoke, he had a habit of looking straight forward over his glasses, a mannerism that seemed to add pertinence to his remarks. His comments in the Council of Bishops were always incisive and almost inevitably brief. He had a sharp sense of humor, which manifested itself from time to time in some penetrating remark. He seemed to take a quiet delight in puncturing the pretenses of sophisticated brethren, and he could do it in a most withering way.

When Bishop McConnell was in his last illness, his daughter, Dorothy, would read to him. One day she decided she would read from a book by a popular religous author of that time. The bishop listened thoughtfully for a little while, pondering what the author was saying, and finally interrupted the reading to say, "That's bunk, Dorothy, that's bunk."

Bishop McConnell, despite his great dedication to scholarship, was a matter-of-fact, down-to-earth man. There was no hypocrisy about him, and he had no use for artificiality in any form. His remarkable balance and sense of fairness, his great concern for those who in some way had failed but who yet could be redeemed, served the church well.

Bishop McConnell was a product of a long line of Ohio

Methodists. His father had also been a preacher. Born on a farm five miles from Trinway, Ohio, August 18, 1871, Bishop McConnell maintained the old home at Lucasville, Ohio, and there life came to its end for him on his eighty-second birthday, August 18, 1953.

Other members of the McConnell family achieved wide prominence in Methodism, especially his wife. Mrs. Francis J. McConnell was for a long while vice-president of the Women's Foreign Missionary Society. Physically of very small stature, in reality she was a giant among women. His daughter, Dorothy, editor of the *World Outlook,* gave valuable service through that distinguished magazine. His brother, Charles, for a quarter of a century was a professor at Boston University School of Theology. His nephew, F. Gerald Ensley, elected a bishop in 1952, inherited his uncle's scholarly and administrative gifts.

Johann Wilhelm Ernst Sommer
(1881–1952)

J. W. E. Sommer was elected by the Germany Central Conference in 1946 after a distinguished career in many fields in the work of the church.

Born March 31, 1881, in Stuttgart, Germany, he was educated primarily in England and Switzerland. With his English wife he served for a period as a missionary in Turkey, then as seminary professor and dean in Germany, as well as filling in as part-time district superintendent. For ten years he was president of Frankfurt Methodist Theological Seminary.

He was an acknowledged scholar of distinction, and a number of writings came from his skilled pen. He was dignified in appearance and quiet in manner.

It was his privilege to take strong and effective leadership in the rebuilding of German Methodism after World War II.

Bishop Sommer was already sixty-five when elected to the episcopacy. Death overtook him after six years of service in that office. His son, Ernst, was elected to the episcopacy in 1968.

V

Toward a Church Without Barriers
1956–1960

The General Conference of 1956, held April 25–May 7, convened in Minneapolis, April 25, with Bishop Purcell in the chair.

The communion service at the opening was in the charge of Bishop Holt.

Recognition was given to the devoted services of those who had died during the previous quadrennium, including eight of the bishops.

The Episcopal Address was prepared and read by Bishop Corson.

Bishops absent at this General Conference were Bishop Arvidson of Scandinavia; Bishops Balloch, Elphick, and Gattinoni from Latin America; Bishops Chen and Kaung of China; and retired bishops Gowdy, Miller, and Peele.

Devotional messages were brought by Bishops Branscomb, Clair, Jr., Dawson, Ensley, Kennedy, Ledden, Subhan, Watkins, and Welch.

Bishops presiding at the sessions were Bishops Purcell, Ledden, A. Frank Smith, Bowen, Lord, W. Angie Smith, Short, Northcott, Arthur Moore, Corson, Wicke, Franklin, Werner, Booth, Harrell, Willis King, Kennedy, Oxnam, Pickett, Paul Martin, and Holt.

The General Conference took recognition of the one-hundredth anniversary of the establishment of work in

India. A whole evening was devoted to "India night." Bishop Pickett of India presided for one session, this being the first time for a Central Conference bishop to preside in a General Conference. The reason that none had presided before was that in the early years Central Conference bishops were regarded as "localized" rather than as "general superintendents" and therefore ineligible to preside in the General Conference. Since 1956 it has been common for Central Conference bishops to occupy the chair.

The 1956 General Conference witnessed the last request by the General Conference for the bishops to sing what had long been termed "the bishops' hymn." This had until then, been a common request by the General Conference.

Several factors contributed to the discontinuance of this practice. One was the fact that some of the bishops long associated with such singing had passed on, such as Bishops Leonard, Mead, and H. Lester Smith. Bishop Lowe had been retired for some time. Again, there was a feeling among the current bishops that musically they were not a particularly gifted group. At the 1952 General Conference Bishop Lowe had made the public suggestion that the Jurisdictional Conferences please elect a few tenors! Moreover the one or two bishops who were musical took the position that the bishops' hymn was not the most desirable music; that a not-too-good hymn, rendered by a not-too-musical group, did not add to the General Conference!

The quadrennium 1952 to 1956 had seen a Youth Emphasis under the leadership of Bishop Lord. A favorable report was made to the General Conference on the churchwide activities that had marked the emphasis.

The Supreme Court decision of 1954 had strong overtones for the 1956 General Conference and gave added emphasis to the conviction long existing among many Methodists that segregation was unwarranted anywhere in Methodism. Thus was begun the long, involved process that in twelve years resulted in the elimination of the Central Jurisdiction from the structure of the church. The first steps taken were disciplinary provisions to make it possible for local churches to transfer from the Central Jurisdiction to other jurisdictions. Little use was subsequently made of this particular legislation. The Episcopal Address at the opening of the conference addressed the existence of racism in the church by taking the position that there was "no place for segregation in The Methodist Church."

Council meeting: Minneapolis General Conference

The Council of Bishops met periodically during the session of the General Conference at Minneapolis during the spring of 1956, with Bishop Purcell presiding.

The council expressed its judgment that for all boards to meet at one time, as had been provided for by the survey report of 1952, was not wise.

It also took exception to the name "Together" for the church's general periodical, feeling that it was not sufficiently meaningful.

Bishop Garber was named to lead the Emphasis upon Higher Education, adopted by the General Conference; and Bishop Short to lead the Emphasis upon the Development of the Local Church.

Bishop Oxnam retired in 1956 as secretary of the Council of Bishops. With his retirement as secretary, a long era in the life of the council came to its end, and certain modifications in procedures were gradually introduced. Bishop Short was elected to succeed him, largely on the basis that before his election as bishop he had served for seventeen years as secretary of his own Annual Conference, the Louisville Conference.

1956 saw the retirement of five bishops and the election of eight new bishops.

Those retiring in 1956 were Bishop Raymond L. Archer from the Singapore area; Bishop J. Waskom Pickett from the Delhi area; Bishop Clement D. Rockey from the Lucknow area; Bishop Costen J. Harrell from the Charlotte area; and Bishop Clare Purcell from the Birmingham area.

The eight new bishops coming into the Council of

Bishops were Bishop Eugene M. Frank from the South Central Jurisdiction; Bishop Nolan B. Harmon and Bishop Bachman G. Hodge from the Southeastern; and Bishop Prince A. Taylor from the Central Jurisdiction for overseas work.

From Central Conferences came Bishop Hobart B. Amstutz; Bishop Ralph E. Dodge; Mangal Singh; and Gabriel Sunderam.

Council meeting: Pasadena, December 10-13, 1956

The Council of Bishops met at the Huntington-Sheraton Hotel, Pasadena, California, December 10-13, 1956, with Bishop W. Earl Ledden presiding. For the first time in sixteen years Bishop Oxnam was not in the secretary's chair. Though nothing was said publicly, all the bishops were wondering how matters would turn out without his invaluable guidance, which had been depended upon so completely for so long.

A Committee on Message was appointed, consisting of Bishops Oxnam, Ensley, Tippett, Bowen, William C. Martin, and Branscomb. The message developed by the committee and released to the church took notice of recent events in Hungary and affirmed that there must be strong resistance to tyranny. It also noted the situation in the Middle East and stated that the United States must rethink its world responsibility. The Committee on Message was ordered continued for the quadrennium.

Bishop Rockey, recently retired in India, was recalled to active service and assigned to the supervision of the work in Pakistan. He was to fulfill this service for a period of eight years, after which Bishop Amstutz, by that time also retired, succeeded him. In 1968 Pakistan elected its own bishop in the person of Bishop John Victor Samuel.

A full morning was devoted to the orientation of newly elected bishops, with addresses by Bishops Oxnam, Frank Smith, Kennedy, Raines, Welch, and Short, each address being followed by a period for questions and discussion.

A considerable block of time was devoted to planning for the implementation of the new quadrennial program with its twin emphases upon Higher Education and the Development of the Local Church.

Another important step taken at this first meeting of the new quadrennium was that of beginning a study of the jurisdictional system, particularly that feature of the system providing for a jurisdiction based upon race.

A social occasion, at which the council members and their wives were guests of Bishop and Mrs. Kennedy and the Los Angeles area, was a dinner at which Cecil B. DeMille spoke on "Why I Made *The Ten Commandments*." A private showing of this notable film was given for the bishops on another evening.

Council meeting: Cincinnati, April 23-26, 1957

The Council of Bishops met at the Netherland Hilton Hotel, Cincinnati, Ohio, April 23-26, 1957, with Bishop Ledden presiding.

The Oberlin Conference on "The Nature of the Unity We Seek" was scheduled for 1957, and the chief feature of the Cincinnati council meeting was a lengthy, carefully planned discussion of ecumenical relations under the guidance of Bishop William C. Martin.

Dr. Robert L. Cushman, as an invited resource person, read a paper on "The Methodist Church and the World Council of Churches"; Bishop Ensley presented a paper on "The Methodist Church and the Ecumenical Church." These two papers became the basis for extended consideration.

In his paper Dr. Cushman had stated, "There ought to be a commission in our church, under the supervision of the Council of Bishops which would call together representative churchmen to discuss the theological and historical basis of our communion and its relation to the various problems of church unity." Bishop Ensley's paper had carried much of the same suggestion. The culmination of this discussion resulted in taking the first steps which led eventually to the establishment of the Commission on Ecumenical Relations by the 1960 General Conference.

Another feature of the Cincinnati meeting was a discussion of appointment procedures. The discussion was guided by Bishop Reed. Participating was a panel composed of Bishops Love, Phillips, Corson, Arthur Moore, and Paul Martin.

Bishop and Mrs. Werner and the Methodists of Ohio entertained the bishops and their wives at a dinner at which the speakers were Mayor Charles P. Taft, Governor C. William O'Neil, and Bishop A. Frank Smith.

Council meeting: Gatlinburg, November 12-14, 1957

The council met at the Mountain View Inn, Gatlinburg, Tennessee, November 12-14, 1957, with Bishop W. Angie Smith presiding. Only once before had the council held one of its regular meetings in the South, and at that time public accommodations were not available for all members of the council, and special entertainment arrangements had to be made for some. There were members of the council who had misgivings about meeting in the South, and the attendance was not quite up to normal. This time there were no problems, and the bishops were lavish in their appreciation for the hospitality received. A few years later the council met again at Gatlinburg, and it has met many times since in the South.

Bishop Flint, shut in by ill health, wrote beautifully in his cryptic style:

> "I wanted to go on account of—
> 1. The Smokies
> 2. The fellowship
> 3. Because it was in the South."

A considerable part of the time at Gatlinburg was devoted to planning for the Emphasis upon the Development of the Local Church.

TOWARD A CHURCH WITHOUT BARRIERS

Plans were laid for emphasizing the growth of the individual church member through development of a series of Lenten booklets written by some of the bishops as follows:

Lent, 1957—"Christ and Ourselves," Bishop Charles W. Brashares

Lent, 1958—"Christ and Our Resources," Bishop William C. Martin

Lent, 1959—"Christ and Our Mission," Bishop Arthur J. Moore

Lent, 1960—"Christ and Our Freedoms," Bishop Lloyd C. Wicke

Plans were also laid for the development of the local congregation through an emphasis upon effectiveness in 1958; expansion in 1959; and enlistment in 1960.

Since Gatlinburg, as well as much of the Holston Conference of which it is a part, lies in the area of the Tennessee Valley Authority, the public program for the bishops consisted of two parts: first, an address by a T.V.A. executive on what T.V.A. had done to change the Tennessee Valley; and second, a pageant, "The Redemption of the Valley," showing what Methodism had done for over a century to change life in the Tennessee Valley.

Council meeting: Ocean City, January 7-8, 1958

The Council of Bishops met in called session at the Flanders Hotel, Ocean City, New Jersey, January 7-8, 1958, with Bishop W. Angie Smith presiding.

The one purpose of the meeting was to consider the matter of the jurisdictional system, particularly the feature of it represented by a jurisdiction based upon race; and to provide input on the part of all members of the council for the benefit of the twelve bishops who were on the Committee on the Jurisdictional System created by the previous General Conference. Every bishop present was asked to share his personal thinking on the matter before the body. The statements were frank and to the point. Where there was difference of opinion, it was voiced with freedom and heard with respect. No formal action of any kind was taken.

Bishop Willis King, in the name of the College of Bishops of the Central Jurisdiction, submitted the following statement: "1. We are in favor of the eventual abolition of the Central Jurisdiction. 2. We approve merger into geographic conferences when and as both groups are ready for such action."

The Ocean City meeting represented the beginning of the bishops' facing together the abolition of the Central Jurisdiction. They would be living actively with the matter for the next ten years until the final dissolution of the jurisdiction would come at last with Methodist-Evangelical United Brethren union in 1968.

Council meeting: Miami Beach, April 8-10, 1958

The Council of Bishops met at the Roney Plaza Hotel, Miami Beach, Florida, April 8-10, 1958, with Bishop W. Angie Smith presiding. Bishop Branscomb had invited the meeting of the council to Havana, Cuba, but a situation developing there necessitated the change to Miami Beach instead.

Since the council could not go to Cuba, Bishop Branscomb arranged to bring a number of the leaders of the church of that country to Miami Beach to meet the bishops. Little was it realized on the festive evening that Bishop Branscomb had arranged what lay ahead for Cuba and Cuban Methodism in a matter of only two years.

Following through on the discussion of the Cincinnati meeting, Bishop Ensley moved the appointment of a Committee on Ecumenical Consultation to be composed of six bishops, six pastors, and six lay persons, one from each jurisdiction. Representatives of the twelve theological schools and persons at large would also be part of the group. The bishops named were Bishops Clair, Ensley, Corson, William C. Martin, Tippett, and Harmon. The committee subsequently organized with Bishop Ensley as chairman and Dr. Ernest Colwell as vice-chairman.

Bishop Ralph A. Ward of China was present at the Miami Beach meeting to voice his concern for the work in Taiwan, particularly Soochow University. The council responded with interest and appointed a committee on Soochow University composed of Bishops W. Angie Smith, Raines, Corson, Arthur Moore, Tippett, King, and Welch.

At this meeting Bishop Harmon raised the question of the constitutionality of legislation adopted by the General Conference to the effect that a bishop cannot transfer a minister from one conference to another without the minister's consent. Back of the question lay the fact that a minister is admitted into the total traveling connection and not just into an Annual Conference. The Council of Bishops decided to ask for a ruling from the Judicial Council. The Judicial Council ruled that the legislation was constitutional. The Council of Bishops later asked for a rehearing, but the request was denied.

The most far-reaching matter on the agenda of the Miami Beach meeting turned out to be a brief report by Bishop Newell, chairman of the Committee on Church Union. Bishop Newell reported that he had received a letter from Bishop George Epp of the Evangelical United Brethren Church asking whether it might be possible to open negotiations on a formal basis for union.

Some of the members of the Methodist committee had met informally with the Evangelical United Brethren bishops in St. Louis for an evening on December 3, 1957. The committees of the two denominations had then had a joint meeting in Cincinnati, March 6-7, 1958. Agreement had been reached upon a common resolution to be presented to the Evangelical United Brethren General Conference in October, 1958, and subsequently to the Methodist General Conference. The resolution called for the establishment of a joint commission to work out a plan of union.

The council heard with great interest Bishop Newell's

HISTORY OF THE COUNCIL OF BISHOPS

report. Ten years of negotiations were yet to lie ahead, but ultimately the two churches were to become one church at the memorable Uniting Conference at Dallas in 1968.

Council meeting: Cincinnati, November 11-13, 1958

The Council of Bishops met at the Netherland Hilton Hotel, Cincinnati, Ohio, November 11-13, 1958, with Bishop G. Bromley Oxnam in the chair. It was good to see him again at the table on the platform where he had sat for so long as secretary. He presided with his usual efficiency and dispatch.

The council heard at this meeting a request from the World Methodist Council for help in purchasing the Epworth Rectory. The bishops agreed to try to raise $46,000 in their areas.

Bishop Garber called attention to the condition of the Negro schools. The bishops committed themselves to an effort to raise a Race Relations Day offering of $1,000,000. A growing concern for these schools appears and reappears in the proceedings of the council after this point, reaching its climax in the commitment of the bishops to the Black College Fund in more recent years.

The council heard with joy a report on the establishment of the Interdenominational Center for Theology in Atlanta.

Another important action of this meeting was the appointment of a committee, composed of Bishops William C. Martin, Ensley, and Garber, to confer with the Methodist Publishing House on a new "History of Methodism." The subsequent result was the production of the now widely accepted three-volume history edited by Book Editor Emory Stevens Bucke.

The year 1958 represented the fiftieth anniversary of the Methodist Social Creed. The message adopted by the council took its cue from this fact, giving formal support to the 1954 Supreme Court decision on integration in the public schools. It also proceeded to speak pertinently on other social problems, including peace, nuclear armaments, juvenile delinquency, and the use and sale of alcoholic beverages.

The holding of a second meeting in Cincinnati, only a year and a half after the meeting there in April of 1957, grew out of necessary cancellation of plans for this session to be held elsewhere.

Council meeting: Washington, April 14-17, 1959

The Council of Bishops met at the Mayflower Hotel, Washington, D. C., April 14-17, 1959, with Bishop Oxnam presiding.

Arrangements had been made for the session to be devoted mainly to meeting with government leaders. Interviews were had with General Nathan Twining, Chairman of the Joint Chiefs of Staff; Chief Justice Earl Warren; Secretaries Neil H. McElroy and Arthur Fleming; Senators Lyndon Johnson, Hubert Humphrey, and John F. Kennedy; and Vice-President Richard Nixon.

A visit was made to the White House where the council was received by President Dwight Eisenhower. Upon this occasion Bishop Oxnam read the message presented to President George Washington by Bishops Asbury and Coke on their visit to him on May 29, 1780, and also President Washington's reply to them. The bishops were cordially received by President Eisenhower and introduced to him one by one.

Sixteen years later when the council met again in Washington, attempt was made by Bishop Mathews, the host bishop, for a similar visit to President Richard Nixon, but the request was denied.

During this session the council visited Wesley Seminary for the dedication of the chapel, Oxnam Chapel, named in honor of Bishop Oxnam. Bishop Welch brought the address, with members of the executive committee participating in the ritual of dedication.

HISTORY OF THE COUNCIL OF BISHOPS

Council meeting: Phoenix, November 17-20, 1959

The Council of Bishops met at the Camel Back Inn, Phoenix, Arizona, November 17-20, 1959, with the president, Bishop Marvin A. Franklin, presiding. This and the spring meeting, just prior to General Conference, were the last meetings in the quadrennium.

The time was given largely to consideration of the Episcopal Address to be given by Bishop William C. Martin. Attention was also given to routine matters related to the forthcoming General Conference.

On one evening, the bishops and their wives were guests of Bishop and Mrs. Kennedy at a dinner at which Governor Paul Fannin and Mayor Sam Mardian were present. The speaker was Dr. Joseph Kaplan, chairman of the Geophysical Year.

Council meeting: Denver, April 19–May 6, 1960

The Council of Bishops met at the Denver-Hilton Hotel, Denver, Colorado, April 19 to May 6, 1960, prior to and periodically during the General Conference. Bishop Franklin presided in the sessions prior to General Conference; Bishop Kennedy, the new president, in the sessions during General Conference.

At the pre-General Conference session the secretary, Bishop Short, placed in the hands of each bishop for the first time a bound workbook outlining the responsibilities to be cared for by the council and the nominations to be made, together with a listing of the previous years of service of each person serving on boards and agencies. The custom of developing such a workbook has been followed ever since.

At the session prior to the General Conference, Bishop Harmon moved that it be suggested that the bishops sing the bishops' hymn during the General Conference, but the motion was defeated. There was some levity attendant upon the defeat of the motion. There are many persons, however, in the church who regret the passing of this custom. There was something deeply moving about a singing episcopacy, even though all were not good singers. The bishops' hymn itself, even though not ideal from the viewpoint of either words or music, did have a marching quality about it that struck a responsive chord with many.

In Memoriam—1956–1960

During the 1956–1960 quadrennium nine of the bishops had run their earthly course:
>John W. Branscomb
>D. Stanley Coors
>Z. T. Kaung
>Frederick D. Leete
>Titus Lowe
>Walter Peele
>Charles C. Selecman
>Ralph A. Ward
>Bascom Watts

John Warren Branscomb
(1905–1959)

John W. Branscomb was elected by the 1952 Southeastern Jurisdictional Conference to the episcopacy. He was assigned to the Jacksonville area, which included Cuba and the Florida Conference, his home conference. He lived to give only seven years of episcopal service.

Born May 11, 1905, in Union Springs, Alabama, Bishop Branscomb was a short, wiry man, but a person of tremendous energy. His enthusiasm was abounding, and he made friends wherever he went. He was always on the positive side of an issue and was an untiring promoter of all Kingdom causes.

He had a great passion for missions and gave strong leadership to making the Florida Conference one of the most missionary-minded conferences in the church.

The responsibility for Cuba brought him great joy, and in the few years he was privileged to serve he took glad leadership in promoting the extension of the work and in building new churches from one end of the island to the other. He likewise took strong leadership in a major church-extension program in Florida to expand Methodism in that fast-growing state.

Bishop Branscomb was a most effective and popular preacher, in large demand for platform appearances throughout the land. Essentially he was an evangelist with a great interest in people. This same interest manifested itself in his pastoral approach, both in his churches and in the episcopacy. Florida Methodism loved him with great devotion. When the day came when with their lips they began to call him "Bishop," in their hearts he remained "John" as always.

Bishop Branscomb had a great sense of humor. He loved a good joke and was adept at telling humorous stories. He was a great "cut-up," so much so that some people who did not know him wondered if he ever had serious moments.

From their days together at Emory University, Bishops Branscomb, Paul Hardin, and Edward J. Pendergrass were fast friends. While in the seminary, the three of them together with Dr. Mack Anthony composed a quartet which became well known for its singing of the gospel.

The bishop never knew how to spare himself or when to stop. He had a killing schedule and gave every passing moment something to keep in store. His tireless activity soon took its toll, and he died of a heart attack January 16, 1959, in Jacksonville, Florida. His body was laid to rest in his hometown of Union Springs, Alabama.

D. Stanley Coors
(1889–1960)

The North Central Jurisdictional Conference elected D. Stanley Coors to the episcopacy in 1952. He had had a distinguished career in Michigan Methodism. For years he and Bishop Marshall R. Reed were close friends and fellow laborers.

Born August 1, 1889, in Pentwater, Michigan, Bishop Coors was a refined, quiet, Christian gentleman, tall and spare in appearance. He commanded great respect wherever he went and was a thoughtful preacher.

Upon his election to the episcopacy he was assigned to the St. Paul area, which proved to be the only area he would serve. He was host to the 1956 General Conference at Minneapolis.

He became ill on an episcopal visit to Germany and never fully recovered. He died in Minneapolis, March 6, 1960, a few weeks before his retirement was due. His body is buried in Lansing, Michigan.

Z. T. Kaung
(1884–1958)

Z. T. Kaung was elected by the Central Conference of China to the episcopacy in 1941.

He was born December 4, 1884, in Shanghai, China, into a wealthy non-Christian family. He became interested in Christianity while a student at the Anglo-Chinese College in Shanghai and was baptized. Later his family members joined him in baptism.

Bishop Kaung was a product of the work of the Methodist Episcopal Church in China. After entering the Christian ministry he was to become one of the giants of the Christian faith in China. While pastor of Allen Memorial Church in Shanghai, of which Madame Chiang Kai-shek was a member, he baptized the Generalissimo. He was also for a period pastor of the great Moore Memorial Church in Shanghai.

It was his fate to serve in the episcopacy during the days of the Communist takeover and to witness the disruption of the church and the attempts to destroy it and other Christian institutions. For years the Methodist Church outside China was out of touch with him, and at times did not know whether he was living or dead.

He died in Peiping, August 23, 1958.

HISTORY OF THE COUNCIL OF BISHOPS
Frederick Deland Leete
(1866-1958)

Frederick D. Leete was elected to the episcopacy by the Methodist Episcopal Church in 1912. He served the Atlanta, Omaha, and Indianapolis areas. Prior to his election he had been pastor of several strong churches, including Central Church, Detroit.

One of the things which spotted him for consideration for the episcopacy was his strong emphasis upon lay work for which he gained nationwide recognition. He also was adept in church efficiency in a day when this emphasis was receiving wide attention.

While he held large pulpits, he was not a particularly moving preacher. He held these churches mainly by hard work, strong organizational emphasis, and dogged determination to accomplish whatever he had set for himself.

Born in Avon, New York, October 1, 1866, of English Puritan and French Huguenot ancestry, Bishop Leete was a direct descendant of Governor William Leete, a colonial governor of Connecticut. Bishop Leete was a tall, spare man. There was little warmth about him, particularly in his later years. He was sometimes abrupt in manner and often crusty in his remarks. He always knew where he wanted to go and how to get there and let nothing stop him. One of the bishops of the Methodist Episcopal Church who was most strongly for Methodist union, he made genuine contribution toward its accomplishment.

Bishop Leete was not the scholar that some of his episcopal colleagues were, but he wrote a number of books covering a rather wide range. He even wrote one book dealing with word studies in the Greek New Testament, a field in which few people have written.

Bishop Leete outlived almost all his contemporaries. When he did appear occasionally at the meetings of the Council of Bishops, he was a lonely figure since there were so few of the bishops any longer that he knew.

The years of his retirement were spent in St. Petersburg,

Florida. He was a regular attendant of Christ Church, where a reserved pew marked by a red velvet cover bore his name.

His absorbing interest in the late years of his life was in episcopal biography. He collected souvenirs of various sorts of the bishops, as well as whatever of their writings or papers he was able to acquire by gift or purchase. In 1948 he published his *Methodist Bishops,* which contained a brief sketch of each bishop elected up to that time, plus excerpts from their correspondence or writings. The book represents a collection of miscellaneous, loosely organized data, but scarcely gives an adequate picture of the bishops as individuals or of their contribution to the church individually or collectively. Bishop Leete's episcopal collection was finally lodged in the library of Perkins School of Theology of Southern Methodist University, Dallas, Texas.

Bishop Leete died February 16, 1958. His body is buried in Syracuse, New York.

Titus Lowe
(1877–1959)

Titus Lowe was elected by the Methodist Episcopal Church to the episcopacy in 1924 after a career as a missionary secretary. His first episcopal assignment was to the Singapore area. There his health broke, and for a time it appeared that he could not continue active service. J. Ralph Magee, who himself became a bishop in 1932, was the leader of the delegation from the Portland area and encouraged the assignment of Bishop Lowe to Portland in 1928. The two men remained fast friends throughout their lives. In 1939 Bishop Lowe was assigned to the Indiana area, where he served until his retirement in 1948.

Bishop Lowe, born in Bilston, England, December 17, 1877, came to the United States at the age of fourteen. He was a large man, somewhat slow and deliberate in his movements. He had a habit of keeping his eyes straight forward and his expression steady as he occupied the chair.

He earned a reputation for being talkative and was often on the floor of the council. His remarks were at times blunt or even caustic. In meetings over which he presided in his area, he did most of the talking. He was sometimes charged with being autocratic as an administrator, and his background as sergeant of a campus military unit during his Ohio Wesleyan student days may have contributed to his unbending attitude. He appeared to have little sense of humor and to be marked by some inflexibility. He had genuine business ability, and for some years the general church looked to him for leadership in financial affairs.

Bishop Lowe was always interested in what was going on and was an active participant not only in the floor discussion of the council, but also in the conversations which often occurred on the side between sessions. He was generally thought of as a rather adroit political leader. Despite his seeming aloofness, he had a capacity for friendship and achieved a record for spotting individuals of promise and bringing them to the attention of the church.

During his retirement he served for a period directing the affairs of the Methodist Committee on Overseas Relief, following Bishop Welch. Toward the end, his health broke badly, and he became a sad figure, often bewildered and confused. He died November 27, 1959, in Indianapolis, Indiana, and is buried there.

William Walter Peele
(1881–1959)

William W. Peele was elected to the episcopacy by the last General Conference of the Methodist Episcopal Church, South in 1938. In that year the Church, South found itself with only five bishops eligible for active service. These were Bishops Darlington, Dobbs, Arthur Moore, Kern, and A. Frank Smith. Accordingly it determined to elect seven more bishops. Bishop Peele was elected on the first ballot, along with Bishop Ivan Lee Holt.

Bishop Peele was a North Carolinian, born in Bigson,

North Carolina, November 26, 1881. He had served leading churches in both the North Carolina conferences. He had also been a district superintendent. His first episcopal assignment was to the Richmond area, which in 1939 was made up of the Virginia, Baltimore, and Western Virginia Conferences. The next year with union, the Western Virginia Conference and much of the Baltimore Conference went into the Northeastern Jurisdiction, and the North Carolina Conference was added to the new Richmond area. Bishop Peele served the Richmond area until he was forced by ill health to ask to be released in 1951. He died in Laurenburg, North Carolina, July 1, 1959, and is buried there in Lytch Cemetery.

Bishop Peele was of average height and trim of figure, bald-headed, and with tender eyes. He was every inch a gentleman, always in full command of himself. He was soft spoken, kind, and gentle. Preachers and people responded to his simplicity, his brotherliness, and his evident pastoral concern.

He was a thoughtful man who seemed to have given long hours to pondering responsibilities before acting to accomplish them. The church often gave him difficult assignments in the confidence that he would prove well able to perform them. He was a master of the *Discipline* of the church. He did not speak too often, but the council always listened carefully when he did speak.

Bishop Peele was not a great preacher, although his messages were thoughtful and helpful. He represented one of the finest choices the church made as the new day came when detailed administration became so great a part of the responsibilities of the episcopacy.

Charles Claude Selecman
(1874–1958)

In 1938 the General Conference of the Methodist Episcopal Church, South elected Charles C. Selecman to the episcopacy. He had had a distinguished career in both pastoral and educational roles, which included the pastorate of Trinity Church, Los Angeles, and of First Church, Dallas; and the presidency of Southern Methodist University. He was already sixty-four at the time of his election. His first assignment was to the work in Arkansas and Oklahoma. In 1944 he went to the Dallas area which he served until his retirement in 1948.

Bishop Selecman was born in Savannah, Missouri, October 13, 1874, and grew up in that state. Much of his ministry was spent in Texas, however, where he held a place of leadership. This was at times a disputed leadership, for there were then rival political schools in Texas Methodism. He would probably have been elected bishop earlier than he was had it not been for this political situation.

Bishop Selecman was of average height and inclined to heaviness. He was broad shouldered and carried himself erect. He was almost wall-eyed and had thinning gray hair which had trouble staying in place.

The bishop was a tremendous preacher, always human and deeply moving in his preaching. His sermons were of the old style and were definitely marked by the hortatory note. He moved his hearers to both laughter and tears. He could "preach out of a hole" as few preachers can. A striking example of this ability came at Savannah in 1938 during the Aldersgate celebration of the Church, South. Two speakers were being used each session. On one evening the eloquent Dr. Merton Rice was the first preacher and Dr. Selecman the second. Dr. Rice's sermon carried the audience to the heights, and almost everyone was feeling sorry for Dr. Selecman for having to follow him. Dr. Selecman started rather slowly, but after a short time struck his stride and before the evening was over matched the glory of the first sermon. There were those who believed that his performance on this occasion made many votes for him for bishop at the General Conference a few months later.

Bishop Selecman had a rare sense of humor which showed itself again and again in his sermons, in his presiding, and in casual conversation. His sense of humor was unexcelled among the bishops of his day. It was always a welcome and refreshing moment when he took the floor. Some of the officers of the council who wanted the meetings to be all business found it impossible to restrain him. He respected the rules and customs of the council, but insisted upon occasionally introducing a few free moves of his own.

At one time when the council was in session and Southern Methodist University was playing Notre Dame University in football, Bishop Selecman first tried to secure adjournment at game time so that the council could follow the game on the radio. Bishop Oxnam, as secretary, insisted that the council stay by its business, and as usual the council followed his advice. Not to be outdone, Bishop Selecman would leave the room periodically, return, and passing down the aisles whisper how the score stood, evidently much to the exasperation of the secretary.

On another occasion Bishop Brashares, as president, had planned a service at which he was anxious to have the bishops share their spiritual experiences. Bishop Selecman had not learned the nature of the service and was quite late coming into the room. Just as he came in, Bishop Brashares said, "Does anyone have a story he would like to share?" There was a long pause as no one said anything. Bishop Selecman then took the floor and said, "If nobody else has anything to say, I'll tell a Texas story about who spit in the cow's eye." The story about ended the experience meeting.

Bishop Selecman was an evangelist. He was president of the Board of Evangelism during the first years of its existence and together with Harry Denman gave a new momentum to evangelism in Methodism, the effect of which to some extent still remains.

The bishop lost his sight almost entirely during the days of his retirement, but this, plus growing feebleness, did not diminish his interest in the welfare of the church, or the radiance of his marvelous spirit.

Bishop Selecman died March 27, 1958, in Dallas, Texas, and is buried there.

HISTORY OF THE COUNCIL OF BISHOPS

Ralph Ansel Ward
(1882–1958)

Ralph A. Ward was elected by the China Central Conference in 1937, in Nanking, China.

Born June 26, 1882, he had been a missionary to China and a field secretary of the Board of Missions.

After his election to the episcopacy, he was first assigned to Chengtu area, which included West China, and then to Shanghai.

It was his lot during World War II to be imprisoned by the Japanese, who charged him with being an American spy. He was kept in prison for three years, during which time he was brutally tortured and not allowed to write to his wife or friends. He also suffered greatly from malnutrition.

Upon his release in 1945 he returned to the United States, but in 1947 he again returned to his duties in China and stayed there even after the Communists took over in that country. In 1951 he finally left China and went to Hong Kong. He devoted the rest of his days to the work in Hong Kong in Taiwan, greatly strengthening and expanding the church there.

Bishop Ward was a spare, somewhat swarthy man, whose face reflected what he had suffered. He literally bore on his body the marks of what he had endured for his Lord.

On his deathbed, December 10, 1958, in Hong Kong, barely able to speak, he ordained three Chinese pastors.

Henry Bascom Watts
(1890–1959)

H. Bascom Watts, born November 6, 1890, in Yellville, Arkansas, was elected to the episcopacy by the South Central Jurisdictional Conference in 1952 and assigned to the Nebraska area.

He had had a distinguished career in the pastorate, serving in five Annual Conferences. He served such strong churches as University Church, Austin; Laurel Heights, San

TOWARD A CHURCH WITHOUT BARRIERS

Antonio; First Church, Little Rock; and Boston Avenue, Tulsa.

Bishop Watts was a congenial spirit who relished good company and who added flavor to any group in which he happened to find himself.

His episcopal career was short. He died November 3, 1959, after giving seven years to the Nebraska area. He is buried in Tulsa, Oklahoma.

VI

A Church in a Changing Day
1960–1964

The 1960 General Conference convened at the Civic Auditorium Theatre in Denver, Colorado, April 28–May 9.

The Episcopal Address was prepared and read by Bishop William C. Martin. Before his address Bishop Martin reverently read the names of the nine bishops who had died during the last quadrennium.

The communion service, with which the conference opened, was in the charge of Bishop Tippett.

Devotional messages were brought by Bishops Dodge, Frank, Hodge, Newell, Northcott, Singh, Taylor, Valencia, and Wunderlich.

Bishops presiding were Bishops Corson, Franklin, W. Angie Smith, Ensley, Tippett, Willis King, Paul Martin, Phillips, Arthur Moore, Oxnam, A. Frank Smith, Werner, Booth, Wicke, Garber, Reed, Lord, Raines, Short, Brashares, Mondol, Harmon, William C. Martin, and Kennedy.

Conference of Bishops

The Conference of Bishops, made up of the council together with the heads of the affiliated autonomous Methodist churches, met first prior to the opening of General Conference. Bishops from Korea, Brazil, and

A CHURCH IN A CHANGING DAY

Mexico were present and a representative of the United Church of Japan (Kyodan). The day was spent in hearing reports from each field.

The plan of having a Conference of Bishops was established in 1939 at the time of Methodist union. It was a means for continuing a relationship with those parts of the church that had become autonomous. It was timed with the General Conference since bishops from the autonomous churches would already be present. The conference never proved effective, either from the viewpoint of the autonomous churches or of The Methodist Church. It appeared to be largely a formality. With the growing number of autonomous churches, the increasing number of bishops in these churches, and the growing number of united churches to which the Evangelical United Brethren had been united, the provision for a Conference of Bishops was dropped from the *Discipline* in 1972. Provision was made for a continued relation with these churches through fraternal representatives which may be seated in the General Conference, any of which may be a bishop if the autonomous church desires.

At present some consideration is being given to the development of concordats with any or all these autonomous churches, similar to the concordat now in effect with the British Methodist Church. Two additional concordats have been concluded: one with Mexican Methodism and one with the Caribbean.

Council meeting: Continuation sessions, General Conference, April 28–May 9, 1960, Denver, Colorado

Before the General Conference adjourned, the council appointed certain members for specific responsibilities in the new quadrennial program, "Jesus Christ Is Lord." Together with their area of responsibility, the following bishops were assigned these responsibilities:

Bishop Kennedy: "Personal Religion and Witness"
Bishop Raines: "Missions"

HISTORY OF THE COUNCIL OF BISHOPS

Bishop Paul Martin: "Stewardship"
Bishop Garber: "Church Extension"
Bishop Short: "Inner City and Rural Churches"
Bishop Werner: "Family Life"
Bishop Wicke: "Social Concerns"
Bishop Tippett: "Recruitment"
Bishop Taylor: "Church and Campus"

The council noted with deep regret that Bishop Robert E. Jones was unable to be present. He had been at each General Conference, either as delegate or bishop, for the last fifty-six years.

The year 1960 saw the largest number of bishops to be elected in any one year since Methodist union in 1939:

Northeastern Jurisdiction: Fred G. Holloway
W. Vernon Middleton
W. Ralph Ward
James K. Mathews
North Central Jurisdiction: Ralph T. Alton
Edwin R. Garrison
T. Otto Nall
South Central Jurisdiction: O. Eugene Slater
W. Kenneth Pope
Paul Galloway
Aubrey G. Walton
Kenneth Copeland
Central Jurisdiction: Charles F. Golden
Noah W. Moore
M. Lafayette Harris
Southeastern Jurisdiction: James W. Henley
Walter C. Gum
Paul Hardin, Jr.
John Owen Smith
Western Jurisdiction: Everett W. Palmer
Central Conference, Latin America: B. Foster Stockwell

Ten bishops retired at the 1960 Jurisdictional Conference:
Northeastern Jurisdiction: G. Bromley Oxnam
W. Earl Ledden
Frederick B. Newell

A CHURCH IN A CHANGING DAY

North Central Jurisdiction: H. Clifford Northcott
South Central Jurisdiction: Dana Dawson
                                    A. Frank Smith
Central Jurisdiction: Willis J. King
                              J. W. E. Bowen
Southeastern Jurisdiction: Arthur J. Moore
                                    William T. Watkins

Council meeting: Chicago, November 15-17, 1960

The first meeting of the Council of Bishops following the 1960 Jurisdictional Conferences, where ten bishops retired and twenty-two new bishops were elected, was held in Chicago at the Palmer House, with Bishop Kennedy presiding.

Among the bishops retiring were some who for twenty years had been among the church's most widely recognized episcopal leaders. In addition, three bishops in active service had died during the previous quadrennium.

By changes in the law, making possible the election of additional bishops, six new areas had come into being: West Virginia, Central Illinois, South Carolina, New Orleans, San Antonio, the Nashville area of the Central Jurisdiction, and the Pacific Northwest. For the first time the number of new bishops in the council practically matched that of those continuing in active service. This represented the largest turnover in episcopal leadership at one time that the council had known since Methodist union.

The first afternoon and evening of the council session were devoted to the orientation of newly elected bishops under the direction of Bishop Kennedy. Papers were read as subjects for discussion by Bishops William C. Martin, Reed, Garber, Raines, Welch, Paul Martin, Ensley, Lord, and Corson.

A change was made in the plan for a standing Message Committee. It was voted that the committee be an annual committee with every bishop assigned for one year of the quadrennium.

HISTORY OF THE COUNCIL OF BISHOPS

Miss Dorothy Magee, daughter of Bishop Magee, presented to each member of the council panels of pictures of all bishops elected from 1784 through 1960. She had collected such pictures as a hobby for some time.

The council sent a telegram to newly elected President John F. Kennedy, assuring him of its prayers.

At the 1960 Central Jurisdiction Bishop Charles Golden had been elected and assigned to the newly created Nashville area of that jurisdiction. Bishop Short of the Nashville area of the Southeastern Jurisdiction had his office in the Publishing House as had all the Nashville area bishops before him in The Methodist Church and in the Methodist Episcopal Church, South for many years. Application was made for office space for Bishop Golden also, and the Publishing House replied that space was not available because of an already overcrowded condition. At the Chicago meeting on motion of Bishop Lord, Bishop Golden and Bishop Short were asked to make statements regarding the situation. Bishop Golden stated simply the facts of the unavailability of space. Bishop Short stated that he could not remain in his adequate office space at the Publishing House when his colleague could not be accommodated there also and that he had contacted other agencies in Nashville to see if the two bishops could be accommodated near each other.

Both the Board of Education and the Board of Evangelism offered space, and Bishop Short told Bishop Golden to make his choice. Bishop Golden chose space in the Board of Evangelism, where his father had been a member of the staff, and Bishop Short took the space in the Board of Education.

After hearing both statements, the council addressed to the Board of Publications a letter of regret that space could not be made available, stating that finding such "would have been an effective witness in this hour of tension between races." The council thanked Bishop Short for his effort to reconcile the matter, and the Board of Evangelism and the Board of Education for their helpfulness. The letter addressed to the Board of Publications was replied to by the president, Dr. F. Murray Benson, expressing regrets, but concurring in the position of management that space problems made the granting of additional office space out of the question.

Bishop Alejandro of the Philippines was present as a bishop elected for the second time. He had served first from 1944 to 1948, had been out of office for twelve years, and now had been elected again.

The council adjourned to Evanston for the dedication of the new student residence hall at Garrett Theological Seminary.

Following several days of business, the council participated in the District Superintendents' Conference.

Council meeting: Boston, April 4-6, 1961

The Council of Bishops met at the Sheraton Plaza Hotel, Boston, April 4-6, 1961, with Bishop Kennedy presiding.

Much of the time was occupied with routine business.

Two moves were made that were to be followed by important developments in the future. A committee had been appointed on the training of new district superintendents, composed of Bishop Garber, chairman, and Bishops Clair and Short. Bishop Garber reported that three sessions had been held in the past, one at Evanston in 1957 with fifty superintendents present, one at Gammon in 1958 with thirty-three present, and one at Wichita in 1959. The council voted that a week of training be provided each year in each jurisdiction, and that such training be inaugurated as soon as possible after the 1962 Annual Conference sessions. From this beginning, the current, annual, churchwide program for the training of new district superintendents has been developed.

The other move leading to important developments was a motion by Bishop Alton that the executive committee schedule at each meeting of the council a consideration of one major issue related to the ongoing life of the church.

HISTORY OF THE COUNCIL OF BISHOPS

A petition was received from some Boston University students regarding the need for the desegregation of the Southern colleges of the church. The council replied that the process was already underway and that Duke University was already open to all.

The message adopted by this session of the council was addressed particularly against the diversion of tax funds to the support of private and parochial schools.

Bishop Brashares raised an interesting legal point asking whether a preacher, who had reached retirement age and who was effectively serving a church that was difficult to fill, could be reappointed to the same church as a retired supply. The reply of the council was that this was technically possible but not wise.

Bishop Kennedy shared with the council a letter he had received from President John F. Kennedy in reply to the message sent him by the council at the previous session.

For one of its devotional services, the council adjourned to Old North Church. The service was in the charge of Bishop Copeland. The council voted to place a plaque in the church in honor of Charles Wesley who had preached there before leaving America in 1736. This was done some months later.

Bishop and Mrs. Mathews and the Boston area arranged for a dinner at which the chief speaker was Dr. W. A. Visser't Hooft, general secretary of the World Council of Churches. He was introduced by Bishop Oxnam. This was the last time this outstanding episcopal leader was to be present at a meeting of the Council of Bishops.

Council meeting: Gatlinburg, November 14-16, 1961

The Council of Bishops met at the Mountain View Inn, Gatlinburg, Tennessee, November 14-16, 1961, with Bishop Paul Martin presiding.

Considerable attention was devoted to the Study of the Episcopacy, referred by the 1960 General Conference to the coordinating council.

A CHURCH IN A CHANGING DAY

An advent message was adopted in which the council restated its opposition to Communism and urged our people to use common sense in considering insidious attacks upon the church. It also cautioned against a panic program of bomb-shelter building.

The council adopted a statement on the recent death of Dag Hammarskjold.

At one of its regular sessions, Governor Frank Clement of Tennessee, himself a Methodist, addressed the council.

Council meeting: Mexico City, April 24-26, 1962

The council met at the Reforma Hotel, Mexico City, Mexico, April 24-26, 1962, with Bishop Paul Martin presiding. This was the one and only time that the council met outside the continental United States.

At the suggestion of the secretary, the custom was begun of having several reports on areas in the United States at each meeting. In an earlier day each bishop reported on his area at each bishops' meeting, but this pattern was abandoned as the number of areas increased and as the business of the bishops in council multiplied. Since 1939 there had been many reports in the council of the work in areas overseas from the United States, but the bishops, as a whole, knew little about the areas in the United States other than their own. The first United States area reports were by Bishops Alton, Golden, Frank, Hardin, and Palmer.

The council devoted a full session to a discussion of appointment-making under the guidance of Bishop Wicke and Bishop Franklin.

Another session, under the guidance of Bishop Ensley, was devoted to reports on the New Delhi Assembly of the World Council of Churches. Brief impressions of the assembly were given by Bishops Barbiere, William C. Martin, Mathews, Amstutz, Corson, Valencia, Lord, Raines, Wunderlich, and Short.

A Committee on Legislation was appointed, consisting of

Bishops Corson, William C. Martin, Nall, Phillips, Harris, Valencia, and Short.

Bishops Love and Lord shared with the council a working agreement that had been developed regarding churches in racially changing neighborhoods in and around Washington and Baltimore. The presentation of this paper represented an introduction to a matter on which all the bishops would be working for many years to come.

The council approved a motion by Bishop Ensley for a day of consultation on the parish ministry between representatives of the council and the heads of the seminaries. This was the beginning of what has now become a regular procedure of consultation between those who train the ministry and those in The United Methodist Church who have the responsibility to deploy it.

The Methodist Church of Mexico on one evening entertained the bishops and their wives at a dinner and afterward attended the National Theater where the Mexican National Ballet performed. The host bishop was Bishop Eleazar Guerra.

Council meeting: St. Louis, November 13-15, 1962

The Council of Bishops met at the Statler Hilton Hotel, St. Louis, Missouri, November 13-15, 1962, with Bishop Reed presiding.

Area reports were given by Bishops Harris, Holloway, Voigt, Galloway, Grant, and Harmon.

Bishop Clair reported for the Committee on the Christian Faith and War in a Nuclear Age. This was a committee ordered by the General Conference to be composed of a group of scholars who would speak to the church upon the subject. The message as developed by the committee was presented by Bishop Clair. On motion of Bishop Ensley the statement was approved for release to the church.

Bishop Ensley moved that the bishops develop a Bishops' Crusade on the Ministry. The motion was approved.

A committee to arrange for the celebration of twenty-five

years of Methodist union was appointed, composed of Bishops Reed, Golden, William C. Martin, Lord, and Short. The celebration never materialized, however.

Bishop Holloway introduced a consideration of divorce in ministerial families with the following statement:

> Our conviction is that for ministers of The Methodist Church divorce be regarded as an obstruction to an effective ministry in all areas of service. We recommend that divorce be regarded as a basis for disqualification for appointment under our system, except when a minister's character and marital status are approved by the resident bishop after receiving a report from the Committee on Investigation and with the consent of the cabinet.

The statement was received and discussed at some length. No action was taken. The subject was one that was to represent a growing concern of the council.

Bishop Nall introduced a resolution regarding the Second Vatican Council that stated, among other things, "We view with interest its proceedings and commend the brotherly spirit manifested in so many ways by Pope John XXIII."

One evening a public dinner was given, sponsored by Bishop and Mrs. Frank and Bishop and Mrs. Clair, at which Bishop Corson was the featured speaker. His theme was Vatican II. He reviewed his experiences on a recent visit to Rome, including an audience with the Pope.

The Central Jurisdiction reported on a recent study conference held in Cincinnati and the set of guiding principles for conference merger that it had developed.

Bishops Ensley, Reed, Mathews, Clair, Tippett, William C. Martin, and Short were appointed as the committee to meet with the seminary heads.

The secretary presented a communication from Bishop Howard, secretary of the Board of Bishops of the Evangelical United Brethren Church, stating that the Evangelical United Brethren General Conference had met in Grand Rapids. The conference had approved by a vote of

310 to 94 the authorization of a Commission on Church Union to work with a similar commission from The Methodist Church to prepare a plan and basis for union.

Bishop Ensley reported an interest upon the part of the heads of certain universities related to The Methodist Church in meeting with representatives of the Council of Bishops to discuss mutual concerns. The council welcomed the suggestions and appointed Bishops Corson, Garber, Voigt, William C. Martin, Harris, and Phillips as the committee. Subsequently, this was made a standing arrangement, and meetings were held profitably for several years.

Council meeting: San Francisco, April 16-18, 1963

The Council of Bishops met at the Californian Hotel, San Francisco, April 16-18, 1963, with Bishop Reed presiding.

Area reports at this session were given by Bishops Henley, Middleton, Noah Moore, Garrison, Walton, and Phillips.

Bishop Harmon read the scholarly paper, "The Role of the Council of Bishops," which was the subject of extended discussion.

Considerable time was given to some pending recommendations of the Committee on the Study of the Episcopacy, which the committee shared with the council, and the council gave its reactions.

The council concurred in the judgment that requests by the conferences for the return of a bishop should be discouraged. It judged that the proposal to fix the retirement age for bishops at sixty-eight was not wise. It affirmed the same judgment with reference to the proposal to prevent the naming of lay persons who were beyond seventy to boards and agencies of the church. It affirmed its conviction that the assignment of its own members to agencies should remain within itself.

Bishop Ensley announced the plans that had been developed for the Bishops' Crusade on the Ministry. This involved deployment of all the bishops across the church, with one or more missions in each episcopal area. The spouses of ministers were to be included as well as ministers because ministerial family matters were to be prominent upon the agenda.

Bishop Alton proposed a statement of support to those persons in racially critical areas who take leadership for the sake of an inclusive church. The motion was unanimously approved.

Bishop and Mrs. Tippett and the San Francisco area hosted a dinner one evening, featuring a dramatic musical program having a missions theme. The program had been previously presented at the assembly of the Women's Society of Christian Service and was repeated at San Francisco under the direction of the author.

Council meeting: Detroit, November 12-14, 1963

The Council of Bishops met at the Statler Hilton Hotel, Detroit, November 12-14, 1963, with Bishop Garber presiding.

Area reports were given by Bishops Mathews, Gum, Slater, Love, J. O. Smith, and Nall.

Attention was given at length to the possibility of union with the Evangelical United Brethren Church. Prepared statements on various phases of the possible union were made by Bishops Newell, Ensley, Harrell, Corson, Ward, and Short. The council engaged in discussion of each statement, but no action was taken.

On motion of Bishop Middleton, a committee was appointed to draw up a compendium of what was being done in race relations. The chair appointed Bishops Middleton, Hardin, Grant, Love, Galloway, and Brashares. The council approved a statement on race, affirming the right of all persons of all races to membership and the privilege of worship in our churches, and likewise the right of oppressed peoples to protest injustice.

Heretofore the naming of bishops to boards and agencies had been by ballot without nomination. The process had been long, cumbersome, and generally unsatisfactory. The secretary, therefore, moved the appointment of a nominating committee composed of the presidents of the colleges, one Central Conference bishop, with the secretary of the council to be available for resource purposes. The motion was approved. It was further ordered that each bishop indicate to the committee his first, second, and third choices for agency assignment, and that as far as possible the nominations be made within these choices.

At Detroit for the first time groups appeared demanding time with the council. The request was not granted, but a committee was appointed to meet with the various groups and hear their requests. In subsequent years other groups appeared making similar requests. Eventually the council devised orderly ways to hear groups that might wish to appear before it. These measures contributed toward the relaxation of tension and the achievement of better understanding.

At a banquet given by the Detroit area, Bishop Reed began the custom of having the secretary introduce the bishops and their wives, a custom that has been generally followed ever since. Governor George Romney was the featured speaker at the banquet. Mrs. Romney also spoke.

The council also shared in the official opening of the Detroit area offices.

Council meeting: Pittsburgh, April 17-25, 1964; Pre-General Conference

The council met at the Penn Sheraton Hotel, Pittsburgh, from April 17 to 25, and whenever necessary during the General Conference session from April 26 to May 8, 1964. Bishop Garber presided at the sessions preceeding General Conference; Bishop Wicke at those during General Conference.

The council heard further area reports by Bishops Brashares, Reed, Clair, William C. Martin, and Franklin.

A CHURCH IN A CHANGING DAY

It was ordered that the committee to meet with the seminary heads become a standing committee, and it has continued so since.

Bishop Palmer moved that the book editor of The Methodist Church be requested to publish in the *Discipline* a listing of all the bishops of the church since 1784, showing the year of their election. The book editor agreed, and the listing has appeared regularly in the *Discipline* since.

Bishop Lord moved the appointment of a committee to explain to certain young people why the sessions of the council are closed. Bishops Galloway, Raines, and Palmer were named as the committee.

On one evening during the pre-General Conference council meeting, Bishop and Mrs. Middleton and Mrs. Love hosted a dinner at which the Wesley Seminary Choir provided the program.

In Memoriam—1960-1964

During this quadrennium sixteen of the bishops had died:
- A. Theodor Arvidson
- Hiram A. Boaz
- John W. E. Bowen
- Ralph S. Cushman
- Roberto V. Elphick
- John Gowdy
- Bachman G. Hodge
- Robert E. Jones
- George A. Miller
- G. Bromley Oxnam
- Clare Purcell
- Julio M. Sabanes
- A. Frank Smith
- John M. Springer
- B. Foster Stockwell
- William T. Watkins

HISTORY OF THE COUNCIL OF BISHOPS

August Theodor Arvidson
(1883–1964)

A. Theodor Arvidson was elected to the episcopacy by the Central Conference of Northern Europe in 1946. He was a native of Sweden, where he was born October 13, 1883, in Jarpas. His parents were Lutherans, but as a young man he was influenced by Methodists and after Seminary at Uppsala became a member of the Swedish Methodist Conference in 1909.

Bishop Arvidson gave strong leadership in the church as pastor, district superintendent, and manager of the Book Concern. He wrote many articles for the press and published several books, as well as translating into Swedish most of the writings of E. Stanley Jones and Leslie Weatherhead. Eight times he was elected as a representative to General Conference. During the Second World War, when no bishop could reach the area, he acted as superintendent of all the work in Scandinavia.

Bishop Arvidson did not become too familiar a figure in the Council of Bishops, as his term was relatively short and his attendance limited. He was a conservative, thoughtful man, who was greatly respected by all who knew him and who made lasting contributions to Methodism in Europe. Of real significance was his help in bridging the gap between the Lutheran and Methodist churches, especially in Sweden.

Hiram Abiff Boaz
(1866–1962)

Hiram A. Boaz was elected to the episcopacy by the General Conference of the Methodist Episcopal Church, South in 1922. At the time he was president of Southern Methodist University in Dallas, Texas.

Bishop Boaz was born December 18, 1866, at Murray, Kentucky, in the Memphis Conference portion of Kentucky; but when he was six years old, his family moved to Texas near

Fort Worth, and he grew up there. He joined the Northwest Texas Conference in 1889. He served as pastor and as a college president and had much to do with the establishment of Southern Methodist University.

From 1922 to 1926 Bishop Boaz administered the work of the Church, South in Japan, Korea, and Manchuria. Following this assignment, he served in Oklahoma and Arkansas for four years, and for eight years in Texas and New Mexico. He retired at the last General Conference of the Church, South in 1938. Following retirement he made his home in Dallas until his death, January 2, 1962.

Bishop Boaz was a strong businessman. This accounted for his selection as a college president and as president of Southern Methodist University. It also accounted for his being chosen to serve as secretary of the Board of Church Extension of the Church, South from 1918 to 1920. He was an unusually effective money-raiser. In retirement he raised each year by personal solicitation thousands of dollars for Southern Methodist University.

At the time of his election as president of Southern Methodist University, Bishop Boaz was secretary of the Board of Church Extension at Louisville. A committee went to Louisville to interview him regarding the presidency, and he indicated his willingness to accept the position. The committee accordingly sent a wire to Dallas. It was during prohibition days, and when the telegram arrived, it read, "Booze is available. Call the trustees."

Bishop Boaz was a preacher of the old school, both in his thought and in his delivery. As an administrator he acquired a reputation for being somewhat severe at times, and some thought him arbitrary. He had some difficulty in getting along with several of his brother bishops in the days when he was on the active roll. He was not what one would call a popular bishop, for he never dodged conflict or taking a stand or doing the unpopular thing. Yet, he did have staunch friends and a large company of admirers.

Bishop Boaz was on the retired list throughout the days of his membership in the Council of Bishops. He attended only infrequently and did not appear too interested in what was going on in the council, his absorbing interest being in what he was doing at Southern Methodist University. The time came when he realized that most of his company had gone on before him, and at eighty-four he wrote and published his memoirs.

He was a giant of a man physically, tall, with a slight stoop. He was an avid golfer and kept his health almost to the end. He died in 1962 at the age of ninety-six. He outlived all the bishops of the former Church, South elected up to the time of his own election.

John Wesley Edward Bowen
(1889–1962)

John W. E. Bowen, born September 24, 1889, in Baltimore, Maryland, was elected by the Central Jurisdiction to the episcopacy in 1948. He was assigned to the Atlantic Coast area, which he served until his retirement in 1960.

He was a well-trained man with a fine mind and an ability to express himself well. He taught at three colleges—Tuskegee, Walden, and Claflin—and at Gammon Seminary. He held strong pastorates in Louisiana and Mississippi. At the time of his election he was editor of the *Central Christian Advocate*.

Bishop Bowen was a quiet, thoughtful man. He talked little in the Council of Bishops; but when he did, he had something important to say. He was the perfect gentleman, immaculate in his appearance and reserved in his bearing. He lived only two years after retirement and died quite suddenly, July 12, 1962, in Atlanta, Georgia, where he is buried.

Bishop Bowen's father, J. W. E. Bowen, Sr., came close to being elected bishop in the Methodist Episcopal Church several times. What was not realized in the case of the father was realized in the son.

Ralph Spaulding Cushman
(1879–1960)

Born November 12, 1879, in Poultney, Vermont, Ralph S. Cushman was elected to the episcopacy in 1932 by the

General Conference of the Methodist Episcopal Church. He had had a distinguished career as pastor in New York State and had attracted much attention by his leadership in the field of stewardship.

Bishop Cushman served the episcopal areas of Denver and St. Paul. He was greatly interested in evangelism and served for a period as the president of the Board of Evangelism.

Bishop Cushman and Bishop Magee were often referred to as "the two Ralphs." They were bishops elected by the General Conference which met at the lowest point of the depression, when the episcopacy found itself under severe fire and when there was some effort to move to term episcopacy.

Bishop Cushman was the poet among the bishops, often quoting his own poetry in his sermons and even sometimes introducing it into his prayers. His little books of religious poems sold in great numbers and were used far and wide. His *Pocket Book of Prayer,* published by "The Upper Room," has reached a total sale of better than two and a half million copies.

Bishop Cushman died August 10, 1960, in Herkimer, New York, and is buried in Manchester in his home state of Vermont.

Roberto Valenzuela Elphick
(1873–1961)

Roberto V. Elphick, born at Antofagasta, Chile, August 28, 1873, was elected to the episcopacy by the Central Conference of Latin America in 1936. He was assigned to supervise the work in Chile, Peru, and Panama, which he did for five years.

Latin America at that time had term episcopacy. Because of his age he was not eligible for reelection in 1941. He continued to serve the church, however, until his death on May 6, 1961, in Santiago, Chile, rounding out a total ministry of sixty-five years.

He was not an active bishop long enough to become a familiar figure in the council. His son-in-law, Pedro Zotelle, was elected in 1962 and served for seven years.

John Gowdy
(1869–1963)

John Gowdy was elected to the episcopacy by the China Central Conference in 1930.

Born in Glasgow, Scotland, December 7, 1869, he came to the United States as a young lad, attending schools and colleges on the East Coast. In 1902 he went as an educational missionary to China, holding the presidency of the Anglo-Chinese College in Foochow for over twenty years. He was a much-beloved missionary in that land.

The previous General Conference had authorized the election of two bishops for China. There was pronounced sentiment for the election of a Chinese. Bishop Birney, who had been resident bishop in China, was strongly in favor of such an election. John Gowdy was elected on the seventh ballot, and in presenting him Bishop Birney showed his disappointment. On the fourteenth ballot a Chinese, Wang Chih-ping, was elected. The work of the episcopacy did not appeal to Bishop Wang, and he abandoned the office in 1934.

It should be noted that while Bishop Gowdy was a missionary, he was not elected by missionary votes. Almost all the missionary delegates had pledged themselves to vote only for a Chinese. The Chinese composed three-fourths of the delegates, and they greatly loved Bishop Gowdy. He was elected originally for a term but was reelected in 1936. He retired in 1940.

Bishop Gowdy was a man of gentle spirit, completely devoted to his work. He attended the council meetings regularly, though in his late years he was a frail man. In retirement he made his home in Winter Park, Florida, where he was unusually active in the local congregation. He died there, September 9, 1963.

A CHURCH IN A CHANGING DAY
Bachman Gladstone Hodge
(1893–1961)

The Southeastern Jurisdictional Conference of 1956 elected Bachman G. Hodge to the episcopacy from the pastorate of Centenary Church, Chattanooga, Tennessee, in the Holston Conference.

He was an Alabamian by birth, born February 21, 1893, in Renfroe, Alabama, and as a young preacher served as associate at First Church, Birmingham, to the famous pastor-evangelist, George R. Stewart. Following such an apprenticeship, he served Settle Memorial, Owensboro, Kentucky; Crescent Hill, Louisville; Belmont, Nashville; and Centenary, Chattanooga. He had one term as district superintendent of the Nashville district.

Bishop Hodge was tall, straight, and most imposing in his appearance. He was a gifted preacher and his messages had about them a deeply moving human quality that attracted a large hearing wherever he went.

His episcopal career was short. He was assigned to the Birmingham area, which heartily welcomed him back as its bishop and native son. The time of his service came in a difficult era in the life of the church, and he was not a person who was temperamentally built to live with controversy. His administrative responsibilities weighed heavily upon him, but he did not shrink from them. He was not well much of the time but continued to give himself without reservation to his work.

In 1960 he was returned to the Birmingham area, but died the next year, January 5, 1961, after a lengthy illness. He is buried in the Jefferson Memorial Gardens in a suburb of Birmingham.

His episcopal area was divided between Bishop Nolan B. Harmon and Bishop Paul Hardin, Jr., for the remainder of the quadrennium.

Robert Elijah Jones
(1872–1960)

Robert E. Jones, born February 19, 1872, in Greensboro, North Carolina, was elected to the episcopacy by the Methodist Episcopal Church in 1920. He was the first Negro bishop elected for service in the United States.

Negro bishops had been elected previously for service in Africa, but with the enthusiasm and vision generated by the Centenary Movement, the church came to the conclusion that two of the bishops elected that year should come from the Negro membership of the church. The two chosen were Robert E. Jones and Matthew W. Clair, Sr.

From 1920 to 1939 Bishop Jones presided mainly over Negro conferences, and in 1939 he became one of the bishops of the Central Jurisdiction. He retired in 1944.

Bishop Jones had a fine mind and for many years was the distinguished editor of the *Southwestern Christian Advocate*. He had an unusually high-pitched voice and was also quite deaf. He was the strong defender of his own people. His continuing urgent demand in writing and in sermons and in debate was "Let my people go." He served faithfully and effectively on the Commission on Interdenominational Relations and Church Union. His conscience would not allow him to consent to the establishment of a jurisdiction based upon race, and he did what he could to prevent it. Nevertheless, though he was not happy about this feature of the Plan of Union, he stayed with the church of his fathers. By and large he was a sad man, who felt deeply what he and his people had suffered.

Bishop Jones took large leadership in the establishment of Gulfside Assembly at Waveland, Mississippi. After his death, May 18, 1960, his body was buried on these grounds sanctified by his toil and love.

A CHURCH IN A CHANGING DAY

George Amos Miller
(1868–1961)

George A. Miller was long connected with the work in Latin America. He was elected bishop by the 1924 General Conference of the Methodist Episcopal Church.

He was born in Mendon, Illinois, July 8, 1868, the son of a Methodist preacher, formerly a Lutheran pastor, who moved to California when George was only five years old.

George Miller joined the Southern California Conference in 1896. After several pastorates in California, he went for a period as a missionary to the Philippines. In 1916 he went as the first missionary to Panama, and a year and a half later he founded the mission in Costa Rica. Subsequently he was enlisted by Bishop Oldham to promote the Centenary Movement throughout Latin America.

Upon his election as bishop in 1924, he was assigned to Mexico, Costa Rica, and Panama. A year later he took over from Bishop Oldham the responsibility for Peru and Bolivia. In 1938 he was given all the conferences of the Methodist Episcopal Church in Latin America, with residence at Buenos Aires. In 1932 he was assigned the work on the West Coast. Bishop Gattinoni, elected that year, was assigned the work on the East Coast.

Bishop Miller retired in 1956. He moved to California and to the end of his days enlisted support for the Latin American work. He was a quiet, unpretentious man, who had little use for show and who paid little attention to the formal dress and conventions that many of the bishops then observed. He died October 12, 1961, and is buried in Oakland, California.

Garfield Bromley Oxnam
(1891–1963)

G. Bromley Oxnam was elected to the episcopacy by the 1936 General Conference of the Methodist Episcopal Church.

HISTORY OF THE COUNCIL OF BISHOPS

Born August 14, 1891, in Sonoro, California, he had a distinguished early career as pastor of the Church of All Nations in Los Angeles for nine years. He then moved East and accepted a professorship at Boston University, where he remained for seven years. At the time of his election he was president of DePauw University in Greencastle, Indiana.

His episcopal assignments were in turn Omaha, Boston, New York, and Washington. He gave a total of twenty-four years active service and retired in 1960. For sixteen years he was the secretary of the Council of Bishops and was largely the guiding hand of affairs during this period.

Bishop Oxnam was a master mind who gave great attention to minute details. His ability to write shorthand and his practice of keeping careful records of what he said and did served him in good stead many times. This was especially true when he appeared before the Committee on Un-American Activities in the Joseph McCarthy era. He proved himself capable of quoting chapter and verse. This story is told in his own book, *I Protest*.

Bishop Oxnam was all business and made every moment count. He was always courteous, but he spent little time in casual fellowship. At the meetings of the council he generally ate his meals alone or in his room. If he did take time to eat with some of his episcopal brethren, it was often to convert the meal into a committee meeting or a conversation on a problem.

In the meetings of the council his face would register his impatience with a brother talking in circles or indulging in frivolity of unnecessary length. He spoke frequently on the floor of the council. He always did his homework, and the council had great respect for the keenness of his mind and the obvious wisdom with which he spoke.

Bishop Oxnam was in great demand on the platform and in the pulpit. His deliverances were masterpieces of thought and logical persuasion. He spoke rapidly and with force, and his mode of speaking was sometimes described as a Gatling gun style.

A CHURCH IN A CHANGING DAY

Bishop Oxnam belonged to the category of the social prophet and will long be remembered as one of the leading advocates of the social gospel. He was the strong opponent of injustice in any and every form, and he did battle for social righteousness until the very end.

He was an ecumenist before devotion to ecumenism was common. His contributions to the National Council of Churches and the World Council of Churches, of which he was one of its first six presidents, were almost beyond calculation.

He continued always the friend of higher education. American University and Wesley Seminary, where his ashes are buried, represented particular concerns for him, especially in his late days as an active bishop.

Retirement did not come easy for one who had been at the center of the church's activity for so long. He lived for only three years after he retired, broken in health but courageous in spirit. He died March 12, 1963, in White Plains, New Jersey. On April 12, 1964, his ashes were interred beneath the altar at Wesley Seminary Chapel, Washington.

He was one bishop who made a lasting impression upon the total church, not only The Methodist Church but the world church as well. His devoted followers are scattered everywhere, and through them his influence continues to live on.

Clare Purcell
(1884–1964)

Clare Purcell was elected by the last General Conference of the Methodist Episcopal Church, South to the episcopacy in 1938.

Born November 17, 1884, in Columbia, Alabama, he was a favorite son of Alabama. He had held some of its strongest churches and was for long years a conference leader. In addition, he enjoyed considerable churchwide recognition and was one of the effective contributors to Methodist union.

His first episcopal assignment was to the Charlotte area, which at that time was composed of two conferences in North Carolina and two in South Carolina. The work performed then by Bishop Purcell is now executed by three resident bishops.

After ten years in the Charlotte area, he was assigned to his home area in Birmingham, where he served for eight years. He was glad to return home, but he often said that he went back too late as he returned at the time when his own contemporaries were facing retirement or sometimes radical adjustments in their appointments. He retired in 1956, continued to live in Birmingham, and gave what hours he could daily to Carraway Hospital.

Bishop Purcell was a distinguished-looking man with blue eyes and snow-white hair. He was of fair size and well proportioned, and followed rigorous eating habits and rigid disciplines. He had a fine sense of humor and often prefaced what he had to say with a delightful chuckle. His face flushed easily and often.

Bishop Purcell was not a moving preacher, but he was a good preacher. He had always been known as an unusual pastor, and in the episcopacy he continued to be a pastor. He had a great heart and wept with those who wept and rejoiced with those who rejoiced. There was a marked tenderness about him. No bishop exceeded him in the capacity for friendship and kindness.

He was an excellent presiding officer who kept calm and remained in command of the parliamentary situation. The conferences felt safe when he was in the chair. His administrative ability was recognized, not only in his own conferences, but in the church at large in the assignments it gave him, particularly in connection with the Council on World Service.

Bishop Purcell was a Southerner of the Southerners. He loved the South out of which he came, but his primary concern was for the emerging new South. He was the perfect Southern gentleman. No one could pronounce "Alabama" the way he could. He was immaculate in his appearance, devoted to the fine amenities of life, reserved in his manner, and the embodiment of courtesy at all times and under all circumstances.

At the General Conference in Jackson, Mississippi, in 1934, Bishop Purcell, then Dr. Purcell, was a delegate. The conference was considering a proposal to make graduation from college mandatory for reception into an Annual Conference. Dr. H. C. Morrison, the rugged, old evangelist from Kentucky, was speaking in opposition to the proposal. He ended his remarks by saying, "Why, friends, under this regulation, Abraham Lincoln couldn't get into a Methodist Annual Conference." Dr. Purcell got the floor and spoke a single brief sentence. He said, "But Robert E. Lee could."

Bishop Purcell died February 8, 1964, in Birmingham and is buried there.

Julio Manuel Sabanes
(1897-1963)

Julio M. Sabanes was elected to the episcopacy by the Central Conference of Latin America in 1952.

He was a native of Uruguay, born July 2, 1897, in Montevideo. He served as pastor in Argentina, at Rosario, for eighteen years and at Buenos Aires for five years. he was assigned after his election to the Santiago area, which included Chile, Peru, Panama, and Costa Rica.

Bishop Sabanes was an evangelist by nature, but he also gave attention to civic concerns, so much so that at one time the Peron regime banned him from his pulpit.

He was a modest, quiet man. During his active episcopacy he did not attend the council too often. This, coupled with his short term of service, meant that he did not become too well known in the episcopal body.

Bishop Sabanes retired in 1960 because of poor health and died, after a long illness, on August 29, 1963, at his home in Buenos Aires.

HISTORY OF THE COUNCIL OF BISHOPS
Angie Frank Smith
(1889–1962)

The General Conference of the Methodist Episcopal Church, South elected A. Frank Smith to the episcopacy in 1930, at the same time as Arthur J. Moore and Paul B. Kern.

All of them had been pastors of large churches in Texas. Bishop Smith and Bishop Moore were once pastors in San Antonio at the same time, and Bishop Kern was a pastor in San Antonio at the time of his election. When Bishop Smith was elected, he was pastor of First Church, Houston. He never moved his residence from that city, where he was so greatly loved. As bishop in the Church, South he resided in Houston and served conferences in Missouri, Oklahoma, and Texas. The Church, South did not require the bishops to reside within the conferences assigned to them.

After union in 1939, Bishop Smith continued to be assigned to the Houston area, but the conferences comprising it were changed on occasion. However, he always kept the Texas Conference. He used to say that he kept this conference so long that a young preacher said to him one day, "Bishop Smith, when I look at you, I think of eternity."

Bishop Smith, a true Texan, was born November 1, 1889, at Elgin, Texas. He was a large man and oversized. He had a jovial nature and an endless fund of stories. No one of the bishops could relieve a tight situation with a play of humor as he could, and the bishops always welcomed his taking the floor. His remarks would be seasoned with humor most of the time, but always they bespoke a remarkable wisdom and balance. After his brother, Angie, came into the council, the two would often tease each other on the floor and tell ridiculous tales on each other. They were almost totally unlike in disposition and in other ways.

Bishop Smith was a great favorite with lay people, and he was essentially a man's man. He knew how to develop leadership among lay people. He had mastered the act of getting them to respond to the calls of the Kingdom.

Though never a profound preacher, Bishop Smith was a popular preacher. Sometimes, especially as he got older, he gave the impression of not having put too much thought into his messages and of speaking impromptu even upon very important occasions. What he had to say was inevitably sprinkled with personal recollections and reminiscences, and keen observations on people and events.

Few bishops have been more genuinely loved than was A. Frank Smith. There was always a tenderness about him, and he was the apostle of the great heart. He knew how to be helpful to those who needed help, and he had his own way of doing it. When one saw a preacher sad and dispirited one day, and the next day in command of himself, even with victory in his face, it used to be said in Texas, "Frank Smith must have put his arm around him."

After thirty years in the episcopacy, retirement did not come too easily for Bishop Smith. Despite his jovial nature he could get moody at times. He and Bishop Moore were elected at the same time, and they retired the same year.

Bishop Smith came to the Southeastern Jurisdictional Conference to pay tribute to Bishop Moore upon the occasion of his retirement. The two men were sitting on the porch at Junaluska talking. Bishop Smith began talking about death in a rather sad way. Bishop Moore said to him, "Frank, you aren't afraid to die, are you?" Bishop Smith replied, "No, I just hope I don't have too much trouble getting out of my body." His wish was granted, for two years later one late afternoon on October 6, 1962, at his home, he said to his wife, "Bess, I believe I would like a cup of tea." She went into an adjoining room to prepare it. When she returned with the tea, she discovered that his spirit had taken its flight. The good Father gave the gentle bishop his wish. He did not have too much trouble getting out of his body.

In 1979 a long-awaited biography of Bishop Smith was published, *Growing a Soul,* by Norman W. Spellmann.

HISTORY OF THE COUNCIL OF BISHOPS
John McKendree Springer
(1873–1963)

John M. Springer was elected a missionary bishop by the 1956 General Conference of the Methodist Episcopal Church to supervise the work in Africa. He was the last of the long line of missionary bishops, beginning with the election of Francis Burns for Liberia in 1856, and including such great names as William Taylor, James M. Thoburn, and Joseph C. Hartzell. The *Discipline* still carries a definition of a missionary bishop but provides no method for the election of such.

Bishop Springer, born September 7, 1873, in Cataract, Wisconsin, went to Africa as a young missionary in 1901. He did pioneer work in Rhodesia and in opening up the Congo. He and his missionary wife became known far and wide for their utter devotion, which in 1907 was dramatized by their following trails across the continent from the Indian Ocean to the Atlantic.

Bishop Springer had behind him thirty-five years of missionary work when he was elected to the episcopacy. He was then sixty-three years of age. He retired in 1944 at the age of seventy-one. Fifteen of his retirement years were spent in Africa.

Bishop Springer was a tall man, well proportioned and with a fine physique even in age. He made a striking appearance in any company. His was an ardent, evangelistic spirit and was generally conservative in his thinking. He attended the meetings of the council with fair regularity, but generally did not speak often. He always seemed to relish greatly the fellowship of the bishops.

Despite his long years in Africa, it is said that he never mastered the languages commonly spoken, but this did not seem to interfere with his effectiveness.

His death, December 2, 1963, at Penny Farms, Florida, represented the final passing of the era of the pioneer missionary bishop. His remains are buried on a beautiful

A CHURCH IN A CHANGING DAY

hilltop in Mulungwishi, which affords a magnificent vista of the Africa he loved.

Bowman Foster Stockwell
(1899–1961)

B. Foster Stockwell was elected bishop by the Latin America Central Conference in 1960.

Born September 17, 1899, in Shawnee, Ohio, as a young man he served for a period as secretary to the great missionary statesman, John R. Mott. In 1926 he was sent by the Board of Missions of the Methodist Episcopal Church to teach at the Union Seminary (now Facultad Evangelica de Teologia) in Buenos Aires. From 1927 to 1960 he was director of the seminary, bringing it up to its present university-degree level.

Bishop Stockwell was strongly committed to ecumenism and was active in ecumenical affairs, both in Latin America and on the world stage. An acknowledged scholar and theologian, he wrote a number of books and edited several papers. He was instrumental in acquiring a valuable library on the little-known Spanish Reformation, which is now housed at the Facultad Evangelica de Teologia in Buenos Aires.

Upon his election to the episcopacy, Bishop Stockwell was assigned to the Pacific area and chose to live in Lima, Peru. His episcopal career lasted only thirteen months as he died on June 5, 1961. He was present at the meeting of the Council of Bishops in Chicago in the fall of 1960, this proving to be the only meeting of the council that he ever attended.

William Turner Watkins
(1895–1961)

William T. Watkins was the last bishop elected by the Methodist Episcopal Church, South, thus bringing to an end a long and distinguished line. His election came at Birmingham in 1938.

Born May 26, 1895, in Maysville, Georgia, Bishop Watkins was a thorough Georgian. After serving several early pastorates in the North Georgia Conference, he became professor of church history at Candler School of Theology, a position that he was holding at the time of his election.

He had only one year as a bishop of the Church South, during which he was assigned the work in Missouri. In 1939 at the Uniting Conference he was assigned to the Atlanta area. From 1940 to 1944 he had the South Carolina work. From there he went to the Louisville area, where he served for sixteen years until his retirement in October of 1959 of physical and nervous exhaustion.

Bishop Watkins was a stocky man, of medium height and well proportioned. He was partially bald and had most penetrating eyes.

He was a true scholar, marked by both the scholar's brooding and to some extent the scholar's forgetfulness. The routine responsibilities of the episcopacy had no charms for him. He had a record of infrequent attendance at the meetings of the Council of Bishops. When he did attend, he often came late and left early. He spent little time in casual fellowship. He was always gracious and kindly, but never intimate and kept largely to himself.

He was one of the greatest minds among the bishops. In the earlier part of his life he did some writing, and his fine book, *Out of Aldersgate*, helped to mark him for the episcopacy. All in all, however, he did relatively little writing for one with his gifts.

His sermons, rather than being written out, were thought out. This was clearly evident when they were delivered. He was truly a great preacher and was advanced in his attitudes, particularly with reference to social problems.

Bishop Watkins was an excellent parliamentarian, but he did almost no presiding in a General Conference in his entire episcopal career.

He centered his attention upon his thought, his books, and his area. One gets the impression that the church as a whole never really discovered what unusual talent he had.

He died February 6, 1961, and is buried in Louisville, Kentucky.

VII

New Structures for Mission
1964–1968

The General Conference of 1964 met at Pittsburgh, April 26–May 8.

The Episcopal Address was written and read by Bishop Kennedy. It noted with solemnity the deaths of the sixteen bishops who had reached life eternal during the 1960-1964 quadrennium.

All the bishops were present at General Conference except Bishops Balloch, Dawson, Flint, Gattinoni, Hammaker, Kelly, and Magee, who were detained because of advanced age or illness, and Bishop Chen, who was unable to leave China.

Bishop Earl Ledden led in the communion service, held at Trinity Episcopal Cathedral.

Devotional messages opening each day of the conference were brought by Bishops Love, Hagen, Reed, Amstutz, W. Ralph Ward, Singh, Pope, Palmer, Holloway, and Wunderlich.

Bishops called to preside were Bishops Garber, Dodge, Wicke, Corson, Tippett, William C. Martin, Ensley, Phillips, Lord, Paul Martin, Booth, Harmon, Gum, Mathews, Werner, Barbieri, Garrison, Taylor, Raines, Middleton, Kennedy, and Short.

The secretary of the council, Bishop Short, presented to the General Conference the fourteen bishops scheduled to

enter the retired relation at the Jurisdictional and Central Conferences later in the summer:
  North Central Jurisdiction: Charles W. Brashares
                                Marshall R. Reed
                                Edwin E. Voigt
  South Central Jurisdiction: William C. Martin
  Southeastern Jurisdiction: Marvin A. Franklin
                                Nolan B. Harmon
  Central Jurisdiction: Matthew M. Clair
                          Edgar A. Love
  Western Jurisdiction: Glenn R. Phillips
  Central Conference of the Philippines: D. D. Alejandro
  Central Conference of Southeast Asia:
        Hobart B. Amstutz
  Central Conference of Southern Asia:
        Clement D. Rockey
        John A. Subhan
        Shot K. Mondol

The Council of Bishops continued meeting throughout the General Conference period whenever it was deemed necessary.

The following new bishops coming into the council by the election of the Jurisdictional and Central Conferences of 1964:
  North Central Jurisdiction: Francis E. Kearns
                                Dwight E. Loder
                                Thomas M. Pryor
                                Lance Webb
  South Central Jurisdiction: W. McFerrin Stowe
  Southeastern Jurisdiction: H. Ellis Finger, Jr.
                                W. Kenneth Goodson
                                Earl G. Hunt
                                Edward J. Pendergrass
  Western Jurisdiction: R. Marvin Stuart
  Central Jurisdiction: James S. Thomas
  Africa Central Conference: Harry P. Andreassen
                               John Wesley Shungu
                               Escrivao A. Zunguze

NEW STRUCTURES FOR MISSION

    Southeast Asia Central Conference: Robert F. Lundy
In 1965:   Southern Asia Central Conference:
        P. C. B. Balaram
        Alfred J. Shaw
        Liberia Central Conference: Stephen T. Nagbe
In 1966:   Southern Europe Central Conference:
        Franz W. Schaefer
In 1967:   Philippines Central Conference:
        Benjamin I. Guansing
        Central Jurisdiction: L. Scott Allen

Bishop Allen was the last bishop elected in The Methodist Church in the United States.

For the first time the orientation for newly elected bishops was held apart from the regular meeting of the council. The meeting was held at Gatlinburg, Tennessee. Bishops reading papers or giving addresses were Bishops Mathews, Nall, Harmon, Reed, Frank, Lord, Clair, Taylor, Walton, Ensley, Slater, Raines, Holloway, Tippett, and Short.

Council meeting: Chicago, November 15-17, 1964

The Council of Bishops met at the Conrad Hilton Hotel, Chicago, November 15-17, 1964, with Bishop Wicke presiding.

Area reports were given by Bishops Lord, Copeland, and Paul Martin.

At the request of the executive committee, Bishop Short presented an analysis of the recent General Conference. This paper dealt specifically with how the General Conference dealt with (1) race in the church; (2) union with the Evangelical United Brethren Church; (3) structure of Methodist overseas; and (4) ecumenical relations.

Each topic was discussed at length. It was realized that the four topics would necessarily set much of the agenda of the council in the quadrennium ahead.

The Central Jurisdiction College shared its thinking

with the council relative to the elimination of the jurisdiction.

Council meeting: Houston, April 18-20, 1965

The council met at the Shamrock Hilton Hotel, Houston, Texas, April 18-20, 1965, with Bishop Wicke presiding.

Area reports were given by Bishops W. Angie Smith, Harris, Booth, and Garber.

Much of the session was devoted to a consideration of race in The Methodist Church. A basic paper was read by Bishop Taylor who was in charge of the discussion. The situation in the various jurisdictions was outlined by Bishops Harris, Hardin, Lord, Pope, and Alton.

Bishop Short read a paper on "The Pastoral Role of the Episcopacy in the Racial Situation." Bishop Raines read one on "Help from Boards and Agencies."

Bishop Middleton moved that the council establish within its membership a committee to work out plans for making the transition to a truly interracial church. The motion was approved. The Bishops' Committee on Race at first consisted of Bishops Wicke, Raines, Golden, Paul Martin, and Short. Subsequently, Bishop Stuart was added to the committee. The committee members forfeited their plans for the coming Fourth of July, and the committee met in Chicago to begin its work. From this point on, the council took active leadership in plans for the elimination of a jurisdiction based upon race, as well as Annual Conferences based upon race. It actively worked for the creation of Christian understanding and forebearance and the practice of full brotherhood as the goal of a truly inclusive church. In every meeting of the council from this point on, reference appears in the minutes to various efforts of the council directed toward the achievement of these goals.

Another period of time was devoted to consideration of matters related to union with the Evangelical United Brethren Church, with Bishops Newell, Ensley, Frank, and Wicke taking the lead in the discussion.

NEW STRUCTURES FOR MISSION

The council also began at this meeting to take a new look at the structure of Methodism overseas. Between this time and the General Conference of 1972, under the guidance of the Committee of the Structure of Methodism Overseas, with the leadership of first Bishop Raines and then Bishop Taylor, alterations were made in relationships which have proved to be far reaching indeed. Such alterations were made with the full participation of the Central Conferences and the conferences in the United States. In effect, what eventually happened was the beginning of a process of dismantling what had been a world church.

By 1972 the Latin America Central Conference was dissolved and made autonomous as union churches were set up in Argentina, Chile, Uruguay, Peru, Bolivia, Panama, and Costa Rica. The same thing happened in the Southeast Asia Central Conference with autonomous churches being set up in Malaya, Sumatra, and Burma. Pakistan also became an autonomous church and later a part of a united church. Cuba, Hong Kong, and Taiwan also became autonomous units.

The Central Conferences in Europe, Southern Asia, Africa, and the Philippines chose to remain with the church of which they had long been an integral part.

The council at this session again sent a message to Vatican II.

At a dinner arranged by Bishop and Mrs. Paul Martin, Governor John Connally of Texas was the chief speaker.

Council meeting: Seattle, November 16-19, 1965

The Council of Bishops met at the Olympia Hotel, Seattle, Washington, November 16-19, 1965, with Bishop Taylor presiding.

The council was shocked as it assembled by the word that Bishop Middleton had died suddenly while enroute to the meeting.

Area reports were made by Bishops Finger and Kearns.

HISTORY OF THE COUNCIL OF BISHOPS

Bishop Paul Martin gave the first report for the Bishops' Committee on Race, established at the last meeting.

Bishops Wicke and Short presented papers on Evangelical United Brethren union which became the subject of general discussion.

Bishop Newell was recalled to active service and placed in charge of the Pittsburgh area, following Bishop Middleton's death.

Bishop Mondol, retired, was assigned for two successive years to the Manila area, since the recent Philippines Central Conference found itself unable to elect a bishop.

Bishop Garber was assigned to care for part of the Geneva area following the death of Bishop Sigg, and Bishop Dodge was to care for the other part until an election could be held.

At a dinner hosted by Bishop and Mrs. Palmer, Senator Henry M. Jackson was the speaker.

A significant step was taken at this meeting with the appointment of Bishops Ensley, Corson, and Mathews and Drs. Albert Outler, Eugene Smith, and Chester Pennington to a committee on consultation with the Roman Catholic Church. Later Bishop Cannon became a part of the continuing conversations.

A further important step was taken with the appointment of Bishops Ensley, Corson, Mathews, and Short, Mr. Charles Parlin, and Mrs. J. Fount Tillman to a committee on consultation with the British Methodist Church. Later Miss Dorothy McConnell took Mrs. Tillman's place. The final issue of the committee's work was the development of the concordat under which delegates from The United Methodist Church are now seated in the British conferences; and delegates from the British Conference were seated in the General Conference of The United Methodist Church for the first time in Atlanta in 1972.

The council received a communication from the Philippines raising the question of the status of Bishop Alejandro, who had been elected a term bishop and had reached retirement age and was therefore not eligible for reelection. On recommendation of the Committee on Law and

Administration, the council requested a decision from the Judicial Council. The Judicial Council subsequently ruled that where term episcopacy prevailed, a bishop reaching retirement age in office was not a retired bishop, but rather a former bishop—and therefore no longer a member of the Council of Bishops. The ruling in Bishop Alejandro's case automatically affected four other bishops in similar circumstances.

Bishop Subhan addressed a letter to the Council of Bishops protesting that as a retired bishop he was not notified of meetings of the bishops in India. The council felt that it had no jurisdiction in the matter; but it did instruct the secretary to write a letter to the college in India suggesting that this procedure be reconsidered. A letter was received in reply from the college through Bishop Shaw stating that "the presence of a retired bishop was likely to prove unhelpful in many ways." There the matter ended.

Council meeting: Louisville, April 11-14, 1966

The Council of Bishops met at Stouffer's Inn, Louisville, Kentucky, April 11-14, 1966, with Bishop Taylor presiding.

Area reports were given by Bishops Galloway and Tippett.

Two sessions were devoted to a consideration of Evangelical United Brethren union, under the guidance of Bishop Wicke.

Another session was devoted to consideration of ways and means to further the quadrennial program.

Still another period was devoted to consideration of certain proposals of the Committee on Structure of Methodism Overseas.

Bishop Henley reported on progress in the special Committee on the Study of the Ministry.

Bishop Corson spoke concerning the new provisions of the *Discipline* for the employment of retired bishops until they reach the age of seventy-two. A committee to deal with such assignments was appointed, composed of Bishops Slater, Mathews, and Short.

At Louisville the Evangelical United Brethren bishops and the Methodist bishops met in joint session for the first time. Bishops Mueller and Wicke shared the chair.

At the public occasion held in a theater the bishops and their wives were seated on the stage. Governor Breathitt, a Methodist, was the featured speaker. The bishops presented to Governor and Mrs. Breathitt a Bible containing the signatures of all the bishops present. Governor Breathitt in his address pointed out with pride that Kentucky had approved the Charter of Human Rights only a week before, being among the first states to take such action.

Council meeting: Chicago, November 5-12, 1966

The Council of Bishops met at the Conrad Hilton Hotel, Chicago, prior to and during the special session of the General Conference, with Bishop Raines presiding.

The council first addressed itself to a review of the Episcopal Address written by Bishop Short.

Bishop Love was reactivated and assigned to the Atlantic Coast area in place of Bishop Harris, deceased.

One of the concerns of this session was the status of Bishop Amstutz, who as a retired bishop had been caring for the work in Pakistan, an arrangement the council wished to continue if possible. Bishop Amstutz was one of those whose situation was affected by the Alejandro decision. The council decided to let him continue in charge of the work for the quadrennium, but to send visiting bishops to care for the ordinations.

Adjourned Session of the General Conference, November 8-11, 1966

The 1964 General Conference voted to meet in adjourned session in 1966 to consider uniting with the Evangelical United Brethren Church, and thus the General

NEW STRUCTURES FOR MISSION

Conference met again, November 8-11, 1966, in the International Ballroom of the Conrad Hilton Hotel in Chicago. Bishop Raines, as presiding officer, opened the conference.

The General Conference of the Evangelical United Brethren Church met at the same time and in the same hotel.

All the bishops were present with the exception of twelve, most of whom were either retired or resident overseas. For the first time the long-honored senior bishop, Bishop Welch, was absent. The same was true also of Bishop Baker and Bishop Holt, long familiar figures at Methodist General Conferences. It was a matter of particular regret that these leaders, who had been so long active in ecumenical affairs, could not be present in this high ecumenical hour for the two churches involved.

Bishop Slater was in charge of the communion service, held in the Chicago Temple the evening before.

The Episcopal Address was prepared and read by Bishop Short. It was the shortest of the episcopal addresses of late years and addressed itself to the matter immediately before the assembly rather than covering the broad range of the usual episcopal addresses.

The devotional messages were brought by Bishops Barbieri, Booth, Loder, Newell, and Stowe.

The bishops presiding were Bishops Raines, Paul Martin, Ensley, Lord, W. Angie Smith, Noah Moore, Kennedy, Short, and Corson.

The 1966 adjourned session of the General Conference lasted for four days. The final vote was 749 in favor of union, 40 opposed, and 5 abstaining. Bishop Short, who was in the chair when the vote was taken, had the honor of declaring that the General Conference had approved the union. The General Conference of the Evangelical United Brethren Church in its session approved union by better than a three-fourths vote.

In the afternoon session on November 11, the members of the Evangelical United Brethren General Conference joined with the members of the Methodist General Conference in a closing service of thanksgiving. Bishop Corson was in the chair. Bishop Newell led in prayer. Bishop Mueller presented the Evangelical United Brethren bishops and made a statement. Bishop Raines brought the closing message. The benediction was pronounced by Bishop Epp.

All seven of the active bishop of the Evangelical United Brethren Church served on the Commission on Union. Methodist bishops serving on the commission were Bishops Wicke, Ensley, Corson, Wunderlich, and Short.

Council meeting: Buffalo, March 27-30, 1967

The Council of Bishops and the Board of Bishops of the Evangelical United Brethren met jointly at the Statler Hotel, Buffalo, March 27-30, 1967, with Bishop Raines and Bishop Mueller presiding.

Much of the session was devoted to matters related to the union of the two churches. Papers were read by Bishops Howard, Loder, Mueller, Pope, Milhouse, Wicke, and Short.

Another period was devoted to the Consultation on Church Union (COCU), with papers by Bishops Mathews, Harmon, Tippett, Ensley, and Short.

The council issued a strong statement against the war in Vietnam, as it had on other occasions.

Bishop and Mrs. Ward had arranged for a public occasion featuring a musical program, and for a dinner at a revolving restaurant above Niagara Falls on the Canadian side.

Council meeting: Miami Beach, November 13-16, 1967

The Council of Bishops met at the Deauville Hotel, Miami Beach, Florida, November 13-16, 1967, with Bishop Tippett presiding. The Evangelical United Brethren bishops were present.

A period was devoted to a consideration of the episcopacy

NEW STRUCTURES FOR MISSION

with papers being presented by Bishops Milhouse, Goodson, William C. Martin, and Holloway.

A large portion of one day was devoted to hearing Dr. John Deschner of Perkins School of Theology on "Current Theological Developments." A period of questions and discussion followed.

Bishops Stowe and Nall were named as a committee to bring in recommendations for credentials and for an episcopal seal for use after union was consummated. The Evangelical United Brethren bishops named Bishop Milhouse and Bishop Howard to the committee. The final issue of the committee's work was a recommendation that credentials follow the Methodist pattern, with a change in the name of the church, of course, and that the episcopal seal carry the emblem of the cross and flame now so familiar to all.

A telegram was sent to President Johnson supporting the Poverty Program.

During this session of the council, a joint session was held also with the members of the Council on World Service and Finance, the coordinating council, the council of Secretaries, and the Administrative Council of the Evangelical United Brethren Church. Bishop Mathews presented the proposal for a quadrennial program from the coordinating council, which he himself had drafted for that council's approval. After some amendment all the above bodies gave their approval to the proposal at this session. (The program was again ratified by these same bodies just prior to the Dallas General Conference the following year. It was presented to and almost unanimously approved by the General Conference as "A New Church for a New World," including the Fund for Reconciliation.)

At the request of the College of Bishops of the North Central Jurisdiction, Bishop Ensley moved the appointment of a committee to consider having a fulltime executive officer for the Council of Bishops. The motion was approved. Bishops Ensley, Ward, Hunt, Slater, Palmer, and Golden were named as the committee.

HISTORY OF THE COUNCIL OF BISHOPS

Bishop Henley, the host bishop, arranged for a public occasion with persons throughout Florida attending. Bishop Tippett was the speaker.

Council meeting: Dallas, April 15-20; April 23–May 4, 1968

The Council of Bishops met prior to General Conference at the Sheraton Hotel, Dallas, April 15-20, 1968, with Bishop Tippett presiding. During the conference sessions, April 23–May 4, Bishop Frank presided at council meetings.

The early sessions were given to a consideration of the Episcopal Address, prepared by Bishop Wicke, and to attention to necessary General Conference details.

Bishop Ward led a discussion on the urban crisis. He also presented a paper entitled, "Commitment in Partnership." This paper helped to shape and accent the quadrennial program, already approved at the council's Miami meeting in November of 1967: "A New Church for a New World"—"A Fund for Reconciliation." The program was approved by the General Conference. Before the General Conference adjourned, the bishops took a firm lead in this program by presenting publicly the total of their individual pledges, affirming that they would not ask the church to do what they had not first done themselves.

It was announced that Bishop Tippett represented the council at the funeral services of Dr. Martin Luther King.

Bishops Mueller and Wicke were name to prepare the episcopal greetings found in the forepart of the *Discipline*.

The committee on a fulltime "executive officer" reported favorably upon the idea. Bishop Alton moved that the term used for the office be "episcopal secretary." His motion was approved. It was moved that the vote on the question be by secret ballot. The recommendation carried by a vote of forty-eight to fourteen. The committee was instructed to prepare a suggested paragraph for the *Discipline* to make possible the office. Bishop Kennedy moved that Bishop Short be requested to assume the office, if created, and his motion was approved. The proposed legislation was

NEW STRUCTURES FOR MISSION

introduced. It involved a constitutional amendment and was approved by the necessary majority in the General Conference.

Upon being handed down for vote in the Annual Conferences, however, the recommendation failed to receive the necessary majority there. Doubtless the reason for this was that Methodism, with its pattern of a general superintendency, has from the beginning been wary of giving to any one bishop anything that every other Methodist bishop does not have. The situation has continued, therefore, of having to ask some bishop to carry area responsibility and at the same time serve as secretary of the council, which by its very nature demands almost fulltime service.

Prior to General Conference, Bishop and Mrs. Pope and Bishop and Mrs. Noah Moore, along with the Dallas area, gave a dinner one evening for the bishops and their wives. Bishop Pope spoke, and Bishop Tippett responded. Bishop Pope presented each bishop with a Texas-style hat.

In Memoriam—1964–1968

During the quadrennium ten of the bishops had died:
P. C. Benjamin Balaram
Dana Dawson
Charles W. Flint
A. Raymond Grant
Marquis Lafayette Harris
Ivan Lee Holt
Edward W. Kelly
W. Vernon Middleton
Alexander Shaw
Ferdinand Sigg

Prabhakar Christopher Benjamin Balaram
(1906–1968)

P. C. Benjamin Balaram was elected to the episcopacy by the Central Conference of Southern Asia in January of

1965, and assigned to the Lucknow area. He had served in various positions in India and was a widely acknowledged leader, especially in education and social work.

Born July 10, 1906, in Hyderabad, P. C. B. Balaram grew up in a home with a remarkably dedicated mother. His ancestors had been of the priestly caste. At a special service held soon after the birth of her son, his mother, then sixteen years of age, made an offering. She put all the money she had into an envelope and wrote on it: "I offer to the Lord these three rupees *and* my son."

Benjamin Balaram was an apt student. He studied engineering at the University of Edinburgh, with further study in Denmark. He was chosen as a Crusade Scholar for higher education in the United States. Completing his B.A. degree, Phi Beta Kappa, he went on to complete his master's degree at the University of Pittsburgh. Upon his return to India, Bishop Pickett enlisted him for development work, both in urban and village Christian work.

Bishop Balaram was a highly creative person, full of ideas. Very articulate and winsome, he won many friends for India wherever he went. He and Bishop Mathews were intimate friends for thirty years. He knew personally many of the political leaders of newly independent India, and helped to offset the damaging image of the Indian Christian Church and community as "foreign."

Bishop Balaram's services in the episcopal office were cut short by death from a heart attack, January 17, 1968, after serving only three years. He is buried in Lucknow.

Dana Dawson
(1892–1964)

Dana Dawson was elected by the South Central Jurisdictional Conference to the episcopacy in 1948, after a distinguished pastorate in larger churches in Arkansas, Oklahoma, and Louisiana.

He was assigned to the Topeka area, and from 1948 to 1952 he had the work in Kansas and Nebraska. From 1952 to his retirement in 1960, because of ill health, he had the work in Kansas alone.

Born in Larrabee, Iowa, April 18, 1892, Dana Dawson was a true preacher and a pastor. His pulpit style was particularly impressive. He spoke in measured tones and scarcely raised his voice in the course of a sermon. He looked straight at his audience as he preached, and the earnestness of his spirit reflected itself in his face. He had a fine command of language, and his sermons were marked by rich content.

Bishop Dawson was the perfect gentleman, quiet, reserved, brotherly, and understanding. He took the floor very little in the Council of Bishops, but when he did, he merited attention.

He enjoyed travel. His reports on his journeys to the far places of the earth were always masterpieces, rich with keen observations. For several years he did not enjoy good health, but he kept to rigid disciplines as prescribed by his physician and continued to travel and to carry on his work.

He died at his home in Shreveport, May 2, 1964, while the General Conference at Pittsburgh was in session. He is buried in Shreveport.

Charles Wesley Flint
(1878–1964)

Charles Wesley Flint, born November 14, 1878, in Stouffville, Ontario, Canada, was elected to the episcopacy by the 1936 General Conference of the Methodist Episcopal Church, which was the last General Conference of that church. He had been the chancellor of Syracuse University. Prior to that he was pastor of outstanding pulpits in New York state.

His first assignment was to the Atlanta area of the Methodist Episcopal Church. In 1939 he was assigned to the Syracuse area and in 1944 to the Washington area, where he served eight years.

Bishop Flint belonged in the category of the scholar

among the bishops. He had the mind, interest, and insight of a scholar. A number of books came from his gifted pen, one of the most interesting of which was a biography of Charles Wesley, for whom he was named.

Bishop Flint was a thoughtful, but not a moving preacher. He was an able and keen administrator. He had the heart of a pastor.

One of the distinguished characteristics of Bishop Flint was his unusual sense of humor. As he sat in the council, it was usually with a smile upon his face. He gave the impression of being a wise old owl, watching the performance of the more vocal brethren. He took the floor seldom; but when he did, it was usually to make some wise observation, couched in few words and more often than not accompanied by a flash of wit. He delighted in passing around little notes that spoke volumes, such as one written in his own retirement days suggesting that the law be changed so that retired bishops be allowed to vote in the council but not speak. He delighted in puncturing episcopal balloons, and he was abundantly able to do it in an adroit way. No one contributed to moments of merriment in the council more than Bishop Flint.

Following the appearance of the article, "Methodism's Pink Fringe," which caused such wide disturbance, he had some stationery printed with a pink fringe.

The bishop was never honored by being elected an officer of the council, nor was he given spotlight assignments, but this did not disturb him. He only smiled at those who wore their ecclesiastical hats too seriously.

Bishop Flint had a habit not followed by any other bishop in these later years. He usually answered his correspondence by longhand and normally in no more than one or two sentences. No one could pack more into a short sentence than could he.

The bishop began to break in health around 1948. Nevertheless he was returned to the Washington area. He developed an impediment in his speech which made it difficult for one to understand him. It also became difficult for him to walk. However, he managed by sheer determination to carry on for the remainder of the quadrennium.

His last years were far from easy ones—with his wife going on before him, with increasing physical incapacity, and with life finally confining him to his room. He still maintained his radiant spirit, however, and continued to the end to send to his friends, and to the council itself, those never-to-be-forgotten, brief, pungent letters, which all who knew him will continue to associate with the name of Charles Wesley Flint.

Bishop Flint died December 12, 1964, and is buried in Syracuse, New York.

Alsie Raymond Grant
(1897–1967)

A. Raymond Grant was elected by the Western Jurisdiction to the episcopacy in 1952 after outstanding pastorates in California. He was born August 24, 1897, in Oshkosh, Wisconsin, but migrated to the western states and spent most of his life there.

Bishop Grant's first and only episcopal assignment was to the Portland area, which then included Oregon, Washington, Idaho, and Alaska. He was not happy when in 1960 the work in Washington and part of Idaho was taken away to form the Seattle area. He was greatly devoted to the work in Alaska, and he gave to it excellent leadership and left a lasting impression upon it.

Bishop Grant did not take the floor too often in the meetings of the council, and he was never one of its officers or too active in its committee affairs. He confined his interests mostly to his area, where he labored effectively and tirelessly.

He was one of the more pronounced liberals of the episcopal company. It was hard for him to understand conservatives or to tolerate their viewpoints. He was rigidly true to his own highest insights.

He was an excellent preacher and a master of language. His prayers were marked by a particular beauty, and a volume of them was issued by friends as a fitting memorial to him.

Much of the time Bishop Grant suffered from ill health. This showed itself occasionally when he appeared to be under strain. He bore his sufferings courageously and carried on bravely when less heroic men would have asked to be excused.

He died August 15, 1967, after a lengthy period of illness.

Marquis Lafayette Harris
(1907–1966)

Marquis Lafayette Harris was elected to the episcopacy by the Central Jurisdiction in 1960, after a twenty-four-year presidency of Philander Smith College. He was assigned to the Atlantic Coast area.

Born March 8, 1907, in Armstrong, Macon County, Georgia, Bishop Harris was a physical giant. As a college boy he had played football, and to the end he looked the part of a gigantic linesman. In fact, he had been All-American.

But Bishop Harris was not only a physical giant. He was also an intellectual giant and had one of the best minds in the council, with a Ph.D. degree behind his name. At the age of thirty-one he was elected president of Philander Smith College in Little Rock, Arkansas. He had a philosophic bent, and his powers of perception were striking.

He did not speak often in the council, but when he did speak, his words were usually gems of wisdom. His great spirit matched his great body and great mind. He was affable, brotherly, fair, and understanding. He took his stand for the rights of his people, but there was no bitterness about him.

It seemed strange that a physical giant such as he should have health problems, but they did develop, and his promising career in the episcopacy was cut short after six years by his death, October 7, 1966, in Atlanta. He is buried there.

NEW STRUCTURES FOR MISSION

Ivan Lee Holt
(1886–1967)

Ivan Lee Holt, born January 9, 1886, in DeWitt, Arkansas, was the first bishop elected by the last General Conference of the Methodist Episcopal Church, South in 1938. He was the pastor of St. John's Church, St. Louis, Missouri, at the time of his election. Previous to that time he had held other pastorates in Missouri and had taught at Southern Methodist University for four years. He was a widely known pulpit and platform speaker.

Upon his election he was assigned to the Dallas area. He was a close friend of Bishop John M. Moore of Texas and apparently had his blessing at the time of his election.

Following his Dallas assignment, he spent twelve years serving Methodism in Missouri, which he so dearly loved. As a young man he came under the influence of the great Missouri bishop, Bishop Hendrix, and for years had close connections with the Hendrix and Scarritt families. He once wrote a small book entitled *The Missouri Bishops,* in which he gave brief biographies of the sons of Missouri who had occupied the episcopal office up to that time.

Bishop Holt was a distinguished-looking man. He was fastidious in his taste and manners. He loved social occasions and did not take too seriously the admonition to take the lowest seat at the table. Most often he was at the head table, either because of some position that he occupied, or because he was the main speaker. He loved good company, and he was good company. He frequently mentioned in sermon and in conversation the distinguished world characters he had known.

He was immaculate in his dress, and he relished dress-up affairs. He knew all the rules of proper behavior for such occasions and observed them scrupulously. He always seemed to enjoy being a bishop.

Bishop Holt lived ahead of his day in the Church, South. He was generally liberal for that time in his theology, though not radically so. He was devoted to liturgy and was a liturgist of the first order. His early stand with reference to liturgical practices frightened some of his older brethren, and he threw some of them into turmoil when he introduced the use of pulpit robes in Southern Methodist University worship services.

Bishop Holt was an early advocate of ecumenism. He took advanced positions with reference to relations with other communions of believers. He had friendly contacts particularly with Roman Catholics before the days when Pope John XXIII opened the doors to wider fellowship. It was largely in recognition of his ecumenical spirit that he was elected president of the World Methodist Council in 1951, an office that he held either active or emeritus until his death.

The bishop was a tireless world traveler. There were few lands on this earth where his feet had not walked. Occasionally there would be a complaint that he traveled to the neglect of his area, but this complaint was never pushed too seriously. He continued to travel after he retired, delighting to walk once again in paths in which his feet had walked in earlier years.

For one who traveled so much, Bishop Holt did considerable writing. He was the author of a number of books and countless articles. He was somewhat eclectic in style and quoted extensively from other writers.

The members of the council used to jest the bishop about his attendance at its meetings, affirming that he came late and left early. There was some exaggeration in this, but it is true that he was ever a man on the run.

In presiding over the General Conference, Bishop Holt liked to keep the business moving quickly, and he was good at this. For several General Conferences he was given the chair at the closing session where there was much to be done and the conference was working against the clock. He always prided himself upon this last session assignment.

Since his death, January 12, 1967, in Atlanta, the council has not had exactly his counterpart within its ranks. His body was taken to St. Louis, Missouri, for burial.

NEW STRUCTURES FOR MISSION
Edward Wendall Kelly
(1880–1964)

Edward W. Kelly was elected to the episcopacy by the Central Jurisdiction in 1944, after popular and most distinguished pastorates. He was getting well along in years at the time of his election. His assignment was to the St. Louis area, which at that time included the Negro conferences in Missouri, Arkansas, and Tennessee, and the Lexington conferences, which represented work in seven states.

Bishop Kelly, born December 27, 1880, in Mexia, Texas, represented the best of the black tradition in preaching. His insight into the Scriptures was keen, the hortatory note was strong in his preaching, and his rich sense of humor seasoned his sermons with salt.

His unique way of expressing what he had to say was well illustrated at the District Superintendents' Conference at St. Louis in 1944, when the Crusade for Christ was being launched. He was pleading for the fullest cooperation in raising the substantial goal that the General Conference had set for the church. Finally he said, "Brethren, you are not going to slip up on raising $25,000,000."

Like many of the older black preachers he would sometimes break into song. His employment of song with his audiences was always deeply moving.

Bishop Kelly was a somewhat heavy man. He had gray hair and wore thick glasses. He had a halting walk, which showed that age was creeping up on him. When he did take the floor in the council, it was usually to make some brief remark that was spiced with humor, however serious the subject. The council always welcomed his assignment to lead a devotional hour, for the members knew he would speak to their hearts as well as to their minds.

Upon retirement, Bishop Kelly made his home in Detroit. He died July 28, 1964. With his passing, the church lost a treasured type in the episcopacy, the like of which will not probably be seen again.

HISTORY OF THE COUNCIL OF BISHOPS

William Vernon Middleton
(1902–1965)

The Northeastern Jurisdictional Conference elected W. Vernon Middleton to the episcopacy in 1960 from the secretaryship of the national division of the Board of Missions. He had given excellent leadership in the field of home missions. His assignment was to the Pittsburgh area, where he was the host to the 1964 General Conference.

Vernon Middleton was born on Christmas Day, 1902, in Baltimore, Maryland. He was a forthright, courageous man of strong convictions, speaking his mind freely when he felt that the occasion demanded it. He knew how to live with difference of opinion without being intolerant toward those who differed from him. He had marked gifts for administration and was known throughout the church as a wise counselor, particularly in difficult situations. He played an important part in the establishment of Alaska Methodist University.

Bishop Middleton's time in the episcopacy did not prove to be lengthy. He was one of the company of Methodist bishops who have died on the road. The end came suddenly for him, November 12, 1965, in Minneapolis, as he was enroute to the meeting of the Council of Bishops in Seattle, Washington. He is buried in Chambersburg, Pennsylvania.

Alexander Preston Shaw
(1879–1966)

Alexander P. Shaw was elected to the episcopacy by the 1936 General Conference of the Methodist Episcopal Church, and he served the New Orleans and the Baltimore areas. He had long been an acknowledged leader among Negro Methodists, had held several strong churches in California, and had been editor of the *Central Christian Advocate*.

Bishop Shaw, born April 18, 1879, in Abbeville, Mississippi, was a deeply moving preacher. He preached with liberation and forcefulness, often reaching high emotional peaks in his preaching. He had full command of his audiences, and inevitably they gave him a welcomed response. There was a strong social note in his preaching. One of the sermons he loved to use most was on the text, "Thy Kingdom come *on earth.*"

Bishop Shaw was a giant of a man physically. He stood straight and tall, and moved with poise and deliberation. By his very presence he made an impression in any company. He kept a good spirit and was always approachable and understanding. He presided well when in the chair and never seemed to become confused.

He retired in 1952 but was called out of retirement in 1953 to serve part of the New Orleans area following the death of Bishop Brooks. He continued to serve for the remainder of the quadrennium. He died March 7, 1966, and is buried in Los Angeles.

Ferdinand Sigg
(1902–1965)

Ferdinand Sigg was elected to the episcopacy by the Southern European Central Conference in 1954. He served the Geneva area until his death in 1965. In many respects, the Geneva area was the most complex area in the church. It included work in nine countries, five of them behind the Iron Curtain.

Born March 22, 1902, in Thalwil near Zurich, Switzerland, Ferdinand Sigg was a Swiss by nationality. Trained as a banker and administrator, he felt a call to the ministry. His training in the business world proved very useful throughout his ministry. He served for some years as secretary to the bishop who more than any other typed European Methodism, Bishop John L. Nuelson.

Bishop Sigg's ministry in the church, his experience with the publishing house in Zurich, his known ecumenical interests and activity, and the confidence which he commanded made him a natural choice to follow Bishop

Garber when he returned to the United States. Bishop Sigg undertook his assignment with devotion and efficiency. No bishop during this period faced greater complications in the social and political situation in which his work had to be done.

Bishop Sigg was a scholar with a finely trained mind. What few observations he made in the council usually represented a scholar's insight. He was a tall, spare man who had difficulty with his sight and had to use strong glasses and hold whatever he was reading close to his face. He was of an exceedingly cordial spirit and was always good company. He was a modest man and tended to underrate himself.

He died October 27, 1965, and was buried in Fluntern Cemetery, Zurich, Switzerland.

VIII

Launching a New Church in a Time of Turbulence
1968–1972

The 1968 General Conference met April 23–May 4, in Dallas Memorial Auditorium, Dallas, Texas. This was actually the Uniting Conference of the two churches, The Methodist Church and the Evangelical United Brethren.

A final session of the General Conference of The Methodist Church was held on April 22, with Bishop Tippett presiding. Attention was given to necessary routine matters to bring to a close the twenty-nine years of the separate existence of The Methodist Church.

A final session of the General Conference of the Evangelical United Brethren Church was also held on April 22. Bishop Heininger presided in the morning and Bishop Howard in the afternoon.

Bishop Heininger asked for the retired relation, and his request was granted. Dr. Paul Washburn was elected as the last bishop to be elected by the Evangelical United Brethren Church. Bishop Mueller invited Bishop Short to participate in his consecration, thus paralleling the action of 1784 when Philip Otterbein, a United Brethren, participated in the consecration of Francis Asbury, the first American Methodist bishop.

The Uniting Conference opened on April 23 with a formal service of union participated in by Bishops Tippett, Mueller,

Wicke, Webb, and Washburn, along with numerous other persons. The message was brought by Dr. Albert Outler.

The Episcopal Address was prepared and read by Bishop Lloyd C. Wicke. It was signed by one hundred bishops of The United Methodist Church, active and retired. Grateful recognition was given to the ten bishops who had died during the last quadrennium of 1964-1968.

The message at the opening communion service was brought by Bishop Harmon.

Devotional messages were brought by Bishops Stuart, Nagbe, Copeland, Kearns, J. O. Smith, Noah Moore, Galloway, Shungu, Sparks, Lundy, and Wunderlich.

Bishops presiding at the conference were Bishops Tippett, Hardin, Corson, Howard, Golden, Henley, Frank, Hagen, Mueller, Lord, Ensley, Loder, W. Ralph Ward, Copeland, Stowe, Raines, Garrison, Kennedy, W. Angie Smith, Thomas, Palmer, Nall, and Mathews.

Evangelical United Brethren Church: Union of United Brethren and Evangelical Churches

Since at the Dallas General Conference The United Methodist Church was formed by the union of The Methodist Church and the Evangelical United Brethren Church, it is appropriate that some word now be said about the Evangelical United Brethren partners in that union. The Evangelical United Brethren Church had been formed in 1946 by a union of the United Brethren and the Evangelical Churches.

At the time of the 1946 union the active bishops of the United Brethren Church were Bishops A. R. Clippenger of Dayton, Ohio; Fred L. Dennis of Indianapolis, Indiana; J. B. Showers of Harrisburg, Pennsylvania; Ira D. Warner of Fresno, California; and V. O. Weidler of Kansas City, Missouri. The retired bishops were G. B. Batdorf of Harrisburg, Pennsylvania; and H. H. Fout of Indianapolis, Indiana.

LAUNCHING A NEW CHURCH IN A TIME OF TURBULENCE

The active bishops of the Evangelical Church were Bishops George E. Epp of Naperville, Illinois; E. W. Praetorius of St. Paul, Minnesota; John S. Stamm of Harrisburg, Pennsylvania; and C. H. Stauffacher of Kansas City, Missouri. There were no retired Evangelical bishops at the time of the merger.

The above-named bishops were deceased when the Evangelical United Brethren and Methodist union was consummated, with the exception of Bishop Epp.

It is appropriate here to mention those bishops who did not live to see the union into The United Methodist Church.

Arthur R. Clippinger (1875–1958) was the senior bishop of the United Brethren Church at the time of the 1946 union. He was elected in 1921. He had a long tenure as bishop in Ohio where he was most influential. He was active in the affairs of Bonebrake Seminary and of Otterbein College. He was remembered for many things, but among others for his habit of always wearing a rose in the lapel of his coat. He retired in 1950 and died suddenly in 1958 while attending a meeting of the Board of Bishops.

Fred L. Dennis (1890–1958) enjoyed the admiration of the entire church. He had a quiet manner of presiding, which set everyone at ease, but he could be firm when necessary. He was adept at healing differences and negotiating the settlement of problems. He was elected in 1941, served the Indianapolis area, and died in 1958.

J. B. Showers (1879–1962) was elected by the 1945 General Conference of the United Brethren Church, which was the last General Conference of that church. He was a Canadian by birth, his father having served as pastor of United Brethren churches in Canada. For many years he served as professor of systematic theology at Bonebrake Seminary. During the depression years he was called to be the agent of the United Brethren Publishing House. Here he wrought a miracle of management and in 1945 was able to announce that the house was free of debt. He served the Eastern area in the episcopacy and then was transferred to the Indianapolis area. He retired in 1954 and died in 1962.

HISTORY OF THE COUNCIL OF BISHOPS

Ira D. Warner (1884–1964), prior to his election to the episcopacy in 1929, was the pastor of First United Brethren Church, Canton, Ohio. At that time this church was the largest in the United Brethren Church. The bishop was known for his strong emphasis upon both evangelism and stewardship. He served the West Coast area, where he established many new churches, and visited personally all the congregations and held revivals in most of them. He also carried the responsibility for the work in Sierra Leone.

V. O. Weidler (1887–1950) was elected to the episcopacy in 1937 and assigned to the United Brethren work in the Southwest. He died suddenly on his way to a churchwide Christian education convocation in 1950 at Kitchener, Ontario, Canada.

E. W. Praetorius (1882–1966) was an outstanding Christian education leader. He was an exacting scholar and writer who served as editor of the *Discipline*. He was also an excellent preacher, who was gifted at interpreting the Scriptures. Elected to the episcopacy in 1934, he served the St. Paul area for twenty years, retired in 1954, and died in 1966.

John S. Stamm (1878–1956) was elected to the episcopacy of the Evangelical Church from the chair of systematic theology of Evangelical Theological Seminary in 1926. He served the Kansas City and the Harrisburg areas and was a recognized scholar. He was known for his ecumenical leadership and served a term as president of the Federal Council of Churches. A memorial room at the headquarters of the National Council of Churches bears his name. He retired in 1958 and died in 1970.

C. H. Stauffacher (1879–1956), elected to the episcopacy of the Evangelical Church in 1934, gave successful leadership to the southwestern work of that church. Upon the death of Bishop Weidler, he took over the United Brethren work also and was able to unite the two. He retired in 1954 and died in 1956.

Two bishops of the former United Brethren Church, retired at the time of the 1946 union, were:

LAUNCHING A NEW CHURCH IN A TIME OF TURBULENCE

B. G. Batdorf (1874–1954) was elected in 1929 to the episcopacy of the United Brethren Church and served the Eastern area of that church, with headquarters at Harrisburg, Pennsylvania. He was a strong churchman, highly respected throughout the church. He always wore clericals at a time when this was not common practice for United Brethren ministers. He retired in 1945.

Henry H. Fout (1861–1947) was a native of West Virginia. After serving for some years in the pastorate, he was elected editor of church school literature, the position from which he was elected to the episcopacy in 1913. He was assigned to the Northwest area of the United Brethren Church. He was one of the most honored and respected bishops of the United Brethren Church. He retired in 1941 and died in 1947 after being struck by a car when crossing a street in Indianapolis.

The eleven bishops elected by the Evangelical United Brethren Church after the 1946 union were D. T. Gregory, 1950; L. L. Baughman, 1954; Harold R. Heininger, 1954; Reuben H. Mueller, 1954; J. Gordon Howard, 1957; Paul E. V. Shannon, 1957; Paul M. Herrick, 1958; Herman W. Kaebnick, 1958; W. Maynard Sparks, 1958; Paul W. Milhouse, 1960; and Paul A. Washburn, 1968, on the eve of the union with The Methodist Church. Bishops Baughman, Gregory, and Shannon died before the union of the Evangelical United Brethren Church with The Methodist Church.

L. L. Baughman (1889–1960) began his ministry in Illinois when still in his teens and was known as "the boy preacher." After serving as pastor of First United Brethren Church of Bloomington, Illinois, he was elected superintendent of the Illinois Conference. Following this he became executive secretary of the General Council on Administration, an office he held for four years before being elected bishop in 1954. His assignment was to the Southwestern area and the work in Sierra Leone. As a bishop he was known for his hard work and his emphasis upon stewardship and tithing. He died from a heart attack in a hotel room while he and his wife were enroute to the Oklahoma Conference, having just held the Kansas Conference.

David T. Gregory (1889–1956) was noted for his emphasis upon stewardship, so much so that in the United Brethren Church he was commonly referred to as "Mr. Stewardship." He was elected by the 1950 General Conference of the newly united church and assigned to the Pittsburgh area. He and his wife were killed instantly in an automobile accident during the Christmas holidays in 1956 while enroute to visit their daughter.

Paul Shannon (1898–1957) served for only one month as a bishop. He was elected in 1957 and assigned to the East Central area. He became ill following his first conference and died a few days later. He had been a highly respected leader in the United Brethren Church and served as superintendent in the Pennsylvania Conference for many years. He was often a delegate to General Conference.

The story of the bishops of the United Brethren Church and the Evangelical Church, who served during approximately the same period of time as that represented by the earlier years of the Council of Bishops of The Methodist Church, has been told at length by Bishop Paul W. Milhouse in his volume, *Nineteen Bishops of the Evangelical United Brethren Church.*

The bishops of the Evangelical United Brethren between 1945 and 1960 gave major attention to consolidation of the union of the United Brethren and Evangelical Churches. They took leadership in rewriting the Confession of Faith, combining the two former confessions into one. They inaugurated the practice of rotating presiding responsibilities in European Conferences. They also began holding regular consultations with the chief executives of program boards and the presidents of institutions. During the sixties all the bishops of the Evangelical United Brethren Church were active in developing the plan for United Methodist union and carrying it to completion. Dr. Paul Washburn was assigned for several years to give his full time to the union.

He carried secretarial responsibilities in the commission and in his capacity did yeoman service. Following his election at the last General Conference of the Evangelical United Brethren Church in Dallas, he was assigned at the North Central Jurisdictional Conference to the Minnesota area.

At the time of the 1968 General Conference the seven active Evangelical United Brethren bishops were assigned one to each of the jurisdictions; with an additional one assigned to the Northeastern and to the North Central Jurisdictions, where the Evangelical United Brethren Church had its heaviest concentration of membership. Bishops Howard and Kaebnick were assigned to the Northeastern Jurisdiction; Bishops Mueller and Washburn to the North Central; Bishop Herrick to the Southeastern; Bishop Milhouse to the South Central; and Bishop Sparks to the Western. Bishops Heininger and Epp, both retired, became part of the North Central College of Bishops.

At the Jurisdictional and Central Conferences following the 1968 General Conference, seventeen bishops were scheduled for retirement. They had been presented at the General Conference by Bishop Short, with Bishop Paul Martin responding for the group. As a group they gave 260 years of episcopal service.

The following bishops retired after the 1968 Jurisdictional Conferences:

Northeastern Jurisdiction:	Fred P. Corson
	Fred G. Holloway
Southeastern Jurisdiction:	Paul N. Garber
	Walter C. Gum
North Central Jurisdiction:	Edwin R. Garrison
	Harold R. Heininger
	T. Otto Nall, Jr.
	Richard C. Raines
South Central Jurisdiction:	Paul E. Martin
	W. Angie Smith
Western Jurisdiction:	Donald H. Tippett

HISTORY OF THE COUNCIL OF BISHOPS

From the Central Conferences:
  Latin America: Sante U. Barbieri
                         P. R. Zottele
  Germany: Friedrich Wunderlich
  Philippines: Jose L. Valencia
  Southern Asia: Mangal Singh
                           Gabriel Sundaram

At the subsequent Jurisdictional and Central Conferences the following bishops were elected and took their places in the Council of Bishops:
  Northeastern Jurisdiction: Roy C. Nichols
                                       D. Frederick Wertz
  Southeastern Jurisdiction: William R. Cannon
  North Central Jurisdiction: A. James Armstrong
  South Central Jurisdiction: Alsie H. Carleton

From the Central Conferences:
  Philippines: Cornelio M. Ferrer
                  Paul L. A. Granadosin
  Africa: Abel T. Muzorewa
  Southern Asia: Ram Dutt Joshi
                        Joseph R. Lance
                        Eric A. Mitchell

Bishop Samuel, elected in Pakistan, and Bishop Pegura, in Latin America, were bishops of The United Methodist Church for only a brief period as their churches shortly became autonomous.

An orientation retreat for the newly elected bishops was held at Mammoth Cave, Kentucky, October 23-25, 1968.

With the final dissolution of the Central Jurisdiction in 1968, the distribution of bishops was implemented, similar to the one that marked the transition of the former Evangelical United Brethren bishops. Bishop Prince Taylor had already been in the Northeastern Jurisdiction. Bishop James Thomas was assigned to the North Central; Bishop Scott Allen to the Southeastern; Bishop Noah Moore to the South Central; and Bishop Golden to the Western. The retired bishops, Bishops Willis King and Edgar A. Love, became members of the colleges where they were resident:

LAUNCHING A NEW CHURCH IN A TIME OF TURBULENCE

Bishop King of the South Central area; Bishop Love of the Northeastern.

The first bishops to be elected by Central Conferences in the new United Methodist Church were Bishop Ole E. Borgen, elected by the Northern European Central Conference; and Bishop Armin E. Hartel, elected by the German Democratic Republic Central Conference. Both of them were elected in 1970.

The Council of Bishops began in June of 1968 the practice of having a one-day meeting of the executive committee to plan the sessions of the council and to care for other items referred to it. The first of such meetings was held at St. Louis, June 24, 1968. Heretofore, the agenda had been planned by the secretary alone in Bishop Oxnam's day, and by the secretary and the president in the earlier years of Bishop Short's secretaryship.

Council meeting: Chicago, November 11-14, 1968

The Council of Bishops met at the Conrad Hilton Hotel, Chicago, Illinois, November 11-14, 1968, with Bishop Frank presiding.

Much of the time was spent planning for the promotion of the Fund for Reconciliation.

Credentials as bishop in the new United Methodist Church were furnished all the bishops of the former Methodist Church and the former Evangelical United Brethren Church.

Council meeting: Charleston, West Virginia, April 8-11, 1969

The council met at the Charleston House, Charleston, West Virginia, April 8-11, 1969, with Bishop Frank presiding.

Bishop Welch died at his home in New York just as the bishops were assembling for their meeting.

A period of time was devoted to hearing Dr. Walter Muelder discuss "Christian Ethics."

HISTORY OF THE COUNCIL OF BISHOPS

The council voted to have a meeting with selected Methodist youth at Kansas City, December 29-30, 1969, with all the bishops requested to attend. This was one more attempt of the council to hear the voice of youth.

A resolution presented by Bishop Nichols opposing the use of state government funds for private and parochial schools was adopted.

The council was given a dinner one evening by Bishop and Mrs. Wertz and the West Virginia area. Governor and Mrs. Moore were present. The address was made by Dr. Franz Shaeffer. Bishop Fred Holloway delighted the council members with a poetry reading, the art of which he was a true master.

The executive committee met in Madison, Wisconsin, July 10, 1969, to plan for the fall meeting.

Council meeting: Columbus, Ohio, November 11-13, 1969

The council met at the Neil House, Columbus, Ohio, November 11-13, 1969, with Bishop Mueller presiding.

Dr. Lyle Schaller led in a full day's discussion of "The Church and Current Sociological Trends."

A period was devoted to a study of the parish system, led by Bishop Garrison.

Bishop Mathews introduced a consideration of the council structure and of ways and means for the council to give increasing leadership to the church.

Bishop Frank reported for the committee appointed by the General Conference to investigate the Publishing House.

Bishops Ensley and Short and Dr. Charles Parlin and Miss Dorothy McConnell were named as the first delegates to the British Conference under the newly approved concordat.

"The Black Manifesto," delivered by James Foreman and others, together with certain confrontations in some churches, had recently captured the headlines. The council gave a considerable block of time to the reaction generated.

Bishop Short presented a paper on the Manifesto from the viewpoint of its effect upon the churches; Bishop Wicke from the viewpoint of the Board of Missions; and Bishop Mueller from the viewpoint of the National Council of Churches. The Council of Bishops issued a statement in which it said: "Some of the demands of the Manifesto are absurd. . . . But [it is] to be understood in the light of centuries of deprivation and exploitation. Black power responsibly used does not allow for violence."

At a public dinner given by the Methodists of the West Ohio area, the council heard an address by the well-known coach, Woody Hayes.

The executive committee met at Hollywood, California, February 27, 1970, to plan for the spring meeting.

The 1968 General Conference had ordered a special five-day session to be held in 1970. The assumption was that there would be numerous matters needing attention that the Uniting Conference would not have time to cover. Once the special session got under way, however, these matters did not prove too many.

Council meeting: St. Louis, Missouri, April 16-20, 1970

The Council of Bishops met at the Jefferson Hotel, St. Louis, Missouri, before the special session of the General Conference, with Bishop Mueller presiding. It also met, of course, during the General Conference.

The pre-General Conference sessions were devoted to a consideration of the Episcopal Address, prepared by Bishop Howard, and to other council responsibilities related to the General Conference.

Retired Bishop Raines was given special responsibility in the area of recruitment, and Bishop Garrison, also retired, in the area of parish development.

An effort was made by way of new legislation, which the council favored, to make it possible for Central Conference bishops who reached retirement age in office to continue as retired members of the council. The proposed legislation was approved by the General Conference, but the Judicial Council ruled that it could not be retroactive in the case of those bishops who had lost their membership through the Alejandro decision.

Bishop and Mrs. Frank and the St. Louis area entertained the episcopal family at a dinner at the Sheraton Jefferson Hotel. The speaker was Bishop Kennedy.

Special Session, General Conference, St. Louis, April 20-25, 1970

The special session met in St. Louis, April 20-25, 1970. All the active bishops were present except one of the Central Conference bishops. The number of absent, retired bishops was unusually large. Eleven bishops had died during the two-year period.

The communion service, with which the 1970 General Conference opened, was in the charge of Bishop Scott Allen.

Devotional messages were brought by Bishops Raines, Nichols, Armstrong, Hunt, and Mitchell.

The bishops presiding were Mueller, Wicke, Mathews, Thomas, Ensley, Loder, Nichols, Slater, Lord, Stowe, Short, Washburn, and Goodson.

The Episcopal Address was prepared and read by Bishop Howard.

The St. Louis Conference met at a time when the pattern of disruption, so frequently followed in the sixties, was still in vogue. The General Conference did not find itself exempt, nor did the Council of Bishops. On one occasion the bishops were locked in their room by one group for a short period. Two of the older bishops were knocked down accidently as a result of some roughing-up tactics to keep the bishops locked in. There were several occasions when there was some disturbance during a conference session. Once an obscene banner was flown across the rear of the auditorium, but it was soon removed by the ushers. The pressure groups

LAUNCHING A NEW CHURCH IN A TIME OF TURBULENCE

were varied and with different concerns. The majority of them were content to distribute literature, talk with delegates, and ask for a hearing. The conference itself, the ushers, and the presiding officers kept calm and took in stride whatever happened.

Expressed to the General Conference at St. Louis in a dramatic and respectful way were the concerns of some of the minorities within its own membership, particularly its Black and Hispanic membership. The General Conference noted this concern and began a process of response that was carried forward at the 1972 General Conference. The response included other minorities also, such as the Oriental and Native American membership of the church.

The General Conference also recognized the desire of the youth of the church for a stronger voice by seating some youth on the floor of the conference, giving them voice but not vote. It was not possible under the constitution to extend the privilege of voting beyond delegates regularly elected by Annual Conferences.

Unhappily the 1970 General Conference came to the unfortunate end of having to adjourn without a quorum.

The executive committee met at Boston, July 13, 1970, to plan for the fall meeting.

Council meeting: Portland, Oregon, November 17-19, 1970

The Council of Bishops met at the Portland Hilton Hotel, Portland, Oregon, November 17-19, 1970, with Bishop Lord presiding.

The council heard Mr. John C. Kimball of the State Department speak on "Projected Issues in Foreign Policy in the Years Ahead." The council also spent a period in discussing "The Methodist Church and Church Union."

Bishops Washburn, Ensley, Taylor, and Short reported on development of the Committee on Structure and functioning of the Council set up by the General Conference.

An important step was taken at this meeting when Bishop

HISTORY OF THE COUNCIL OF BISHOPS

Armstrong was requested to take the initiative in developing a program looking to the achievement of world peace, and to report back to the council.

It was announced that Bishop Herrick had asked to be relieved of his area for health reasons, and that Bishop Cannon would assume responsibility for the Richmond area in addition to the Raleigh area.

The council took note of the organization of the Central Conference of the German Democratic Republic and the election of its first bishop, Bishop Armin Härtel.

Bishop and Mrs. Palmer and the Portland area entertained at a dinner at which the speaker was Senator Mark Hatfield.

The executive committee met at New Orleans, February 11, 1971, to plan for the spring meeting.

Council meeting: New York City, March 1-4, 1971

The Council of Bishops met in New York, March 1-4, 1971, in observance of the twenty-fifth birthday of the United Nations. The Secretary General and a number of United Nations personnel addressed the bishops and their wives. There was full and free discussion of the various subjects presented. Some of the sessions were held at The United Methodist United Nations Building.

The council took time out to attend a performance of *1776* as guests of Bishop and Mrs. Wicke and the New York area.

Council meeting: San Antonio, April 13-15, 1971

The council met at the St. Anthony Hotel, San Antonio, Texas, April 13-15, 1971, wih Bishop Lord presiding.

Bishop Mathews read the paper, "The Role of the Council of Bishops in the Future"; and Bishop Short one on "The Major Problems of the Council of Bishops as Seen by the Secretary." Both papers were discussed at length. On

LAUNCHING A NEW CHURCH IN A TIME OF TURBULENCE

motion of Bishop Nichols, a committee was appointed to consider the major points in the two papers and to report back recommendations. This was the beginning of the new pattern of operation developed within the next year and currently followed by the council.

The Native American Caucus was granted a thirty-minute hearing.

Bishop Wertz was named chairman of a task force on the orientation of newly elected bishops.

Bishop Sparks was given responsibility for the Portland area, following the death of Bishop Palmer, this responsibility to be exercised in addition to his responsibilities in the Seattle area.

A unique feature of this session was a Mexican dinner served on boats in the river that winds through San Antonio. The program for the evening was given from a stage on one side of the river, and the audience was seated on the other side. Bishop and Mrs. Slater were the hosts.

The executive committee met at Covington, Kentucky, July 20, 1971, to plan for the fall meeting.

Council meeting: Des Moines, November 15-18, 1971

The council met at the Fort Des Moines Hotel, Des Moines, Iowa, November 15-18, 1971, with Bishop Hardin presiding.

A major topic for consideration was the place of minorities in The United Methodist Church. Bishop Short read the paper, "Dealing Administratively with Minority Situations." The purpose of the paper was to precipitate the question of how minorities could be dealt with in the most constructive way. Written comments on the basic paper were submitted by Bishops Golden, Milhouse, and Slater. The council discussed the whole question at length. The result of the discussion was the appintment of the Committee on Response to Minorities composed of Bishops Goodson, Golden, Nichols, Slater, and Loder.

HISTORY OF THE COUNCIL OF BISHOPS

Before the council adjourned, the committee recommended holding a special conference with minority representatives in Atlanta on April 8, 1972. The council approved the recommendation.

A call for peace was also approved by the council.

Another session was devoted to two papers on church and state relationships, one by Bishop Finger and the other by Bishop Garrison.

At another session the council heard an address by Bishop David E. Richards of the Office of Pastoral Development of the Episcopal Church.

Bishop and Mrs. Thomas and the United Methodists of Iowa were hosts at a dinner at which Senator Harold Hughes was the speaker.

Council meeting: Epworth-by-the-Sea, Georgia, April 10-13, 1972

The council met in its final meeting of the quadrennium at Epworth-by-the-Sea, Georgia, April 10-13, 1972, just prior to the opening of General Conference, with Bishop Hardin presiding. It met periodically during the General Conference with Bishop Slater presiding.

At the Epworth meeting attention was devoted to the perfecting of the Episcopal Address prepared by Bishop Ensley.

The block and gavel, used for thirty-three years in The Methodist Church by the president, were retired. A new block and gavel for The United Methodist Church were put into use at this meeting. The block was made of wood taken from the steeple of the old Otterbein Church in Baltimore, and the gavel of wood from Barratt's Chapel in Delaware, where Coke and Asbury met in 1784. The block and gavel were made by the Rev. D. R. Gant, a retired minister of the Louisville Conference living at Drakesboro, Kentucky.

Bishop Wicke reported for the Committee on Structure and Functioning of the Council. Among other things, the report recommended the division of the council into four

LAUNCHING A NEW CHURCH IN A TIME OF TURBULENCE

committees: (1) teaching; (2) pastoral concerns; (3) administration; and (4) relational concerns. Each member of the council, active and retired, was to be assigned to one of the committees, preferably that of his choice. It also provided for an executive committee, larger than executive committees heretofore, with each jurisdiction and each council committee represented. Regulations were also adopted providing for a time limit for service on the executive committee or as chairman of one of the four council committees. The report further recommended that some sessions of each council meeting be open to the public. The recommendations of the committee were approved.

Bishop Armstrong reported on his assignment to develop a program looking to the achievement of world peace. He proposed an emphasis entitled "Peace and the Self-Development of Peoples," to be carried forward under the leadership of the Council of Bishops. The council approved the emphasis, as did also the General Conference. Bishop Armstrong was named to lead the emphasis, and Bishop Lord, retired, was assigned to help in its promotion.

Bishop and Mrs. J. O. Smith and the Atlanta area entertained the council at Jekyll Island on one evening. Bishop Arthur Moore and Bishop Smith spoke on Georgia Methodist history.

At this meeting of the council, Bishop Short completed sixteen years of service as secretary, and Bishop Alton was elected to the office.

The council met at Atlanta on April 8, 1972, with representatives of the Asian, Black, Indian, and Hispanic minorities, as had been planned at the Des Moines council meeting, November 18.

In Memoriam—1968–1972

The quadrennium of 1968–1972 saw the death of seventeen of the bishops of The United Methodist Church:

Raymond L. Archer
James C. Baker
Newell S. Booth
W. Y. Chen
Matthew W. Clair, Jr.
George E. Epp
Juan E. Gattinoni
Benjamin I. Guansing
Walter C. Gum
Odd A. Hagen
Wilbur E. Hammaker
Costen J. Harrell
J. Ralph Magee
Everett W. Palmer
Glenn R. Phillips
Raymond J. Wade
Herbert Welch

Raymond Leroy Archer
(1887–1970)

Raymond L. Archer was elected to the episcopacy by the Southeast Asia Central Conference in 1950. He had for thirty-one years been an honored missionary in Java, Sumatra, and Malaya. Returning to the United States in 1942, he served eight years on the staff of the Board of Missions. He was elected from that post to the episcopacy and was assigned to the Singapore area, where he gave six years of service as bishop.

Born October 21, 1887, in Adonis, West Virginia, he was a heavy man who moved deliberately and always approached matters thoughtfully and in a scholarly manner. He was indeed a scholar with a specialty in Islamic studies.

Bishop Archer attended the meetings of the council with interest, but sat through them quietly and usually did not speak unless someone called upon him. He was marked by an almost extreme modesty.

After retirement he moved to Pittsburgh, the conference

he had come from originally. In 1966 he was caught in the Judicial Council decision that held that Bishop D. D. Alejandro, who had reached retirement age as a term bishop and was not therefore subject to reelection, was no longer a member of the Council of Bishops. The status of other retired Central Conference bishops where term episcopacy prevailed was likewise affected.

Bishop Archer was greatly disappointed to lose his Council of Bishops privileges, but he took the decision without a murmur and had nothing to say. It is said that he did not even tell his wife who was ill at the time, for he knew what a disappointment this would have been for her.

He died July 4, 1970, in Pittsburgh and is buried there.

James Chamberlain Baker
(1879–1969)

James C. Baker was elected by the 1928 General Conference of the Methodist Episcopal Church to the episcopacy from his home state of Illinois, where he was born June 2, 1879, in Sheldon. For some years he had been in student work, following successful pastorates in smaller and larger churches in Illinois.

Bishop Baker was the father of the Wesley Foundation Movement, and his interest in this continued throughout his life. His first episcopal assignment was to Japan and Korea, and afterward he served the Los Angeles area until his retirement.

Bishop Baker was tall and had all the appearance of the scholar that he really was. He was widely read, loved good poetry, and was a master of diction.

He was a liberal in thought and was strongly committed to social progress. He kept fully abreast of world affairs and was always insisting that the council take note of what was happening and speak its mind accordingly. A word often upon his lips was "relevant." He often asked the council whether what was said or done or proposed was actually "relevant." He had little patience with preachers and people whose thinking, as he saw it, was too otherworldly.

Bishop Baker was a thoughtful preacher and his messages were designed to provoke active, intelligent response. He was not too effective in occupying the chair at General Conference since he sometimes had difficulty in controlling his personal reactions to what was happening on the floor.

The bishop had a great interest in the realm of missions and ecumenical affairs. He attended a number of the great world councils and conferences, which met in the earlier half of the century. For six years he was the distinguished chairman of the International Missionary Council.

Bishop Baker had an enviable record in administrating his area in California. He had a particular ability for spotting promising young preachers. He used to visit the seminaries regularly seeking preachers for California. He knew how to encourage young preachers and help them grow. Eight of his "preacher boys" to date have taken their place in the Council of Bishops in the person of Bishops Kennedy, Phillips, Tippett, Grant, Palmer, Stuart, Wheatley, and Choy.

There was a very tender side to Bishop Baker, which showed itself increasingly as he grew older. He would offer, as he had opportunity, the kindly word. All of us were conscious of his sustaining prayers. The last years were difficult for him. He was lonely for his beloved Lena, who had gone on before him. His increasing blindness and his failing strength added to his problems. He continued his interest, however, in the things that had long engaged his attention and made use of younger eyes to read for him. Having loved the church, he loved it unto the end.

He spent his last years in a retirement home in Claremont, California, where he died September 26, 1969. He is buried in Pasadena, California.

LAUNCHING A NEW CHURCH IN A TIME OF TURBULENCE
Newell Snow Booth
(1903–1968)

Newell S. Booth was elected to the episcopacy by the Northeastern Jurisdiction in 1944 to serve the work in Africa.

Born June 14, 1903, at Belchertown, Massachusetts, he had been a missionary in the Belgian Congo for some years previous to his election. He was admirably equipped to supervise the work of his episcopal area. The vast territory, which was his area and which he traveled, was of continental proportions and is now served by five resident native-born bishops.

The period during which Bishop Booth served was a time when the new Africa was emerging. Colonialism was passing, and new nations were being born in a day. On occasion there was violence, competition for leadership, and mistakes, all of which naturally go along with inexperience upon the part of those who have found new freedom. Bishop Booth welcomed every change which meant freedom for Africans, and he was himself no little part of the process. He believed the time had come for the election of national bishops. When this process began in 1964 with the election of Bishop John Wesley Shungu and Bishop E. A. Zunguze, he greatly rejoiced.

The Judicial Council in 1964 ruled that while Bishop Booth was elected by the Northeastern Jurisdictional Conference for service in Africa, he was nevertheless a bishop of that jurisdiction. In 1964 he returned to the United States and was assigned as resident bishop of the newly created Harrisburg area, which he served until his death.

Bishop Booth was a quiet, devoted man, marked by deep earnestness in all he had to say and do. He was well trained and had an analytical mind. When he spoke in the council, he usually stood holding in his hand some carefully thought-through notes. He set a good example of thinking first and then speaking.

His health was much impaired during the last years at

HISTORY OF THE COUNCIL OF BISHOPS

Harrisburg, but he kept struggling nobly to carry on his work. His last appearance before the Council of Bishops was a deeply moving one, as he tried so bravely to communicate his great concerns to the brethren and found himself reaching for words and dropping into repetition. It was clearly evident that his body was breaking, but that his brave and noble soul was still pressing on.

Bishop Booth died May 17, 1968. His body was returned to his hometown of Belchertown, Massachusetts, for burial.

Wen Yuan Chen
(1897–1968)

The China Central Conference of 1941 elected W. Y. Chen to the episcopacy.

Born in Foochow, China, July 16, 1897, the only son of a Chinese magistrate, W. Y. Chen came under the influence of President John Gowdy (later bishop) at the Anglo-Chinese College in Foochow and was baptized a Christian. He had an unusually fine education, having studied as a young man in America, England, and Germany, as well as in China.

He served as a pastor, a university teacher, and a dean, as well as executive secretary of the National Christian Council of China. Even after his election to the episcopacy he continued as the N.C.C. executive secretary during the very difficult days China was experiencing. His episcopal assignment was the Chungking area.

After the Communist take-over of China, Bishop Chen disappeared from sight. The report was that he was under house arrest. This situation apparently continued for some years. Finally it was reported that he had died of cancer, November 8, 1968, and was buried in Chungking.

Matthew Walker Clair, Jr.
(1890–1968)

Matthew W. Clair, Jr., was one of only two bishops whose father had also been a bishop, the other being Bishop Ernst

Sommer. Matthew W. Clair, Jr., was elected to the episcopacy by the Central Jurisdiction in 1952 from the pastorate of St. Marks Church in Chicago. He was assigned to the St. Louis area, where he served throughout his active episcopacy and where he resided after his retirement in 1960 and until his death, July 10, 1968.

Born August 12, 1890, at Harper's Ferry, West Virginia, Bishop Clair was a distinguished-looking man whose fine appearance made an impression wherever he went. He was genial in disposition and had a fine sense of humor of the quiet kind. His chuckle was unforgettable. He was a strong preacher, able to move his audiences deeply. His administration was firm but at the same time kindly.

His brother bishops had great confidence in him and often sent him on highly important and sometimes difficult missions, particularly in Africa. In some of these he found himself walking in the footsteps of his sainted father.

Bishop Clair was a member of the executive committee of the council for more years than perhaps any bishop except Bishop Oxnam and Bishop Short, each of whom had sixteen years as secretary.

George Edward Epp
(1885–1970)

George Edward Epp, born June 15, 1885, in Sheboygan, Wisconsin, was elected to the episcopacy by the Evangelical Church in 1930, after being executive secretary of the Missionary Society of that church. His commanding interest throughout his career was in missions.

It was the lot of Bishop Epp to be a bishop in three different churches: the Evangelical Church from 1930 to 1946; the Evangelical United Brethren Church from 1946 to 1968; and The United Methodist Church from 1968 to his death, May 7, 1970. He took the retired relation in 1958.

His episcopal colleagues in the Evangelical United Brethren Church held him in great love. His new associates

HISTORY OF THE COUNCIL OF BISHOPS

in The United Methodist Church felt that his presence at the meetings he was able to attend was a benediction to all.

Juan Ermete Gattinoni
(1878–1970)

Juan E. Gattinoni was elected by the Latin American Central Conference to the episcopacy in 1932.

Born June 24, 1878, in Italy, his Roman Catholic family migrated to Argentina while he was very young. There he was influenced by the Methodists and joined their church, eventually bringing most of his family also into the Methodist Church.

He trained for the ministry in Buenos Aires and served pastorates in Uruguay and Argentina. He was the first Central Conference bishop to be elected in Latin America. He gave twelve years of service as an active bishop.

Bishop Gattinoni's family have been strong leaders in Argentina Methodism. A son, Carlos Gattinoni, was elected in 1972 as the first bishop of the autonomous Methodist Church of Argentina.

Bishop Juan E. Gattinoni died January 7, 1970, in Buenos Aires.

Benjamin I. Guansing
(1908–1968)

Benjamin I. Guansing was elected by the Philippines Central Conference in 1967 to the episcopacy. He had come near to election at a session of the Central Conference several years before, but had fallen short by a small number of votes. After what seemed like a hopeless deadlock, the conference had adjourned to try again later for an election.

Bishop Guansing was born February 24, 1908, at Melabon, Rizal, the Philippines. He was a tall, quiet, scholarly man. After serving pastorates in the Philippines, he taught at the Union Theological Seminary in the Philippines, becoming its president in 1951. He had been a Crusade Scholar, earning his Master's degree from Columbia University in New York City.

After his election to the episcopacy, Bishop Guansing was assigned to the Manila area, composing the Philippines and Middle Philippines Conferences. An attractive new residence was built for him in Manila. He did not get to live in it long, however, and was able to attend only one or two meetings of the Council of Bishops. Upon returning home to Manila from the General Conference of 1968, he suffered a fatal heart attack and died June 3, 1968.

Walter Clark Gum
(1897–1969)

Walter C. Gum was elected to the episcopacy by the Southeastern Jurisdictional Conference in 1960. He was a favorite son of the Virginia Conference, and indeed a son of Virginia, where he was born at Monterey on July 4, 1897.

Bishop Gum had been a district superintendent and also a pastor of some of Virginia's strongest churches. His first assignment as bishop was to the Louisville area, where he served four years; and then the Richmond area, where he served another four years, retiring in 1968. His retirement period was brief, for he died March 31, 1969.

Bishop Gum was a fairly large man, trim in his proportions. He was athletic and had a great interest in sports, not only as an observer but also as a participant. He was a man's man and was particularly well liked by laymen. He was good natured and an incurable optimist. He was a promoter by nature, and he believed strongly that whatever needed to be done could be done.

He was fervently committed to evangelism and to missions. In these fields he took leadership not only in Virginia but throughout the Southeastern Jurisdiction and the church at large. He was a great money-raiser and an administrator who delighted in carrying a banner. One of his particular concerns was Alaska Methodist University.

HISTORY OF THE COUNCIL OF BISHOPS

Odd Arthur Hagen
(1905–1970)

The Northern European Central Conference elected Odd A. Hagen to the episcopacy in 1953. He was a native of Norway, born in Trondheim, December 16, 1905. He had served as pastor and as seminary president of the Union Scandinavian Theological School in Gothenburg. He was a scholarly man with several earned degrees and a number of honorary degrees. He wrote some six books.

Bishop Hagen was a man of medium height and trim build. He was of a genial disposition and almost always wore a smile. He was good company. He worked his area untiringly, administering faithfully the work in the four countries that comprised his area—Sweden, Norway, Denmark, and Finland. He also established contact with the work in Estonia and Latvia, which for the years following the Russian occupation had had no contact with the rest of Methodism.

In 1966 he was elected president of the World Methodist Council at their meeting in London, a position he filled until his death in 1970. As president he traveled widely, making a fine impression wherever he went. He and Mrs. Hagen were splendid hosts at the Oslo meeting of the tenth World Methodist Council, meeting there in 1961.

Bishop Hagen made it a habit to attend the council of Bishops meetings on an average of once a year. He was greatly respected by the entire council, and his interesting reports from the field were always welcome.

He died suddenly on January 28, 1970, in Stockholm, before his term as World Methodist Council president was to end in 1971.

Wilbur Emery Hammaker
(1876–1968)

Wilbur E. Hammaker was elected to the episcopacy by the 1936 General Conference of the Methodist Episcopal

LAUNCHING A NEW CHURCH IN A TIME OF TURBULENCE

Church from a distinguished pastorate of First Church, Youngstown, Ohio. A son of Ohio, born February 17, 1876, at Springfield, he had long been a participant in Annual Conference affairs in Ohio and in General Conferences and was known for being a good strategist.

Bishop Hammaker's first assignment was to Nanking, China, for three years. He was the last of the long line of general superintendents sent to reside in that long-loved early foreign mission field of the church. His three-years service in China witnessed the further development of the Central Conference and vast and far-reaching changes in the country itself. At the Uniting Conference in 1939 he was assigned to the Denver area, where he served until retirement in 1948.

Bishop Hammaker was a portly man who carried himself with great dignity and who looked the part of one who was conscious of his office. There were those who thought of him as being pompous, though he did not intend to be. He moved slowly and deliberately and spoke the same way. There was a slow drawl in his speech, whether in preaching or in conversation. He was always formal in his bearing, but kindly in spirit and always brotherly. He was definitely old style in his thinking and in his preaching. He was a cautious administrator, somewhat persistent, and usually sure of the end he had in mind. When in the chair in the General Conference he usually had the situation well in hand.

One of his major interests was social reform, particularly the battle against the liquor traffic. For some years he was connected with the Board of Temperance, and upon his retirement he became a part of its staff. He took up residence in the Methodist Building in Washington and lived there until his death, August 11, 1968. He was also connected with the old Anti-Saloon League and other dry organizations. One could, at each council meeting, expect some resolution either from him or from Bishop Cannon concerning the liquor traffic.

Bishop Hammaker's passing signified the end of an era. He was almost the last of that once large company in

HISTORY OF THE COUNCIL OF BISHOPS

Methodism, the foes of alcohol, who helped bring into being the Eighteenth Amendment to the Constitution.

Bishop Hammaker's body was returned to his hometown of Springfield, Ohio, for burial.

Costen Jordan Harrell
(1885–1971)

Costen J. Harrell was elected by the Southeastern Jurisdictional Conference to the episcopacy in 1944. At the time he was pastor of West End Church, Nashville.

Born February 12, 1885, at "Holly Grove," Gates County, North Carolina, Bishop Harrell had served strong churches in the North Carolina and Virginia Conferences before being transferred to the Tennessee Conference. His first assignment as bishop was to the Birmingham area where he served four years; following that he was assigned to the Charlotte area for eight years.

Bishop Harrell was a man of medium size who was somewhat stiff in his movements. Generally he gave an impression of being aloof. He was decidedly formal and observed all the amenities with scrupulous care.

There was much of the old South in the bishop. He was every inch the gentleman as conceived by the South of the day in which he grew up. Bishop Harrell was a man of sterling integrity and deep convictions. He did not hesitate to face problems or unpleasant situations. He entered without fear or hesitance any battle where he was convinced that truth and righteousness were involved.

The bishop was a finished preacher. He devoted long hours to the preparation of his messages, and every sentence was carefully weighed. He was perhaps the last of the Victorians in the episcopacy. Those who heard him preach soon discovered that he was fully familiar with Tennyson and Browning and similar popular spirits of the day in which he was young.

Bishop Harrell did a great deal of writing and had a number of books published, chiefly in the devotional field.

LAUNCHING A NEW CHURCH IN A TIME OF TURBULENCE

One of the hymns in *The Book of Hymns,* often used on dedication occasions, "Eternal God and Sovereign Lord," came from his hand. The little poem which he wrote upon the death of his son and only child is a gem of rare beauty.

As an administrator Bishop Harrell kept in full command of the situation. His adminstration was firm, and there were those who felt that he leaned too much toward being arbitrary. Actually he had a tender heart and a great concern for people, but he was fully confident of the validity of his own judgments. He was perhaps nearer in pattern of operation to some of the bishops of another generation than to most of the episcopal colleagues of his own day.

Bishop Harrell was an unusually able man. He was a master in writing church law. Only those who knew him well and the story of the development of the *Discipline,* particularly in the years beginning with 1939, can realize how many paragraphs in their original form were written by his hand. He was particularly interested in the sections that deal with the local church, with church finance, with church property, and with the judicial system.

Bishop Harrell was in reality the father of the Advance Program, which has added so richly to the life of the church for now some thirty years.

Following his retirement, Bishop Harrell moved to Atlanta, where for a number of years he taught in the Candler School of Theology until his health and that of his wife would not allow him to continue longer. He made a tremendous impression upon the young ministers who sat in his classroom, and thus in the eventide of his life made what was perhaps his most lasting contribution to The Methodist Church.

Bishop Harrell died in Atlanta, November 29, 1971.

Junius Ralph Magee
(1880-1970)

J. Ralph Magee was elected bishop by the Methodist Episcopal Church in 1932, at the bottom of the depression, from the pastorate of First Church, Seattle. He was originally a native of Iowa, born in Maquoketa, June 3, 1880, and his early ministry was spent in that state. Later he served churches in Massachusetts and Washington state. As bishop he served in turn the St. Paul, Minnesota, area; Des Moines, Iowa, area; and Chicago area, retiring in 1952.

Bishop Magee was a man of fair size who walked with something of a swagger. He was a matter-of-fact type of man, who had about him a certain ruggedness. He lacked the polish and finesse of some of his episcopal colleagues and had an utter disdain for anything he regarded as artificiality. He was forthright in speaking his mind and utterly sincere. He was courageous to the point of fearlessness and never shrank back from conflict if he thought it necessary. He was eminently fair, but he could be positive and even hard when he felt the occasion demanded it.

Bishop Magee was an acceptable but not an unusual preacher. His strong forte was administration. From 1944 to 1948 he gave efficient leadership to the Crusade for Christ throughout the entire church.

In 1944 the state of Iowa honored him by placing a portrait of him in the state capitol, thus recognizing him as one of its own sons who had the honor of heading the Methodism of the state he called home.

In the late years of his life, Bishop Magee was confined to his home by severe arthritis. After the death of his wife, he and his daughter, Dorothy, made their home together.

Bishop Magee died December 19, 1970, in Morton Grove, Illinois.

Everett Walter Palmer
(1906–1971)

Everett W. Palmer was elected to the episcopacy by the Western Jurisdictional Conference in 1960 after pastorates in the Dakotas, New Jersey, and California. His assignment as bishop was to the newly created Seattle area, where he served for eight years. He was then assigned to the Portland, Oregon, area. He found himself challenged particularly by the Alaska Mission and had thrown himself wholeheartedly into finding solutions for its concerns when death found him all too quickly.

Bishop Palmer was every inch a man. He was tall, athletic, and looked like a football player, which he had been in earlier days. He was the one bishop who wore a crewcut throughout his episcopacy. There was an expression of earnestness upon his face. He had a cheerful spirit, a fine sense of humor, and a twinkle in his eyes. He had about him something of the freshness of the western country, out of which he came, though he was born in Menomonie, Wisconsin, January 25, 1906. He grew up in South Dakota and was at one time a lumberjack and a miner.

Bishop Palmer was an excellent preacher. He had a unique preaching style. It was interesting to watch his face and his features. As he preached, he seemed to be reaching for words with his eyes, his facial expression, and his hands. This added to the charm of his delivery. He was always a popular preacher.

Bishop Palmer loved athletics and exercised regularly. The end came quite suddenly while he was on vacation in Palm Springs, California, on a day when he had been playing golf and jogging. He managed to get back to his car, but there the earthly journey ended for him, January 5, 1971. He had entertained the Council of Bishops at Seattle only a few weeks before.

Glenn Randall Phillips
(1894–1970)

Glenn R. Phillips was elected by the Western Jurisdictional Conference to the episcopacy in 1948. Though a midwesterner by birth, in Paulding County, Ohio, May 21, 1894, Bishop Phillips moved West and held various charges in California, where he was a very popular pastor. He and Bishop Donald Tippett were elected the same year from the same conference, Bishop Phillips from the pastorate of First Church, Hollywood, and Bishop Tippett from the pastorate of First Church, Los Angeles. They were great friends and in a way friendly rivals.

Bishop Phillips was assigned to the Denver area, which he served with great credit until his retirement in 1964. Following the death of Bishop Grant, he was recalled to active service and served the Portland area, comprising Oregon, Idaho, and Alaska, for the remainder of the quadrennium, retiring again in 1968 in San Diego, California.

Bishop Phillips was tall, trim, and bald. He had expressive blue eyes that had a light in them. He was genial by disposition, loved a good laugh, and had a dry sense of humor. He believed that good fun had a proper role to play in life. He was liberal but not extreme, understanding but not compromising. He was social minded and the strong champion of the rights and aspirations of all God's children.

For some several years before he died, Bishop Phillips was greatly incapacitated by illness. When he attended the General Conference for his last time, he was in a wheelchair, pushed by his pastor son. It was fully evident that his radiant spirit was still in full control despite his physical affliction. His episcopal brethren loved him with an abiding love.

Bishop Phillips died October 6, 1970. He is buried in Los Angeles.

Raymond J. Wade
(1875–1970)

Raymond J. Wade was elected by the Methodist Episcopal Church to the episcopacy in 1928. He had spent his ministry in Indiana, where he was born May 29, 1875, at Lagrange. He was secretary of the General Conference at the time of his election.

Bishop Wade's first episcopal assignment was to the Stockholm area, which he served from 1928 to 1940. At one time the area included work from the North Pole to the

LAUNCHING A NEW CHURCH IN A TIME OF TURBULENCE

Madeira Islands. In this area Bishop Wade rendered noteworthy service. He had to deal, however, with two particularly difficult problems. One was the aftermath of the case of Bishop Anton Bast whom he followed, who was suspended and who later withdrew from the ministry after both civil and church trials. The other was the problem of depleted resources growing out of the collapse of the Centenary Movement and the coming of the depression. The inevitable result was retrenchment at many points and even the final abandonment of the work in Madeira. Bishop Wade tried personally to collect funds from friends to make up for financial losses, but it was an impossible task.

From 1940 to 1948 Bishop Wade served the Detroit area.

After retirement he maintained a winter residence at St. Petersburg, Florida, and a summer residence at Bay View, Michigan. For almost all his retirement years he was the executive secretary of the Bay View Assembly in Michigan.

Bishop Wade was a heavy, rather slowly moving man. He had large eyes that were unusually expressive. He spoke with a somewhat deep voice. His preaching was thoughtful and earnest, but not animated. As his secretarial assignment would suggest, he was very careful of detail and always anxious to have everything exactly correct. He was a good parliamentarian and was at ease when presiding. He never appeared anxious or confused.

Bishop Wade did not take the floor too often in the council, but when he did, it was always to make some pertinent but brief observation. He was a diligent observer. He always took a front seat at the council and kept an attentive eye and ear on everything that went on. Usually he was to be seen making careful notes on what was being said.

Bishop Wade's last days were days of great affliction, but he maintained in his suffering his poise of soul. The writer visited him the late afternoon of the day he died, January 24, 1970.

Memorial services were held several days later at Christ Church, St. Petersburg, with Dr. Paul R. Horton in charge and Bishop Edward R. Garrison, also a bishop from

Indiana, and Bishop Short representing the Council of Bishops. The interment was in Petoskey, Michigan.

Herbert Welch
(1862–1969)

Herbert Welch was elected to the episcopacy by the Methodist Episcopal Church in 1916 from the presidency of Ohio Wesleyan University. He had been a leader in the establishment of the Methodist Federation for Social Action, an early exponent of the social gospel, and a strong advocate of the church's participation in all types of social reform.

His first episcopal assignment was to Korea and Japan, where he served for twelve years. He rendered significant service and was highly instrumental in bringing into being the autonomous church in Korea. He was the primary author of the now widely used Korean Creed.

From 1928 to 1932 he supervised the Pittsburgh area, but service in the states did not appeal to him. In 1932 he went gladly to China for his last assignment. He retired in 1936 but was recalled to serve the Boston area for two years following the death of Bishop Burns. After the Methodist Committee on Overseas Relief was organized in 1940, he gave eight years as its executive secretary, despite the fact that he was then in his late seventies and early eighties.

Born November 7, 1862, in New York City, Bishop Welch was a well-proportioned man who stood erect and walked with steady step even as he approached the century mark. He was immaculate in his dress, impressive in his bearing, and reserved in his manner. He knew how to relax and always gave the impression of being fully in command of himself physically, mentally, and emotionally. He loved life and enjoyed its proper pleasures. He was fully observant and was intensely interested in current events and new developments. He had a childlike curiosity. When he reached one hundred years of age, he found great pleasure in making a cross-continent trip to the Seattle World's Fair in 1962.

LAUNCHING A NEW CHURCH IN A TIME OF TURBULENCE

Bishop Welch was of a genial and kindly disposition with a fine sense of humor. There was a twinkle in his eye and usually a smile upon his face. He was the soul of graciousness and ever a source of encouragement, particularly to the younger bishops. An optimist by nature, rather than looking back at the past, as older persons are so often prone to do, he was forever looking to the future.

Bishop Welch did not take the floor too often in the Council of Bishops' meetings, but when he did, it was always to speak words of wise counsel, and his episcopal brethren valued his observations most highly.

In 1966 when the council met in Louisville, he had overlooked the fact that he was at this session completing fifty years in the episcopacy. He had sent notice of his intention not to be present. With some effort he was induced, however, to change his plans. An episcopal family dinner was arranged in his honor at which he spoke. There was no indulging in reminiscences but rather, as always, a looking to the future. There was considerable excitement at the time over the death-of-God theology. The bishop with his usual poise counseled his hearers that they did not need to be too excited about needing to defend the Almighty.

In 1962, upon the occasion of his one-hundredth birthday, he wrote the book, *As I Recall My Past Century*. While he embodied some recollections in it, in the main he made it an occasion to express his philosophy of life.

The end, so far as this world is concerned, came for Bishop Welch April 4, 1969, at his home in New York City, in his one hundred-seventh year, just as the bishops were assembling for their first meeting of the new quadrennium at Charleston, West Virginia.

Bishop Welch had been a Methodist minister for seventy-eight years and a bishop for fifty-two. It was a record unmatched by any bishop of The Methodist Church, or The United Methodist Church. Many of his episcopal colleagues thought of him as "the noblest Roman of them all."

IX

A Restructured Council in a Restructured Church 1972–1976

The General Conference of 1972 met in Atlanta, April 16-28. All the bishops were present except Bishops Straughan, W. Angie Smith, Reed, and Werner, all of whom were retired.

The communion service with which the General Conference opened was in the charge of Bishop Pryor, with Bishop Brashares bringing the message.

The Episcopal Address was given by Bishop Ensley. Grateful recognition was given to the seventeen bishops who had died during the quadrennium of 1968–1972.

Devotional messages were brought by Bishops Wicke, Alton, Kaebnick, Golden, Pope, Borgen, Webb, Pryor, Goodson, and Milhouse.

The bishops presiding were Bishops Hardin, Mathews, Stowe, Nichols, Wertz, W. Ralph Ward, Alton, Thomas, Slater, Pendergrass, Washburn, Copeland, Allen, Loder, Goodson, Golden, and Short.

The Council of Bishops met periodically during the General Conference whenever it was necessary.

The 1972 General Conference had its tense moments, but overall it was able to do its work with greater smoothness and less interruption than the two previous General Conferences. The larger part of the time of the conference was consumed in a consideration of total restructure of the

A RESTRUCTURED COUNCIL IN A RESTRUCTURED CHURCH

agencies of the church, following a quadrennium-long study by a special commission.

The first delegates from the British Methodist Conference, authorized under the concordat initiated in 1968 and approved by the Annual Conferences, were present and took their seats in the body for the first time. They were Dr. Eric Baker, Mr. John Kellaway, Dr. Norman Woolridge, and Dr. Pauline Webb.

Governor Jimmy Carter of Georgia, later to be elected President of the United States, was presented and addressed the conference.

At one session of the General Conference Bishop Alton presented the bishops scheduled to retire at the coming jurisdictional conferences:

Northeastern Jurisdiction:	J. Gordon Howard
	Hermann W. Kaebnick
	John Wesley Lord
	Lloyd C. Wicke
Southeastern Jurisdiction:	Paul Hardin
	James W. Henley
	Edward J. Pendergrass
	Roy H. Short
	J. O. Smith
North Central Jurisdiction:	Reuben R. Mueller
	Thomas M. Pryor
South Central Jurisdiction:	Paul V. Galloway
	Noah Moore
	W. Kenneth Pope
	Aubrey G. Walton
Western Jurisdiction:	Gerald H. Kennedy
	W. Maynard Sparks

Bishop Sommer was also due for retirement at his Germany Central Conference.

At the 1972 Jurisdictional Conferences the following bishops were elected:

Northeastern Jurisdiction:	James M. Ault
	Edward C. Carroll

HISTORY OF THE COUNCIL OF BISHOPS

	John B. Warman
	Joseph H. Yeakel
Southeastern Jurisdiction:	Robert M. Blackburn
	Joel D. McDavid
	Frank L. Robertson
	Carl J. Sanders
	Mack B. Stokes
	Edward L. Tullis
North Central Jurisdiction:	Wayne K. Clymer
	Jesse R. DeWitt
South Central Jurisdiction:	Finis A. Crutchfield
	Ernest T. Dixon
	Robert E. Goodrich, Jr.
	Don W. Holter
Western Jurisdiction:	Wilbur W. Y. Choy
	Jack M. Tuell
	Melvin E. Wheatley, Jr.

The Africa Central Conference elected Emilio de Carvalho and Onema Fama to the episcopacy.

The Southern Asia Central Conference elected Elia Peters.

The Liberia Central Conference in 1973 elected Bennie Warner.

Council meeting: Cleveland, Ohio, September 22-25, 1972

The Council of Bishops met at the Cleveland Sheraton Hotel, Cleveland, Ohio, September 22-25, 1972, with Bishop Slater presiding. Bishop Alton began his service as secretary at this meeting. Nineteen newly elected bishops took their place in the council. An orientation conference had been held for them at Lake Junaluska the previous August.

This meeting of the council was held a few weeks earlier than usual to coincide with the meeting of the district superintendents also held in Cleveland.

The new committee structure of the council was put into operation at this meeting.

A RESTRUCTURED COUNCIL IN A RESTRUCTURED CHURCH

Bishop Lord reviewed developments in and further plans for the Bishops' Call for Peace and the Self-Development of Peoples.

The program of visitation was extended to include visits by Central Conference bishops to areas in the United States and to Central Conferences other than their own.

The new episcopal insignia composed of the Greek letters Chi, Rho, Alpha, and Omega, plus the shepherd's staff was adopted. The insignia had been originally developed for use in the Evangelical United Brethren Church by Bishop Praetorious and Dr. Ralph Holderman, the secretary of evangelism, who had a particular interest in symbolic art.

The Philippines Central Conference failed to elect a bishop at its recent session. Bishop Short, retired, was appointed to care for the work there until the situation could be worked out.

Council meeting: Washington, D. C., April 24-27, 1973

The Council of Bishops met at the Statler Hilton Hotel, Washington, D. C., April 24-27, 1973, with Bishop Slater presiding.

This was the first session of the council at which the practice of having some meetings open began to be observed.

The council was greatly disappointed that the efforts of Bishop Mathews to arrange a meeting with President Richard Nixon had been rebuffed. A number of political leaders, however, made presentations on issues related to the Bishops' Call for Peace and the Self-Development of Peoples.

One of the matters brought to the attention of the council at this meeting, to which considerable attention was devoted, was a strike at the Methodist Hospital in Pikeville, Kentucky. The hospital board had chosen not to recognize the choice of some employees of the hospital to identify with the Communications Workers of America Union.

The Communications Union had addressed an appeal to

the council and had representatives present at Washington to request a hearing. The council realized that it had no authority over the trustees of the hospital. Nevertheless, it was anxious to be helpful in a Methodist institution situation of this kind, if at all possible. To this end it did several things. First of all, it arranged for a hearing in Washington of the union, the trustees, and the administration. It reminded all concerned that our Social Creed had long included an endorsement of the process of collective bargaining and the right of workers to choose their own union. It also took note of the seriousness of a strike in an institution such as a hospital. Furthermore, it appointed a committee to be as helpful as possible to Bishop Robertson, the bishop of the Kentucky area, in his efforts to resolve the situation. Bishops Wicke, Allen, and Holter were named as the committee. The committee made numerous trips to Pikeville, and the matter remained open for some time, during which both Bishop Robertson and the committee reported periodically to the council.

Bishop Hunt reported on the development of two studies requested by the General Conference, one on the Holy Spirit and the other on Christian experiences.

The book on the Holy Spirit was edited by Bishop Hunt and was entitled *Storms and Starlight*. It contained chapters by Bishops Thomas, Goodrich, Nichols, Clymer, Wheatley, Loder, Borgen, and Goodson.

The book on Christian experience was written by Bishop Stokes and was entitled *The Holy Spirit and Christian Experience*.

Bishop and Mrs. Mathews and the Washington area hosted the council at a dinner at which Miss Pauline Frederick was the featured speaker.

On another evening the members of the council and their wives were the guests of Bishop and Mrs. Ledden at a symphony concert at the Kennedy Center, where they heard a remarkable presentation of Mahler's *Resurrection Symphony*.

A RESTRUCTURED COUNCIL IN A RESTRUCTURED CHURCH

Council meeting: Nashville, November 12-15, 1973

The Council of Bishops met at the Holiday Inn, Nashville, Tennessee, November 12-15, 1973, with Bishop Golden presiding.

The council devoted one session to hearing the concerns of a panel from the Commission on the Status and Role of Women.

Two papers were presented at this meeting, one by Dr. James Laney of the Candler School of Theology on "The Decline and Fall of Character"; and the other, "The Loss of Integrity as a Threat to Peace," by Dr. Walter Muelder of Boston University.

During this session the council paid a visit to Meharry Medical College, where they were guests for dinner. The program lifted up the services of the black colleges.

Bishop and Mrs. Finger and the Nashville area entertained the council with a country dinner, where there was a program of songs by country music singers and an address by Governor Winfield Dunn.

Council meeting: Los Angeles, April 15-18, 1974

The council met at the Los Angeles Hilton, Los Angeles, California, April 15-18, 1974, with Bishop Golden presiding.

Members of the Commission on the Study of the Episcopacy and District Superintendency were present, and a full day was devoted to discussion of the study, both in the council as a whole and in small groups.

Dr. Albert Outler was present as a guest speaker and brought a paper entitled "The Changing Human Condition and the Eternal Christian Hope." He invited questions and discussion at the conclusion of his address. The address dealt effectively wih the theme of evangelism.

A message was addressed to the church entitled "The Bishops' Call at Mid-Passage."

It was voted that the order of episcopal appointment to the British Conference would be: (1) past president, (2) president, (3) president designate.

Bishop Hunt reported on the wide acceptance of the two study books written by members of the council.

Bishop Dodge was named to replace Bishop Lord on the assignment for promotion of the Call for Peace and the Self-Development of Peoples, since Bishop Lord had asked to be excused.

Bishop and Mrs. Golden and the Los Angeles area entertained the council with a dinner on one evening at the Los Angeles Hilton. Dr. Randall Phillips, son of Bishop and Mrs. Phillips, presided. The chief feature of the evening was a television documentary on United Methodist work in southern California, Arizona, and Hawaii.

Council meeting: Lake Junaluska, November 10-14, 1974

The Council met at Lambuth Inn, Lake Junaluska, North Carolina, November 10-14, 1975, with Bishop Loder presiding.

A telegram was addressed to President Gerald Ford, who had recently taken office, assuring him of our prayers.

Bishop Kearns presented for initial consideration a proposed statement on evangelism.

Papers presented at this session were "Confidentiality in the Clergy," by Bishop Garrison; "Episcopal Accountability," by Bishop Ward; and "How Jesus Christ Frees and Unites," by Bishop Mathews.

A paper was received from the Council of the United Methodist Central Conferences of Europe entitled "The Central Conferences and the Connectional United Methodist Church."

Lake Junaluska had been for fifty years the unofficial capital of Methodism in the Southeast. Many of the bishops had made platform appearances there, but that was the first time for the council to meet at the lake.

On one evening the bishops and their wives journeyed to Asheville to be the guests of Bishop and Mrs. Hunt and the Charlotte area at a dinner at the Great Smokies Hilton Inn. The program included music by the Junaluska singers, a

A RESTRUCTURED COUNCIL IN A RESTRUCTURED CHURCH

presentation of the new *Encyclopedia of World Methodism,* and a documentary on the Charlotte area.

Council meeting: Minneapolis, March 31–April 4, 1975

The council met at the Sheraton Ritz Hotel, Minneapolis, Minnesota, March 31–April 4, 1975, with Bishop Loder presiding.

The council granted interviews to representatives of Black Methodists for church renewal and to the Native American Caucus.

A full day was given to a discussion of matters pending before the special Committee on the Ministry ordered by the General Conference. The consideration was under the guidance of Bishop Cannon. Members of the committee were present and participated in the discussions. Particular attention was given to problems represented by special appointments.

Papers were read by Bishop Nall on "Autonomy and Beyond"; by Bishop Hunt entitled "The Council of Bishops and the Emphasis Upon the Holy Spirit"; and by Bishop Ward, "Manifesting Corporateness in the Council of Bishops."

At this session the council reaffirmed the General Conference statement on human sexuality and stated its opposition to an amendment to the Constitution that would define the personhood of the fetus.

It also issued an appeal to the government to cease intervention in Southeast Asia.

Bishop Hunt moved that we express ourselves as being receptive to a new episcopal forum succeeding the former Conference of Bishops. The motion was approved.

At this meeting Bishop Ledden, who had been pianist for the council for thirty-one years, asked to be relieved. The council expressed its gratitude for his long service and appointed Bishop Borgen as pianist.

A "United Methodist Night in Minnesota" was observed on one night with Bishop and Mrs. Clymer as hosts. The address was brought by Justice Harry A. Blackmun. A unique feature of the evening was that United Methodists came from all over Minnesota and brought with them an offering for hunger, which reached an unusually large total.

Council meeting: New Orleans, November 10-14, 1975

The council met at New Orleans at the Roosevelt Hotel, November 10-14, 1975, with Bishop Ward presiding.

Dr. Ralph Houston, president of the Judicial Council, was present as a guest. This was the first time the president of the Judicial Council had ever met with the Council of Bishops. Dr. Houston spoke briefly.

Bishop Barbieri brought a paper on "The Message of Evangelism for Today."

Bishop Webb reported on the Grain Belt Consultation.

Much of the meeting was devoted to an urban study for which Bishop Pryor carried responsibility. Bishop Pryor had invited a number of urban specialists as resource persons, and the entire day was spent in consultation with them.

Bishop and Mrs. Crutchfield and the United Methodists of Louisiana entertained at an unusual banquet one evening. The famous Mardi Gras costumes were taken out of storage and used by a group of professional performers staging a mini Mardi Gras. There was also ragtime music by a nationally famous local band.

On another evening the council enjoyed a creole dinner, followed by an old-fashioned Methodist love feast at beautiful Rayne Memorial Church.

Council meeting: Lincoln City, Oregon, April 20-25, 1976

The Council of Bishops met at the Dunes, Lincoln City, Oregon, April 20-25, 1976, with Bishop Ward presiding.

Much time was employed considering the Episcopal Address written by Bishop Thomas and attending to details relative to the General Conference.

A RESTRUCTURED COUNCIL IN A RESTRUCTURED CHURCH

The role of the bishops in the General Conference was considered under the guidance of Bishops Allen, Alton, and Short.

At the request of the Committee on Pastoral Concerns, Bishop Short read a paper entitled "What We As Bishops Owe to Our Successors."

In lieu of the Conference of Bishops, it was decided to have a dinner for all the bishops of autonomous churches present at the General Conference. Bishop Choy was assigned responsibility for the dinner.

Bishops Allen, Tullis, and Short were assigned to meet with the bishops of the Southern Asia Central Conference. The bishops in that conference were concerned about the decision of the Judicial Council on church union in India since recent developments had changed the situation there.

Early in the meeting a motion was made to recommend to the Council on Finance and Administration that episcopal salaries remain the same in the new quadrennium. In lieu of this motion, a motion was adopted that it be recommended to the Council on Finance that a study be made of all episcopal and general agency salaries.

At this meeting Bishop Alton requested that he not be reelected as secretary. Bishop Mathews was elected as the fifth secretary of the council since its organization.

A high occasion for the council was the privilege of hearing at a dinner Senator Frank Church of Idaho in a thought-provoking address. For this privilege the council was indebted to Bishop and Mrs. Tuell.

In Memoriam—1972–1976

During the quadrennium, 1972–1976, fourteen of the bishops had gone to life eternal:
    D. D. Alejandro
    Kenneth W. Copeland
    Marvin A. Franklin
    Paul N. Garber
    Paul M. Herrick

HISTORY OF THE COUNCIL OF BISHOPS

J. Gordon Howard
Edgar A. Love
Paul E. Martin
Arthur J. Moore
Stephen T. Nagbe
Marshall R. Reed
Clement D. Rockey
W. Angie Smith
James H. Straughn

Dionisio Deista Alejandro
(1893–1972)

D. D. Alejandro was elected a term bishop by the Philippines Central Conference in 1944 and served for four years. He was elected a second time in 1960 and served until 1964.

Born at Quiapo, Manila, February 19, 1893, he was the first native Filipino to be elected to the episcopacy. He was well educated, with a distinguished career as pastor and teacher. He proved himself fully capable of the administrative responsibilities to which the church called him, giving unusual service during the war years, despite harassment and arrest by the Japanese Occupation Army. After the war he was instrumental in the reopening of Union Theological Seminary in Manila.

Bishop Alejandro did not attend the council too frequently and therefore did not become too familiar a figure in the episcopal family. When the Judicial Council decision ruled that term bishops were no longer members of the council after retirement, under the law at that time, the bishop was disappointed but took the decision humbly. His Filipino friends continued to think of him as bishop and to call him "Bishop" until the end.

After retirement he continued to live in Manila and to teach and preach as opportunity afforded. He died November 18, 1972.

A RESTRUCTURED COUNCIL IN A RESTRUCTURED CHURCH

Kenneth Wilford Copeland
(1912–1973)

Kenneth W. Copeland was elected by the South Central Jurisdictional Conference to the episcopacy in 1960 from the pastorate of Travis Park, San Antonio, Texas. His first episcopal assignment was to the Nebraska area, where he served eight years, and from which he was sent to the Houston area, where he served until his death in 1973. Bishop Paul Galloway was called out of retirement to care for the Houston area for the remainder of the quadrennium.

Bishop Copeland, born April 3, 1912, in Bexar, Arkansas, was originally a Methodist Protestant. At the age of only twenty-six he was made president of the Methodist Protestant Texas Conference. He, together with Bishops Broomfield, Straughn, Holloway, and Warman, are the former Methodist Protestants in the episcopacy.

Bishop Copeland was of medium height and agile in his movements. He was a man of great energy and was forever busy. He had a warm, friendly spirit and always wore a kindly smile. He was good company and was well liked wherever he went.

The bishop was a popular preacher, as his eleven years at Travis Park testified. He was in wide demand for seminars and preaching engagements. His administration was careful and democratic in spirit. His great interests were evangelism and missions. For a period he was chairman of the World Division of the Board of Global Ministries. Throughout his days of membership in the council he was the assistant to Bishop Ledden as pianist.

Bishop Copeland died August 7, 1973, as a result of a heart attack after attending a conference on evangelism in Mexico City. His burial was in Houston, Texas.

Marvin Augustus Franklin
(1894–1972)

The Southeastern Jurisdiction elected Marvin A. Franklin to the episcopacy in 1948 from the pastorate of Highlands Church, Birmingham, Alabama.

He was a native of Georgia, born in White County, January 19, 1894, and began his ministry in the North Georgia Conference. He also served in the Florida and Alabama Conferences.

His first episcopal assignment was to the Jackson, Mississippi, area, where he remained the entire sixteen years of his active episcopacy. For five years of this time he had responsibility for the Memphis Conference also. He had this responsibility for one year during the illness of Bishop Watkins, 1959 to 1960. The Memphis Conference was then added to the Jackson area for one quadrennium.

Bishop Franklin was a greatly loved pastor-preacher. He was not given to depth in his preaching, but there was a warmth and a humanness about it that quickly won people's hearts. His preaching had a strong evangelistic emphasis. He was in popular demand as an after-dinner speaker and was active in civic club and fraternal circles.

The bishop was a tall man who walked with a shuffle and a slight stoop. He never seemed to be in a hurry. He had a decided southern drawl. He possessed a delightful sense of humor and made full and frequent use of his rich store of humorous stories. He had a pleasant disposition and a winsome smile. He did not concentrate on administration, but he took his administrative responsibilities in stride.

It was the lot of Bishop Franklin to have responsibility in one of the states of the deep South during the days when the South was having to adjust to a new pattern of life as the Civil Rights movement reached full tide. He, himself, was conservative but not reactionary. By nature he shrank from controversy and tension. He found himself caught between those who felt that almost anything he attempted that was constructive and forward looking was going too far, and those, on the other hand, who criticized him for not going far enough.

After retiring in 1964 Bishop Franklin continued to live in Jackson and to engage in preaching missions for which he had many invitations. His rare capacity for friendship marked him to the end. He died August 23, 1972, in Jackson.

A RESTRUCTURED COUNCIL IN A RESTRUCTURED CHURCH
Paul Neff Garber
(1899–1972)

Paul N. Garber was elected to the episcopacy by the Southeastern Jurisdictional Conference in 1944. He was at the time dean of the Divinity School of Duke University, where he had taught for some years in the field of church history.

His first assignment was to the Geneva area, which included all the work in Southern Europe and North Africa. The war was still raging at the time of his election, and it was some months before he could travel to Geneva and an even longer time before he could visit some of his conferences. When he finally was able to visit most of them, he found the people scattered, hungry, without adequate clothing, and showing plainly in body and spirit what they had suffered. Often he discovered that the churches, the homes of the people, and church institutions had been destroyed. Many of the pastors had been called into the army, some never to return, and personnel for leadership in the church represented a most serious problem.

Bishop Garber plunged immediately into a program of relief, rehabilitation, and rebuilding. The story of what he accomplished during these difficult years is one of the magnificent chapters in the story of the Methodist episcopacy. He went through the experience of seeing much of the work in countries behind the Iron Curtain severely curtailed and at points destroyed by Communist governments.

In 1948 he was returned to the Geneva area where he served two more years. He was then appointed to the Richmond area in February, 1951, when Bishop Peele had to ask to be relieved because of ill health. He served the Richmond area until 1964, when he was sent to the new Raleigh area, which he served for four years. He retired in 1968.

Bishop Garber was a short, somewhat stocky man, who never seemed to tire. He made it a habit to work for almost endless hours and to write out everything in a running, often almost illegible hand. He kept careful and voluminous records and maintained a daily account, not only of his doings but of his thoughts as well. He continued throughout his episcopacy and retirement to follow the research techniques that he had developed in an earlier day as a university professor.

Bishop Garber was not a preacher and never served in the pastorate. He wrote out his messages and read them, but read them effectively. His sermons were more of the nature of a professor's lecture than what is usually thought of as a sermon.

Bishop Garber was an acknowledged scholar, particularly in the field of church history. Numerous articles and books came from his gifted pen.

He was a strong administrator and wrote an unusual record in Virginia and North Carolina. He developed and took leadership in a program of church extension in his conferences that was not exceeded anywhere in the church. He also took strong leadership in the field of education and was instrumental in the establishment of three colleges, two in North Carolina and one in Virginia. He served as president of the General Board of Education from 1960 to 1964.

Bishop Garber, born July 27, 1899, at New Market, Virginia, grew up in the Church of the Brethren and was ordained in that church. He made scant, if any reference to these early days. After going to Duke, he became both a Methodist and an authority on Methodist history. With this major interest, apparently he felt there was no point in calling attention to the fact that his own roots were in another tradition.

Bishop Garber was a genial personality, warm and friendly with all. At least so far as his public expression was concerned, he was an optimist. He was often effusive in his praise of others when he was in the chair. If he disagreed, he kept his disagreements to himself. His biographer, quoting somewhat extensively from the bishop's private journal,

A RESTRUCTURED COUNCIL IN A RESTRUCTURED CHURCH

affirms that often the bishop's private reactions and public reactions did not always coincide. Generally speaking, he was more conservative on social questions than most of his Southern colleagues in the episcopacy.

After retiring, Bishop Garber moved to Geneva to serve the World Methodist Council. He also worked on a *History of Methodism in Europe*. He was well along in this labor when death came suddenly for him on December 18, 1972.

The Council of Bishops requested Bishop Short to go to Zurich, where his papers were, and to finalize the manuscript of his book.

Paul Murray Herrick
(1898–1972)

Paul M. Herrick was elected to the episcopacy by the Evangelical United Brethren Church in 1958 from the pastorate of First Church, Dayton, one of the strongest of the Evangelical United Brethren churches. He continued to reside in Dayton. He had the responsibility for conferences in Ohio and Tennessee as well as the Red Bird Missionary Conference in Kentucky.

Bishop Herrick was a popular preacher. He made much use of poetry in his preaching, particularly poetry of the popular, religious type. He paid attention to the conduct of worship and could handle a ritual with particular effectiveness.

Born in rural Kansas, April 3, 1898, Bishop Herrick was of medium height and trim of figure. He exercised regularly and played golf the day of his death. The end came unexpectedly as he died quietly in his sleep, November 23, 1972. His burial was in Dayton, Ohio.

Bishop Herrick was a modest, quiet, unpretentious man, who sometimes gave an impression of being not too sure of himself. He was always the gentleman and never self-seeking.

In the distribution of the Evangelical United Brethren bishops among the jurisdictions in 1968, he was assigned to the Southeastern Jurisdiction. His colleagues in the college soon came to regard him as a brother beloved. He was assigned to the large Richmond area. He received this heavy assignment with some misgiving, but entered into it with humility and soon won the hearts of the Methodists of Virginia.

Both his own health and that of his wife were such that after two years he had to ask his College and Council of Bishops to relieve him. This they did with regret. He returned to his beloved Dayton to live out his remaining days.

John Gordon Howard
(1899-1974)

J. Gordon Howard was elected to the episcopacy by the Evangelical United Brethren Church in 1957 and served the Pittsburgh area of that church. Upon union in 1968 he was assigned to the Philadelphia area, to which he gave four years of devoted service. He retired in 1972 and made his home in Winchester, Virginia.

Bishop Howard had been a strong leader in the Evangelical United Brethren Church. He came of a missionary background and was born December 8, 1899, in Tokyo, Japan, where his parents were missionaries. He served for five years as editor of church school literature and for twelve years as president of Otterbein College. He was secretary of the Board of Bishops of the Evangelical United Brethren Church.

The bishop was a portly man who carried himself with dignity. He had a genial disposition and felt that fun had a proper place in life. He relished a good joke and was adept at making humorous but at the same time telling observations. He was a well-trained and thoughtful man. The papers that he read on occasion in the council bore witness to his earlier editorial activity. He was a wise and cautious administrator, fully democratic in his spirit.

As he came into the council in the new united church, he came bearing the full confidence of the church out of which he came. His brethren in the new council of the new church soon discovered why it was that he was so greatly appreciated. Puerto Rico was a part of his Philadelphia area, and he was greatly loved there. One of the reasons was that he did not hesitate to try out his Spanish and delighted to eat rice and beans with his pastors and tried to identify with them.

Edgar Amos Love
(1891-1974)

Born September 10, 1891, in Harrisonburg, Virginia, Edgar A. Love was elected to the episcopacy by the Central Jurisdictional Conference in 1952, after having served as one of the secretaries in the national division of the Board of Missions for the previous twelve years. He was a member of the Washington Conference, where he served churches and districts. He was a chaplain in World War I. After his election to the episcopacy, Bishop Love was assigned to the Baltimore area and served it until retirement in 1964.

Bishop Love was a short, slender man, and was bald-headed. He was energetic, and what he did he did well. He had a strong social consciousness and was the champion of his people and of justice for all. He was gentle in spirit and manner but rose to the heights of indignation when he felt something was wrong. On such occasions he had the capacity to speak with withering words. He looked forward to desegregation in the church and was one of the bishops who contributed most to its accomplishment. He had a pleasant disposition and delighted in good fellowship.

Bishop Love played an active role in the council, and his administrative ability brought him many special responsibilities.

Upon his retirement he continued to live in Baltimore until his death, May 1, 1974. He is buried there.

The last meeting of the council Bishop Love was able to attend was that in Nashville in November of 1973.

HISTORY OF THE COUNCIL OF BISHOPS
Paul Elliott Martin
(1897–1975)

Paul E. Martin was elected by the South Central Jurisdictional Conference to the episcopacy in 1944 from the pastorate of First Church, Wichita Falls, Texas. He was assigned to the Little Rock area, which included the conferences in Arkansas and Louisiana. He served this area until 1960 when he was assigned to the Houston area, serving until his retirement in 1968.

Bishop Martin was a greatly loved son of Texas, where he was born December 31, 1897, in the little town of Blossom, which he referred to lovingly over and over again. He went to Texas schools and to Southern Methodist University. He served churches and districts in the North Texas Conference. He and Bishop W. Angie Smith were both members of the North Texas Conference when they were elected together in 1944.

Bishop Martin was a popular preacher, usually low key, and quiet in his style. His sermons were replete with human interest and therefore held his audiences well. The bishop was a careful administrator who was democratic in spirit. He seemed to have particular ability to handle tense and delicate situations and to contribute to resolving of conflict. The church at large soon discovered his administrative talents. He served, in turn, as president of the Board of Temperance, president of the local church section of the Board of Education, and for eight years president of the Council on World Service and Finance.

Bishop Martin was a man of average size, who almost always wore a smile. He walked with a slight stoop and with his head thrust slightly forward. He had a most genial disposition and was uniformly brotherly, courteous, and kind. He had a fine sense of humor and a rich fund of anecdotes. He was an unusually effective after-dinner speaker. No one among his episcopal brethren could exceed him as a master of ceremonies. When in the chair of a conference he was always careful, fair, and relaxed.

A RESTRUCTURED COUNCIL IN A RESTRUCTURED CHURCH

The bishop was above all else a kindly friend to all. In return he was cordially loved everywhere. He died February 13, 1975, and was buried in Dallas, Texas.

Arthur James Moore
(1888–1974)

Arthur J. Moore was elected to the episcopacy by the 1930 General Conference of the Methodist Episcopal Church, South from the pastorate of First Church, Birmingham. He was only forty-one years of age and had had a meteoric rise to prominence. He had already been pastor of two great churches—Travis Park in San Antonio and First Church, Birmingham. He also had a striking career as an evangelist. His name had become a household word in much of Southern Methodism. His first episcopal assignment was to the supervision of the small and widely scattered Southern work in California, Arizona, and the Pacific Northwest.

In 1934 the Church, South found itself deep in the depression. It was losing three bishops by retirement and had lost two active bishops by death during the previous quadrennium. The decision was not to elect any new bishops and to double the assignments of the bishops remaining active. Bishop Kern was returned from the Orient for assignment to home service; and Bishop Darlington from Europe for the same purpose. The episcopal assignment of the entire mission field of the Southern Church was placed on the shoulders of Bishop Moore, and he carried it for six years. In the years to come he was to know more assignments for temporary service in mission fields than any other bishop of the church.

In 1940 he was assigned to the Atlanta area, which he served for the next twenty years. He was a native son of Georgia, where he was born December 26, 1888, in Argyle. He grew up in Georgia, was converted there, and began his ministry in the South Georgia Conference. The two great Georgia bishops of that period, Bishop Candler and Bishop

Ainsworth, were in a sense his spiritual fathers. They gave him great encouragement throughout their lives.

Bishop Moore was particularly active in the affairs of Emory University, in the establishment of Epworth-by-the-Sea, in the promotion of all Georgia Conference educational and other institutions. He also furthered the work of Paine College, long a joint enterprise of the Christian Methodist Episcopal Church and the Methodist Episcopal Church, South.

Everything in Georgia Methodism in the last forty years still carries the mark of Bishop Moore's influence and will continue to do so for years to come. The whole of Georgia regarded him as one of its first citizens. It is indeed fitting that Atlanta should have been the final resting place upon his departing this life on June 30, 1974.

Bishop Moore was primarily a preacher, with a warm heart. His preaching was scriptural, fervent, and deeply moving. He had an unusual command of language, and words flowed from his lips and pen in a torrent of beauty. Vast audiences waited upon his preaching. One of the striking facts about him was that he was such a master of speech when his school days had been so limited. As a young man he was a railroader, as his father had been before him. He was largely self-taught; an avid reader, and a close follower of current affairs. He had no earned academic degree, but the day came when great educational institutions showered honorary degrees upon him.

Following his retirement he went back to his first love, evangelism, and followed a full schedule of evangelistic meetings all over the country that would have taxed the strength of a far younger evangelist.

Bishop Moore's companion interest was missions. As a young man he applied for missionary service but was turned down by the Mission Board of the Church, South. He lived to see the day when he was bishop of the very fields to which he sought once to go as a missionary. He served as president of the Board of Missions of The Methodist Church for twenty years. He never visited Cuba, perhaps because it was nearby, but he visited every other mission field of the church. His feet walked literally in the far places of the earth. On countless occasions the Council of Bishops or the Board of Missions sent him on special missionary journeys. He raised millions for missions, and the map of the world was stamped upon his heart. He used to say that should he find himself stranded overnight in almost any large city of the world, he would be able to call someone he knew who would open the door of his home in hospitality to him. The statement was no exaggeration.

Bishop Moore was a large man with striking blue eyes that seemed to have in them the element of wonder. He moved with a rapid gait and never seemed to tire. All his movements were quick. He had a genial and warm disposition, and his emotions ran deep. He cultivated friendships and was particularly popular with laymen. He challenged them for the Kingdom and usually met with ready response.

Bishop Moore was a strong personality. Without purposely doing so, he dominated any group he was in by the sheer weight of his personality. He always had something to say, and he spoke his mind freely on any and every occasion. He was fully self-confident. Bishop John Branscomb, whom he loved devotedly and who loved him, used to refer to him humorously in his absence as "King Arthur." Bishop Moore was aware of this, and it afforded him amusement. The term did not miss the mark too far. He was not, however, an autocrat. Rather, he was simply an unusually strong man.

He spoke often in the council. In his active days he had much to do with determining whatever work was done. He will long be remembered as one of the greats of the episcopal body.

Stephen Trowen Nagbe
(1933–1973)

Stephen T. Nagbe was elected by the Liberia Central Conference to the episcopacy in 1965. He was the first citizen of Liberia elected to the episcopacy since Bishop John W. Roberts, who was elected ninety-nine years before. Bishop Roberts died in 1875. From that time on the Liberian work was cared for by white American-born bishops such as Bishops William Taylor, Joseph C. Hartzell, and John Springer; or by black American-born bishops such as Bishops I. B. Scott, Alexander P. Camphor, and Matthew W. Clair. All of these were elected by the General Conference. Central Jurisdiction bishops had also served the Liberia area—such as Bishops Willis King and Prince Taylor.

The conference at which Bishop Nagbe was elected was held at Cape Palmas. The five bishops present—including Bishops Taylor, Barbieri and Short, and two bishops of other denominations—were entertained at the summer palace of President Tubman.

Bishop Nagbe was elected on the second ballot. He was only thirty-two years of age and was perhaps the youngest person ever elected bishop in The Methodist Church. He studied at the college of West Africa and received a B.D. degree from Gammon and an S.T.M. degree from Boston.

Bishop Nagbe was a quiet, thoughtful, modest man. He had little to say in the Council of Bishops unless called upon. However, in his area he gave positive, statesmanlike leadership. He enjoyed the confidence and friendship of the president of the country, President Tubman.

Bishop Nagbe, born in Betu, Sinoe County in Liberia, October 23, 1933, was a "Bushman." He came from one of the up-country tribes, rather than from among the descendents of the ex-slaves who were colonized in Liberia and who represented a more privileged class in the national makeup.

The bishop was able to give only little more than seven years of service in his episcopal office as he died of cancer, February 2, 1973.

Marshall Russell Reed
(1891–1973)

Marshall R. Reed was elected by the North Central Jurisdictional Conference to the episcopacy in 1948 from

A RESTRUCTURED COUNCIL IN A RESTRUCTURED CHURCH

the pastorate of Nardin Park Church in Detroit. He had been a favorite son of Michigan, where he was born September 15, 1891, at Onsted. Before being elected a bishop, he had served some of the leading churches and had been a strong leader in conference affairs. He had the high honor of being appointed to the area from which he came, and he served it for the full sixteen years of his active episcopacy.

Bishop Reed was a large man and in his earlier days had been an athlete. He had both marked physical and mental strength. He carried whatever assignment was given him through to perfection. The general church knew his strength, and it gave him some assignments that were far from easy. He was a matter-of-fact type of man who spoke his mind freely and sometimes perhaps a bit bluntly. He had a fine sense of fairness and was above anything small. He always did his work carefully, and the papers he presented in the council on occasion were masterpieces of thoroughness.

Upon retirement he and Mrs. Reed returned to live in the modest Michigan town he called home. The quietness of life there was in striking contrast to life in a turbulent urban center where he had lived, particularly in the late fifties and early sixties.

Before too long the bishop's eyes began to give him trouble, and in time his strong body, too, began to give way. For long months he was an immobilized invalid until release came on March 1, 1973.

Clement Daniel Rockey
(1889–1975)

Clement D. Rockey was elected by the Southern Asia Central Conference to the episcopacy in 1941. He had been born of missionary parents in India, September 5, 1889, in Cawnpore, United Provinces. He was himself a missionary for many years prior to his election. His episcopal assignment was the Lucknow area, where he served until his retirement because of age in 1956.

HISTORY OF THE COUNCIL OF BISHOPS

Bishop Rockey's command of several of the Indian languages was considerable. He was a master of Urdu, especially scholarly Urdu. He spoke it as fluently as he did English and preferred to preach in it. He translated much devotional literature and many hymns from English into Urdu.

The Council of Bishops called him out of retirement to oversee the work in Pakistan for eight years. In 1964 he retired for a second time and made his home in Eugene, Oregon.

Bishop Rockey was a quiet man, fully devoted to his work. He had a good mind and was well trained, holding a Ph.D. degree from the University of Chicago as well as three other earned degrees.

In the Council of Bishops he spoke little, except when matters arose connected with his own work. He was intensely interested, however, in everything that went on. In his retirement days he seemed to relish particularly attending the meetings of the council and having fellowship once again with his episcopal brethren. In his later years, however, he found it difficult to concentrate on issues before the council, but he was still profoundly concerned for the church to which he had given his life. His brethren honored him for his work's sake.

Bishop Rockey was the last missionary to be elected and consecrated to the episcopacy by the Central Conference of Southern Asia. Twelve missionaries had been elected by the various Central Conferences of Methodism between the original provision for Central Conferences made in 1928 and the present. The last missionary to be elected a bishop from a Central Conference was Bishop Robert Lundy in 1964. All Central Conference bishops elected since that date have been national bishops, and the indications are that such will continue to be the pattern in the future. Of the missionaries elected bishop only Bishops Pickett, Amstutz, Dodge, Andreassen, and Lundy are still living as of this date.

Bishop Rockey died August 15, 1975. His interment was in Eugene, Oregon.

A RESTRUCTURED COUNCIL IN A RESTRUCTURED CHURCH
William Angie Smith
(1894–1974)

W. Angie Smith was elected to the episcopacy by the South Central Jursdictional Conference in 1944 from the pastorate of First Church, Dallas. He was assigned to the Oklahoma City area, which included Oklahoma and New Mexico. He served there for his entire active episcopacy of twenty-four years.

Bishop Smith was a popular preacher. Prior to serving First Church, Dallas, he had filled the distinguished pulpit of First Church, Birmingham, which Bishop Arthur Moore had filled not too many years before him. His preaching was not profound, but it was plain, human, and earnest, and it had a reasonable degree of emotional appeal. He placed strong emphasis upon evangelism. He wrote an enviable record of reaching large numbers of people for Christ, not only in the churches that he served but also through the definite evangelistic plans that he developed constantly for his area. For eight years he served as president of the General Board of Evangelism and gave devoted attention to this assignment.

As an administrator, Bishop Smith was a bishop who was always in full command of the ship. He knew where he wanted to go and how to get there. Decision-making had no terrors for him, for he had a large measure of self-confidence. There were some who thought him arbitrary, but he did not intend to be. While there was much firmness about him, at the same time he had a tender heart. He was a good presiding officer and was often placed in the chair at the General Conference at sessions that promised to represent ticklish situations.

Bishop Smith was a large man, perhaps the heaviest of the bishops in his day in the council. Born in Elgin, Texas, December 21, 1894, he could show a bit of the roughness of the open spaces in which he was born. But again, when the occasion demanded, he would display the finest observance of the amenities and courtesies that are the hallmarks of gentility. He had a fine sense of humor and like his brother, Frank, had an endless fund of humorous stories.

In the South at the time when Bishop Smith was elected, preachers were not supposed to evidence interest in being elected to the episcopacy, and were rather to let the office seek them, or to come through the efforts of their friends and admirers. Bishop Smith, however, did not attempt to conceal his interest in joining the episcopacy or the fact that he enjoyed the office after he was elected. He received a substantial vote at the last session of the General Conference of the Methodist Episcopal Church, South, which he hosted in Birmingham in 1933. At the second South Central Jurisdictional Conference in 1944, after he had been elected along with Bishop Paul Martin, the bishops were discussing the order for a certain service in which one of the new bishops was to pray and the other read the lesson. The question was who should do what. Finally Bishop Selecman said, "Let Angie read the lesson and Paul offer the prayer, because Angie has had only one prayer for a long time, and that has already been answered by this Jurisdictional Conference."

Bishop Smith took the floor often in the council and did not hesitate to object to something when he thought objection ought to be made. He probably had more influence in shaping many decisions in the council than was sometimes realized. He was never merely an observer but always a participant, though he always chose a seat in the back row at the council meetings. This location never deterred him from getting into the game. He was a strong defender not of himself nor his brother bishops as such, but of the office of the episcopacy in Methodism. He believed that whatever weakened the episcopacy in Methodism weakened the church.

One of Bishop Smith's great commitments was to the American Indian work. Throughout his active career he administered the Indian Mission. The Indians loved him, and he loved them.

For all of his days Bishop Smith was a busy bishop. He

kept on the road, served actively on several of the boards and agencies of the church at large, and on the World Methodist Council. He managed at the same time to give attention even to small details in his own area.

For one who had been so busy and so much in the middle of things, retirement did not come easy. In addition, his health was breaking. He began to attend the meetings of the council only infrequently. The last occasion that a number of his episcopal brethren saw him was when he spoke at the funeral of Bishop Copeland. In a matter of only a brief time the long journey came to an end for him on March 15, 1974. His burial was in Houston, Texas.

James Henry Straughn
(1877–1974)

James H. Straughn was elected by the Methodist Protestant Church to the episcopacy at the time of the Uniting Conference in Kansas City in 1939. He was president of that church at the time. The Methodist Protestants had no episcopacy and at one time were decidedly opposed to the office.

From 1939 to 1940 Bishop Straughn was assigned to give leadership to helping the Methodist Protestant churches adjust to life in the new church. In 1940 he was assigned to the Pittsburgh area, which he served until retirement in 1948.

Born June 1, 1877, in Centreville, Maryland, Bishop Straughn was a strong scriptural, evangelistic preacher, whose preaching was always marked by great earnestness and great helpfulness. He was a short man with most expressive eyes and a pleasant countenance and was partially bald. He had the energy that often characterizes men of smaller stature. He had to get used to being a bishop, insofar as the office was so different from the beloved tradition in which he grew up.

There were no guarantees for the merging denominations in Methodist union as there were for the first twelve years of the Methodist-Evangelical United Brethren union.

Bishop Straughn soon began to fear that the Methodist Protestant group was just about to sink without trace in the larger Methodist Church. He felt this more as time went on. In his later days he came close to barely escaping the bitterness of disillusionment, if indeed he did escape it. In addition, he also found it difficult to appreciate some changes coming with a new age, particularly some radical changes, as he saw them, taking place in Methodism itself. He maintained, however, his loyalty to the church for whose union he had labored even when he was not too happy with what might be occurring.

Bishop Straughn spoke often in the Council of Bishops in the earlier days, usually to voice some typical Methodist Protestant conviction.

After retirement he did not attend the council often. When the General Conference met in Pittsburgh, he put in an appearance. Many of the younger bishops did not know him and inquired who he was. The bishops who had known him in other years found it difficult to recognize him at first, so much had his appearance changed with the coming of his late years. He let it be known that he felt very much alone as he had outlived the early proponents of union.

Bishop Straughn was indeed a choice spirit who loved God and loved God's church. He was a man of sterling integrity, rich religious experience, and tireless devotion. Having been elected so late in life and having such a relatively short term of active service, he did not have the opportunity to develop the degree of leadership in the new Methodist Church, which had so long been his in the Methodist Protestant Church.

Bishop Straughn died September 9, 1974, just three years short of his hundredth birthday. He is buried in Baltimore, Maryland.

X

New Problems Responsibilities, and Opportunities 1976–1979

The 1975 General Conference met at Portland, Oregon, April 27–May 7.

The address at the communion service that opened the General Conference was brought by Bishop W. Ralph Ward.

The Episcopal Address was written and delivered by Bishop James S. Thomas. Solemn recognition was given to the fourteen bishops who had died during the previous quadrennium, 1972–1976.

Devotional messages each morning were brought by Bishops Cannon, Holter, Borgen, Nichols, Choy, Stowe, Washburn, and Mathews.

The bishops presiding were Bishops W. Ralph Ward, Stowe, Kearns, Milhouse, McDavid, Allen, Tuell, Wetz, Frank, Taylor, Goodson, Mathews, Alton, Nichols, Thomas, Slater, Hunt, Washburn, Yeakel, Golden, Finger, and Loder.

The Council of Bishops met periodically as necessary during the General Conference upon call of the president.

Much of the attention of the General Conference centered upon the report of the Commission on the Study of the Episcopacy and the District Superintendency that had functioned throughout the quadrennium. Many of the recommendations of the committee were approved,

HISTORY OF THE COUNCIL OF BISHOPS

including an eight-year limitation upon episcopal assignment to an area, lowering the retirement age of bishops, optional procedures for nominations in episcopal elections, and specifications regarding appointment-making. A minority report favoring term episcopacy failed by a vote of 625 to 345.

The 1976 Jurisdictional and Central Conferences saw the retirement of bishops:

Northeastern Jurisdiction: Prince A. Taylor
North Central Jurisdiction: F. Gerald Ensley
    Francis E. Kearns
South Central Jurisdiction: Eugene M. Frank
    Don W. Holter
    O. Eugene Slater
Germany Central Conference: C. Ernst Sommer

Election to the episcopacy by the Jurisdictional and Central Conferences saw the following bishops joining the Council of Bishops:

Northeastern Jurisdiction: C. Dale White
North Central Jurisdiction: Edsel A. Ammons
    Leroy C. Hodapp
South Central Jurisdiction: A. Monk Bryan
    Kenneth W. Hicks
    J. Chess Lovern
    J. Kenneth Shamblin
Germany Central Conference: Hermann L. Sticher
Africa Central Conference: Almeida Penicela
    N. K. Wakadilo
Philippines Central Conference: LaVerne D. Mercado

Council meeting: Philadelphia, November 16-19, 1976

The Council of Bishops met at the Warwick Hotel, Philadelphia, November 16-19, 1976, with Bishop Goodson presiding.

A letter of support was addressed to President-elect Jimmy Carter.

A session was devoted to the situation in Southern Africa with Bishops Dodge, de Carvalho, Wakadilo, and Warner speaking to the situation and the council asking questions. A statement pleading for majority rule was adopted.

A full day was devoted to a consideration of the General Conference-approved "Three Missional Priorities," led by Bishop Cannon, and of "The Seven Vital Concerns," led by Bishop Nichols. The general secretaries of the boards and agencies were present for this period and joined in the discussion.

Still another session was devoted to a consideration of higher education with Bishop Thomas speaking on "The Educational Ministry of the Church"; and Bishop Ault on "The Future of Church-Related Higher Education."

The council approved a resolution in opposition to capital punishment.

Bishop Webb reported that at the Grain Belt Consultation at Overland Park, Kansas, twenty-three episcopal areas were represented.

A notable feature of this meeting of the council was an evening session in Independence Hall, where Bishop Goodson brought the message.

On another evening the council assembled at historic St. George's Church for a service, followed by an opportunity to visit the building and examine its historic treasures.

On still another evening, the council joined in a great public worship service at Tindley Temple, with Bishop Goodson bringing the message. The service was preceded by a dinner at the Union League Club as the guests of Bishop and Mrs. Ault and the United Methodists of the Philadelphia area.

Council meeting: Williamsburg, Virginia, April 12-15, 1977

The council met at Hospitality House, Williamsburg, Virginia, April 12-15, 1977, with Bishop Goodson presiding.

Bishop Hermann L. Sticher, recently elected by the Germany Central Conference, was present for the first time and was introduced to the council. Bishop Sticher had been an Evangelical United Brethren minister in Germany prior to the union in 1968.

It was announced that Bishop Mercado, recently elected by the Philippines Central Conference, had resigned shortly thereafter for health reasons. It became necessary for Bishop Granadosin to carry the responsibility for both the Baguio and Manila areas for the remainder of the quadrennium.

It was also announced that Bishop Penicela, who had been elected by the Africa Central Conference and assigned to care for the work in Mozambique, had shortly thereafter been seriously injured in an accident. There was no hope of his being able to function at least for some time. Bishop Zunguze, retired, was named to oversee the work.

A period was devoted to a consideration of the subject, "The Ethnic Minority Local Church," under the guidance of Bishops Thomas, Choy, Carleton, Allen, and Ward.

Another period was devoted to consideration of the Consultation on Church Union under the guidance of Bishop Cannon. Dr. Gerald F. Moede, the executive secretary of the consultation, and Dr. Robert W. Huston of the Division of Ecumenical Ministries presented papers.

Bishop Stowe outlined the plans of the World Methodist Council for a worldwide emphasis upon evangelism, and the council offered its cooperation.

Bishop and Mrs. Goodson and the Methodists of the Richmond area arranged for tours of Williamsburg and for a colonial dinner at Williamsburg Lodge. The address of the evening was given by Governor Mills E. Godwin, Jr.

Council meeting: Milwaukee, November 15-18, 1977

The council met at the Red Carpet Inn, Milwaukee, Wisconsin, November 15-18, 1977, with Bishop Milhouse presiding.

It was announced that Bishop Warner, who was present, had been elected vice-president of the Republic of Liberia.

Notice was taken of the fact that another member of the

NEW PROBLEMS, RESPONSIBILITIES, AND OPPORTUNITIES

council had also found prominent place in national affairs in another African country in the person of Bishop Muzorewa.

A session was devoted to evangelism with Dr. George Hunter of the Board of Discipleship speaking on "United Methodist Bishops and the Propagation of the Faith."

The council gave attention to a paper by Bishop Carroll on "The Role of a Bishop in Crisis Intervention."

An entire morning and afternoon were given to a session on "Ministry and Management," under the guidance of Dr. James D. Glasse.

The Native American Caucus was again granted an interview.

Guidelines for renewal leaves for the bishops were developed and approved at this meeting.

The bishops and their wives were guests of Bishop and Mrs. DeWitt and the Wisconsin area at a program celebrating the United Methodist heritage in Wisconsin. They were also guests at a German dinner at a typical mansion of a money baron of earlier days, which is now a museum. On another occasion they were guests at a luncheon at Wesley Park Retirement Center.

Council meeting: Oklahoma City, March 28-31, 1978

The council met at the Sheraton Center Hotel, Oklahoma City, March 28-31, 1978, with Bishop Milhouse presiding.

The first several days were devoted to a seminar on "Marriage and Divorce," under the chairmanship of Bishop White. Particular attention was addressed to the growing problem of divorce in ministerial families. The bishops' wives were asked to participate in the seminar. A number of leaders recognized in the field of marital counseling had been invited as resource persons. It was agreed that the consultation represented only a first approach to the problem. There would be further times when the subject would be again on the agenda of the council.

Following a suggestion by Bishop Mathews, the council

HISTORY OF THE COUNCIL OF BISHOPS

agreed to meet as a body in Atlanta in March of 1979 with the bishops of the African Methodist Episcopal Church; the African Methodist Episcopal Church, Zion; and the Christian Methodist Episcopal Church.

Bishop Stowe was elected to write the Episcopal Address to the 1980 General Conference.

The bishops and their wives were guests of Bishop and Mrs. Milhouse and the Oklahoma area at two dinners, one at First United Methodist Church and the other at the Petroleum Club. At one of these dinners selections from New York musicals were given by local singers, *Oklahoma* being among them.

Council meeting: Colorado Springs, November 14-18, 1978

The Council of Bishops met at the Antlers Hotel, Colorado Springs, Colorado, November 14-18, 1978, with Bishop Stuart presiding.

The session began with a communion service at the Air Force Academy Chapel, at which Bishop Mathews gave the meditation. It was followed by a chuck-wagon family dinner, at which Bishop Tippett spoke concerning various personalities of the council since its inception in 1939.

In the standing committee and college meetings and in the full council sessions there were a larger number than usual of administrative items demanding attention.

Bishop Washburn presented a paper on "Power in the Church," which was discussed at some length and then sent back for further consideration.

Bishop Mathews presented a paper on "The Portland General Conference and the Council of Bishops."

The council released to the church a mid-quadrennial message, prepared by Bishop Mathews and read by Bishop Stuart.

On one evening the bishops and their wives were the guests of Bishop and Mrs. Wheatley and the Denver area at dinner. The program was in the form of a concert.

Following the adjournment of the council, a consultation

was held under the direction of Bishop Pryor for retired bishops and bishops scheduled for retirement in 1980.

Council meeting: Boston, April 17-20, 1979
Fortieth Birthday

The Council of Bishops reached its Fortieth Birthday meeting at the Copley Plaza Hotel, Boston, Massachusetts, April 17-20, 1979, with Bishop Stuart presiding.

On the evening before the opening business session, the bishops and their wives were the guests of Bishop and Mrs. Carroll at a clambake at the New England Aquarium. After dinner Bishop Short reviewed highlights of the council's first forty years.

Preceding the dinner a communion service was held at Marsh Chapel of Boston University, at which Bishop Carroll brought the message.

Dr. Albert Outler addressed the council on "The Governance Crisis in The United Methodist Church." The address was followed by a full discussion. The insistence of the address was that the council should make full use of its historical mandate found in the Constitution of the church.

The council received a presentation from the General Commission on the Status and Role of Women under the direction of the president, Carolyn R. Oehler.

Important matters to which attention was given included the proposed new pension plan before the coming General Conference; a report on the new proposal for Africa, submitted by the African Task Force; a disaster call to the churches in the amount of one million dollars; plans for The United Methodist Bicentennial in 1984; and further proposals regarding the World Hunger program.

A letter was addressed to President Jimmy Carter growing out of the accident at Metropolitan Edison's Nuclear Power Plant, Unit 2, on Three-Mile Island in the Susquehanna River. The letter recommended the delay of construction of any nuclear energy power plants until assurance can be given that the health and well-being of

HISTORY OF THE COUNCIL OF BISHOPS

American people have first priority. It further recommended that the federal government focus its resources upon renewable and non-nuclear forms of energy; and that a comprehensive national program of conservation of energy resources be implemented fully.

On one evening the bishops and their wives were the guests of Bishop and Mrs. Carroll and the Boston area at a dinner at which an oratorio, *New Land, New Covenant,* was presented. The Right Honorable George Thomas, speaker of the House of Commons in Great Britain, brought the address.

The council brought its first forty years to a close with the election of Bishop Ralph Alton as president, and Bishop Roy Nichols as president-elect.

In Memoriam—1976–May, 1979

Eight of the bishops died between the 1976 General Conference and the close of the first forty years of the Council of Bishops, May, 1979:

> F. Gerald Ensley
> R. D. Joshi
> Willis J. King
> H. Clifford Northcott
> J. Owen Smith
> John A. Subhan
> Edwin E. Voigt
> Aubrey G. Walton

Francis Gerald Ensley
(1907–1976)

F. Gerald Ensley was elected to the episcopacy by the North Central Jurisdictional Conference in 1952, from the pastorate of Broadway Church, Columbus, Ohio. Previous to that he had held other pulpits and had been a professor at Boston University. He was assigned to the Iowa area, which he served for twelve years, and then he served the Ohio West area for twelve years.

NEW PROBLEMS, RESPONSIBILITIES, AND OPPORTUNITIES

Bishop Ensley was a gifted preacher whose sermons were marked by penetrating insight. He had the capacity to make his audiences think as well as feel. He was in great demand, not only in churches but also in college and university chapels, and he filled almost countless lectureships on campuses everywhere. His sermons reflected the ponderings of his mind in hours of study and solitude and the wide range of his reading. No bishop had a finer library than did he, and he knew the rich contents of the books that lined his shelves. At odd moments one would often come upon him with his nose buried in a solid book.

The bishop was an able administrator who knew how to take administrative responsibilities in stride. He never panicked under pressure or asked to be excused from a difficult task. Therefore the church sometimes gave him administrative responsibilities that were not easy. When occupying the chair, he gave the impression of being at ease and of being fully able to handle any parliamentary situation that might arise.

Born August 17, 1907, in Morrow County, Ohio, Bishop Ensley was a short man. He had a habit of sometimes holding his glasses in his hand, or if he chose to wear them, he would look over them as he spoke. He had a fine sense of humor. His messages and his conversation were often characterized by wit. He was a nephew of Bishop McConnell, and he had some of the bishop's mannerisms as well as his type of mind.

Bishop Ensley spoke often in the Council of Bishops as matters were under discussion. He was especially interesting when he differed with a colleague. He would walk to the front, swing his glasses, and in a slow drawl begin his remarks with the words, "Now, brethren." Often he entered a plea for balance and for not getting too tense about what at the moment appeared to be alarming.

Bishop Ensley was particularly interested in higher education, in ecumenical cooperation and dialogue, in Christian social problems, and in evangelism. The latter became a mounting concern for him in his later days. He voiced this concern in the central committee of the World Council of Churches of which he was a member, and in the executive committee of the World Methodist Council, of which he was also a member. The World Methodist Council responded to his plea at this point and made him chairman of a Worldwide Evangelistic emphasis, a responsibility he carried until the time of his death.

Bishop Ensley was one more Methodist bishop who died on the road. He was stricken while attending the World Methodist Council in Dublin, Ireland. His last public appearance was before the council when he entered a moving plea for a fresh emphasis upon evangelism throughout Methodism. A few hours later he had to be taken to the hospital where he died within a few weeks, September 21, 1976. He knew less than two months as a retired bishop.

Ram Dutt Joshi
(1916–1976)

Ram Dutt Joshi was elected by the Southern Asia Central Conference to the episcopacy in 1969. He was assigned to the Bombay area. He was privileged to serve as a bishop for only seven years, as he died December 26, 1976, at the time of the Central Conference in Lucknow.

Prior to his election as bishop, Bishop Joshi had served with distinction in India as pastor, district superintendent, seminary professor, and educational secretary.

Born November 16, 1916, in Dwarahat in the Kumaon Hills of northern India, Bishop Joshi was a thoughtful man, with a gift for analyzing situations. In dialogue groups he was noted for his calm, pertinent contributions. He was broad in his sympathies and fully devoted to seeing the church in India fulfill its destiny.

Willis Jefferson King
(1886–1976)

Willis J. King was elected by the Central Jurisdiction to the episcopacy in 1944 and assigned to Liberia, where he served until 1956. He was then assigned to the New Orleans area. He retired in 1960 and continued to make his home in New Orleans.

Bishop King was a well-trained man, holding a Ph.D. degree from Boston University. He also studied at Oxford.

Most of his life was spent in the field of education. For two years he was the president of Samuel Houston College, Austin, Texas; and for twenty-eight years he served as professor or president at Gammon Seminary. He was recognized as a master teacher. Five of his students became his colleagues in the Council of Bishops.

Bishop King, born October 1, 1886, in Rose Hill, Texas, was a kind man, with a genial disposition. He had a fine sense of humor, which occasionally came through when he was in the presiding officer's chair.

The bishop was a strong advocate of justice and equality. He knew how to work creatively with other people in achieving social ends.

Bishop Scott Allen, in his memorial tribute to Bishop King, as his former teacher, said, "He knew how to stoop to conquer. For his noble acts of sacrifice, while maintaining and supporting principles, Willis Jefferson King will be widely acclaimed in the future."

Full of years and greatly loved, Bishop King died June 17, 1976, and is buried in Atlanta. Mrs. King followed him in death by only a few days.

Harry Clifford Northcott
(1890–1976)

H. Clifford Northcott was elected by the North Central Jurisdictional Conference to the episcopacy in 1948 from the pastorate of First Church, Champaign, Illinois, where he had served for twenty years. His earlier ministry had been in and around Chicago. Upon election he was assigned to the Wisconsin area, which he served until retirement in 1960.

Bishop Northcott was a Canadian by birth, born October 16, 1890, in Exeter, Ontario. He was a warm-hearted, human preacher. He exercised his duties in his area in a dedicated, pastoral way, and it was in being a pastor that his strength lay. He was thought of as the bishop of the great heart among his episcopal brethren. The Minutes of the council show that most of the motions he made were courtesy motions—to send flowers to someone who was ill, or to remember someone's birthday, or to show kindness in some other way. He seldom took the floor of the council for any other purpose. He was not made to be a presiding officer, and a difficult parliamentary situation was entirely beyond him. His colleagues in the council always referred to him lovingly as "Cliff." He was a large, well-proportioned man, impressive in his appearance, and most outgoing in his disposition.

Bishop Northcott suffered a stroke in the dining room of the hotel while attending the council meeting at Cincinnati in 1956. He managed by sheer willpower to oversee his area for the remainder of the quadrennium, at the close of which he took the retired relation. For a while he continued to live in Madison, Wisconsin, and then moved to Evanston, Illinois.

No bishop perhaps ever relished the meetings of the council and the fellowship they afforded more than did Bishop Northcott. He continued to attend even when he was hardly able to do so. He became severely handicapped physically with speech difficulties. Finally, he was unable to control his emotions and needed assistance to get about. But he was so evidently eager to talk with anyone and everyone who could spare him a few minutes of time. He loved his brethren and the church.

His release from his physical handicaps came July 18, 1976. His interment was in Hillside, Illinois.

John Owen Smith
(1902-1978)

John Owen Smith, familiarly known as "J. O.," was elected by the Southeastern Jurisdictional Conference to the episcopacy in 1960. He was assigned to the Atlanta area, which he served under his retirement in 1972. He was a native of South Carolina, born in Johnston, September 21, 1902, and had served as pastor and district superintendent in that conference until his election.

Bishop Smith was a short man, bald, with a fringe of gray hair, with eyes that had a light in them and seemed to speak of richness of soul. He was delightfully informal—informal in his tastes, in his dress, in his preaching, in his manner, and even informal in his prayers. He was a man who knew and loved the out-of-doors. He was constantly insisting that everyone should get as much of what he termed "fun" out of life as possible. He was an incurable optimist and often met difficult problems by asserting that they were not to be taken too seriously.

Bishop Smith was a social liberal. In his earlier ministry he was in the vanguard of those younger ministers of the South working for a new society. His passion for social righteousness marked him throughout his life. He was also a man of refinement and a speaker of the well-chosen word.

He was the host to the General Conference in 1972, which was the first General Conference to meet in the South since union in 1939. After his retirement in 1972 he continued to live in Atlanta and taught for several years in Candler School of Theology. He died December 3, 1978. His body was laid to rest in the churchyard of the rural church in South Carolina which he attended as a boy.

John Abdus Subhan
(1899–1977)

John A. Subhan was elected to the episcopacy by the Southern Asia Central Conference in 1944. He was assigned to the Bombay area, which he served for twelve years; and then to the Hyderabad area, which he served for eight years, retiring in 1964.

Bishop Subhan, born August 8, 1899, in Calcutta, came from a Muslim family, and in his early years he was an ardent Muslim and a Sufi, or mystic. When he was a young man, a copy of the Gospels fell into his hands, and this aroused in him an interest in becoming a Christian. He was confirmed in the Church of England, but in 1921 joined the Roman Catholic Church. After four years in that church he became a Methodist. He became head of the department of Islamic studies at Bareilly Theological Seminary in northern India.

Bishop Subhan was a short man with a light brown complexion. He had a fine mind, was well educated, and continued as a student all his days. He was strong in his convictions and fast in his reactions. He had the intensity of a fanatic or a new convert; he was said to have been almost violent in his Muslim fanaticism in his younger days. Like Paul, he showed the same devotion to the new religion he had found that he once showed for the earlier religion in which he had been raised. He could be quick in his retorts and was not too predictable in what positions he might take.

In a way he was something of a "loner," both in the College of Bishops in India and in the council itself. Perhaps no Methodist bishop in the history of the church has represented a wider range of ecclesiastical attachments across his lifetime than Bishop Subhan.

His fourteen retirement years were spent in Hyderabad, during which he had only infrequent contact with his episcopal colleagues. He died May 20, 1977, and is buried in Hyderabad.

Edwin Edgar Voigt
(1892–1977)

Edwin E. Voigt was elected by the North Central Jurisdictional Conference to the episcopacy in 1952 from the presidency of Simpson College. He was assigned to the newly created Dakotas area, which he served for eight years; and then to the Illinois area, which he served for four years. Following his retirement he served for four years as president of McKendree College in Illinois.

NEW PROBLEMS, RESPONSIBILITIES, AND OPPORTUNITIES

Bishop Voigt was an unusually well-trained man and is properly to be ranked among the scholars in the episcopacy. For example, he was well-trained in Islamics. Most of his ministry was spent as a university or seminary professor or as a college president. For six years he was engaged in Wesley Foundation work.

A midwesterner by birth—born near Kankakee, Illinois, February 13, 1892—Bishop Voigt was tall, trim, scholarly looking, with a fine bearing and immaculate in dress. He had a bearing of reserve that he carried with dignity. He was modest and never coveted the spotlight. The bishop had a good sense of humor and was marked always by a kind, brotherly spirit. Yet he had a high sense of indignation at anything cheap, unjust, or hurtful, and he could express his scorn both by the expression upon his face and in a few well-chosen words. He was, all in all, the Christian gentleman.

The bishop in his younger days had been associated with Ernest Freemont Little at First Church, Evanston, and with such figures at Garrett as Harris Franklin Hall and Horace G. Smith. He belonged to the liberal school of thought. He had a keen interest in the overseas work of the church, particularly the work in India, where his sister and nephew were missionaries.

Bishop Voigt was one of the more quiet members of the council. One could see him sitting and listening thoughtfully to all that was being said. When he did speak, it was to voice some pronounced conviction or to add genuine wisdom to what was being said. He never aspired to holding office in the council, and never did so. Likewise, he never presided in a General Conference, and this represented his preference. Yet, he did preside well in his Annual Conference sessions.

Bishop Voigt was chairman of the Commission on Worship. It was in this capacity that the whole church will feel his influence for years to come. He was chairman of the commission that produced the 1964 *Hymnal.* He gave it skilled and devoted guidance, enlisting the aid of resource persons who could make genuine contributions. His own sense of good taste in poetry and music and Scripture was reflected again and again in the hymns selected, the text of the hymns, and the Scripture selections and aids for worship.

After retirement Bishop Voigt attended the council meetings only about once a year, feeling in his modesty that his presence hardly warranted the expenses of a lengthy trip. The council sessions were poorer when he was not there, for his very presence in any group was always a steadying force and a benediction.

Bishop Voigt died August 31, 1977, and his earthly remains were buried in the family plot at Kankakee, Illinois.

Aubrey Grey Walton
(1901–1978)

Aubrey G. Walton was elected to the episcopacy by the South Central Jurisdiction in 1960 and assigned to the Louisiana area, which he served until his retirement in 1972. He was a native of Mississippi, where he was born June 20, 1901, in Clarksdale, but he spent his ministerial life prior to his election in the North Arkansas Conference. There he was a greaty beloved favorite son.

Bishop Walton was a Christian gentleman, quiet and reserved in manner. He had a fine sense of humor, a contagious smile, and a cordial, outgoing spirit. He was thorough in all he undertook and something of a perfectionist.

He was the resident bishop in Louisiana at the time of the dissolving of the Central Jurisdiction. New Orleans had long been one of the strongholds of black Methodism, and there was a strong necessity that whatever values and gains had been inherent in the former racial conferences should not be lost. Bishop Walton enjoyed the confidence of both conferences. While some difficult problems were involved, he brought the two together in a way that won the admiration of the entire church.

Bishop Walton died April 11, 1978, and is buried in Little Rock, Arkansas.

XI

Council Sidelights

During the past forty years there have been other persons regulary associated with the meetings of the council beyond the bishops themselves.

"Behind every good bishop . . ."

First of all there have been the bishops' wives. Of the wives of the bishops at the time of union in 1939, only Mrs. J. Waskom Pickett and Mrs. William C. Martin are still living. Mrs. Bruce Baxter, whose husband was elected in 1940, is still living at this date (1979), but her husband died shortly after his election, and she never became a familiar figure at the council meetings. Some of the wives have attended council meetings regularly with their husbands for twenty-five years or more. Among them are Mrs. Fred Corson, Mrs. Paul Martin, Mrs. Angie Smith, Mrs. Gerald Kennedy, Mrs. Richard Raines, Mrs. Marshall Reed, Mrs. Donald Tippett, Mrs. Gerald Ensley, Mrs. Lloyd Wicke, Mrs. Frederick Newell, Mrs. Roy H. Short, Mrs. Shot Mondol, Mrs. Clement Rockey, and Mrs. Newell Booth. Wives of Central Conference bishops have usually attended at the time of General Conference and occasionally at other times.

In the early days of the council it was not too common for

the wives of the bishops to go with them to the council meetings. This was because travel was by train and because during the war years travel not absolutely necessary was discouraged by the government. With the return of more normal travel conditions, and particularly when airlines began to offer half fare for a wife traveling with her husband, the attendance of wives began to increase. This attendance was also accelerated as travel by car became easier. By about 1952 it became much more common for wives to go with their husbands to the meetings of the council. It must be remembered, however, that some of the wives had younger children at home and found it very difficult to attend.

The wives of the bishops in the early days of the council tended to be a rather sedate, dignified group, marked by considerable formality. The same, of course, was true also of the bishops themselves in that period.

One of the bishops' wives who was always on hand at the time of the council meetings was Mrs. Oxnam, who made her husband's task as secretary easier by attending to many small details for him. He was a quick, easily irritated man who wanted everything in exact order. Some of his fellow bishops used to relate the story about Bishop Oxnam that on one occasion, after speaking, he went quickly to his car where Mrs. Oxnam was already seated behind the wheel. He seemed to be miffed, and she said, "Bromley, what did I do wrong? Wasn't I parked where I was supposed to, and didn't I have the car headed in the right direction?" He replied, "Yes, but you didn't have the motor running." The story is apocryphal, but it does speak eloquently of the role Mrs. Oxnam played with reference to details. She was an attractive person, of gentle bearing, who appeared to be quietly proud of her husband's accomplishments, but not inclined to magnify them out of due proportion.

Some other wives of bishops usually present in the beginning days were Mrs. Baker, Mrs. Flint, Mrs. Hammaker, Mrs. Wade, and Mrs. Cushman. These were to be seen often in each other's company, and apparently there were strong

COUNCIL SIDELIGHTS

bonds of friendship between them. Their husbands had been elected in the same general period. They were all marked by poise, by a certain reserve, and by an obvious concern for the church. Mrs. Wade had a lot of sparkle and laughter about her, but it was always subdued.

The wives of some of the bishops who were very active in the affairs of the council attended only infrequently. This was true of Mrs. Arthur Moore, Mrs. Paul Kern, Mrs. A. Frank Smith, Mrs. John Wesley Lord, and others.

Of the bishops' wives in the first years of the council, Mrs. Nicholson and Mrs. McConnell, in particular, were active in women's work at the general church level. Both of them held national office. Most of the episcopal wives were not too active in the women's work as a rule. Mrs. Northcott, however, was quite active and died while addressing a society meeting at First Church, Evanston.

For the first thirty years of the council's life, there were two occasions when the wives were regularly invited to join with the bishops in their session.

The first of these was the annual memorial services, which come at the spring meeting. These services have been tender, unforgettable, family occasions marked by triumph and celebration. Those members of the council, wives, or widows who have died during the previous year are remembered one by one. The tributes are usually recollections of those experiences that the group and the one who has gone on have shared together.

The second occasion when the wives have shared sessions with the bishops have been those when reports on episcopal visitations have been given.

Since 1972 the council has followed the practice of having most sessions open, and the majority of the wives have chosen to drop in on them from time to time when their own schedule of activities has allowed. They have attended the early morning devotional services regularly in a body.

Beginning in the 1960s, there appeared in the council a tendency to be less formal and more relaxed with each other. This informality has extended, on the part of some of the episcopal family, even to the point of a friendly embrace and kiss upon meeting. A few of the older brethren have not proved too good at this and are embarrassed by their awkwardness. Nevertheless, the council does appear to be becoming more of an episcopal family rather than just an episcopal body. Since 1972 the wives have been included in the orientation experience following the episcopal elections.

Secretaries

A second group of persons associated with the meetings of the Council of Bishops has been the secretaries to the secretary of the council. These have always been present to assist the secretary and to render secretarial service for the other bishops as needed. Only in the last six years, since the practice of open meetings has been followed, have they been in the council room during sessions.

For sixteen years Miss Christine Knudson of Boston and Washington served as secretary to Bishop Oxnam. For eight years Mrs. Frances Meeker of Nashville, and for eight years Mrs. Jane Williams of Louisville served as secretaries to Bishop Short. Mrs. Jean Pickett and Mrs. Barbara Niswonger McCallie of Indianapolis assisted Bishop Alton during his years as secretary. Mrs. Faith Richardson of Washington and Boston has assisted Bishop Mathews. The value of the services of these women to the council has been beyond calculation.

The Church Press

A third group of persons long associated with the meetings of the Council of Bishops has been the directors of *Methodist Information*. These have always been on hand at the time of the council meetings, but not present in the sessions themselves until the open meeting policy was adopted. For long years until his retirement, Dr. Ralph Stoody represented *Methodist Information,* and then Dr. Arthur West until his retirement.

COUNCIL SIDELIGHTS

Since the retirement of Dr. West, Miss Martha Mann has represented *Methodist Information*.

Methodist Information representatives have regularly served as a liaison with the press for the council, both for other church press and secular press. Since only bishops could be present in the council sessions, Bishop Oxnam instituted the custom of having the council name a bishop as press representative with whom *Methodist Information* could counsel. Usually bishops who had seen some editorial service were assigned this responsibility. These included Bishops Hartman, Nall, Harmon, and Taylor. Bishops Finger and Frank have also carried this assignment on occasion.

Local Arrangements Committee

Still a fourth group associated with the meetings of the council has been the local arrangements committee. These persons have done a commendable job regarding arrangements for the council. They have made hotel arrangements, often furnished transportation from airports, placed flowers and fruit in the rooms, arranged for a hospitality room and for coffee at intermission time, and often provided the bishops and their wives with local souvenirs.

For some years local arrangements committees have planned for some public occasion to give the people of the area and the bishops opportunity to meet each other. These have all been gala occasions with programs including music and other forms of entertainment, and often an address by a local dignitary. On such occasions the council has heard from United States senators, representatives, governors of states, and mayors, as well as from other distinguished persons.

At some of the public occasions the bishops and their wives have been seated on the platform at long tables facing the audience. At others they have been scattered among the tables, one episcopal couple at each table, in order to afford contact with local United Methodists. Sometimes there have been receiving lines prior to the dinner.

In recent years it has become customary to have an episcopal family dinner on the first evening. Usually these family dinners have been held at a nearby church.

Often the local arrangements committees have arranged for visits to United Methodist institutions of the area, such as colleges, seminaries, homes, hospitals, community centers, urban projects of various types, and retreat centers. Visits have also been arranged at times to historic sites, as well as to significant social projects that are not United Methodist sponsored.

In every case a program has been arranged for the bishops' wives. Leadership in such programs has been taken by the wife of the host bishop and by the officers of the bishops' wives organization.

Meeting Places and Hosts

Regular or called meetings of the Council of Bishops have been held in the Northeastern Jurisdiction at Atlantic City seven times; at New York four times; at Buck Hill Falls four times; at Washington and Boston three times; at Philadelphia twice; and at Springfield, Buffalo, Pittsburgh, Charleston, and Ocean City once each.

In the North Central Jurisdiction the council has met at Chicago twelve times; at Cincinnati three times; at Cleveland three times; at Columbus and Minneapolis twice; and at Grand Rapids, Indianapolis, Detroit, Des Moines, and Milwaukee once each.

In the Southeastern Jurisdiction the council has met at Nashville five times; at Epworth-by-the-Sea, Gatlinburg, and Miami Beach twice; and once each at Sea Island, Lake Junaluska, Louisville, and Williamsburg.

In the Western Jurisdiction the council has met twice at Portland, Seattle, and San Francisco; and once each at

COUNCIL SIDELIGHTS

Riverside, Grand Canyon, Pasadena, Los Angeles, Phoenix, Denver, and Colorado Springs.

In the first twenty years of the life of the council, it was hosted eleven times by Bishop and Mrs. Corson; six times by Bishop and Mrs. Oxnam; four times by Bishop and Mrs. Richardson, Bishop and Mrs. Kern, Bishop and Mrs. Werner, and Bishop Magee and daughter; twice by Bishop and Mrs. Moore, Bishop and Mrs. Baker; and once each by Bishop and Mrs. McConnell, Bishop and Mrs. Mead, Bishop and Mrs. Lester Smith, Bishop and Mrs. Leonard, Bishop and Mrs. Broomfield, Bishop and Mrs. Wade, Bishop and Mrs. Raines, Bishop and Mrs. Tippett, Bishop and Mrs. Watts, Bishop and Mrs. Newell, Bishop and Mrs. Brashares, Bishop and Mrs. Grant, Bishop and Mrs. Coors, and Bishop and Mrs. Short.

During the second twenty years the council has been entertained three times by Bishop and Mrs. Pryor; twice by Bishop and Mrs. Kennedy, Bishop and Mrs. Frank, Bishop and Mrs. Clair, Bishop and Mrs. Mathews, Bishop and Mrs. Palmer, and Bishop and Mrs. Short; and once each by Bishop and Mrs. Tippett, Bishop and Mrs. Branscomb, Bishop and Mrs. Phillips, Bishop and Mrs. Brashares, Bishop Henley, Bishop and Mrs. Middleton, Bishop and Mrs. Love, Bishop and Mrs. Reed, Bishop and Mrs. Paul Martin, Bishop and Mrs. Noah Moore and Bishop and Mrs. W. Ralph Ward, Bishop and Mrs. Pope, Bishop and Mrs. Ensley, Bishop and Mrs. Slater, Bishop and Mrs. Thomas, Bishop and Mrs. Wertz, Bishop and Mrs. J. O. Smith, Bishop and Mrs. Kearns, Bishop and Mrs. Finger, Bishop and Mrs. Golden, Bishop and Mrs. Hunt, Bishop and Mrs. Clymer, Bishop and Mrs. Crutchfield, Bishop and Mrs. Tuell, Bishop and Mrs. Ault, Bishop and Mrs. Goodson, Bishop and Mrs. DeWitt, Bishop and Mrs. Milhouse, Bishop and Mrs. Wheatley, and Bishop and Mrs. Carroll.

While most of the sessions of the council have been held separately, a few of these, particularly in the early period when Methodist union was just getting underway, were held in connection with other meetings such as those of the Board of Missions or the Board of Education. This accounts for most of the short sessions held at New York, Buck Hill Falls, Chicago, Nashville, and Atlantic City.

Some regular sessions have been held prior to, or immediately following, certain national meetings such as the Women's Assembly at Cleveland or several District Superintendents' Conferences held at Chicago or Cleveland.

Connectional Officers

Some mention may properly be made at this point of some of the connectional officers of the church with whom the bishops had frequent contact, particularly in the beginning days of the council. These officers did not, of course, attend the meetings of the council, but they had significant informal and personal contacts with the bishops, which were far reaching in their influence.

One of these connectional figures was Dr. Ralph E. Diffendorfer of the Board of Missions. For many years he was the gifted "foreign minister" of Methodism. He was a man of great administrative ability, large vision, strong commitment, and an iron will. All the bishops of the earlier period had dealings with him, particularly those who had responsibility for administration in what were then known as mission fields. He could be very understanding, but again he could be rigid. He did not hesitate to take issue with any bishop if he differed in judgment. Many of the bishops of the early period had some story to tell of a personal encounter with Methodism's strong missionary statesman. Dr. Diffendorfer retired in 1949.

Another connectional man with whom the bishops had frequent contact in the earliest years was Dr. John Q. Schisler of the Board of Education. Dr. Schisler was a man who operated quietly but kept in constant touch with the bishops and was greatly respected by them. His great concern was quality Christian education through the church school. He was always carrying a banner for the cause that

COUNCIL SIDELIGHTS

claimed his heart, and the bishops gladly responded to his leadership, as did the entire church.

With the coming of union in 1939, the secretary of the Council on World Service was Dr. O. W. Auman, who was followed by Dr. Thomas B. Lugg, Dr. Don Cooke, and Dr. Bryan Brawner. All of these were unfailingly kind to the bishops and did all in their power to make the episcopal task easier. The Council on World Service not only paid the bishops' salaries and travel accounts, but it went the second mile. It took care of such details as providing episcopal seals, helping with transportation problems, and arranging for episcopal accommodations at the General Conference.

Two of the publishing agents of the earlier period who were close to the bishops were Dr. Fred Stone and Dr. Roy L. Smith. Dr. Stone was a particularly able minister, and the bishops always found him especially helpful. He was a man of great balance, coupled with a fine sense of humor and fair play. He brought to the affairs of the Publishing House the perspective of the clerical mind. He was always a General Conference delegate, and there he gave excellent floor leadership. In a tangled situation more than once a bishop occupying the chair has cast an eye in Dr. Stone's direction and found him a very present help in time of trouble.

Dr. Roy L. Smith was a great friend of the bishops, and they were to him. As editor of the *Christian Advocate* he used them often in its pages, and as publishing agent he sought their advice. He was a popular speaker, having been one of the best known of the downtown preachers of the twenties and thirties. The bishops used him largely in the conference sessions and area meetings.

Dr. John O. Gross was another connectional man with whom the bishops had frequent dealings for some years. He was Methodism's chief spokesman for higher education, and he was the father of a new and more vital relationship between the church and its colleges. Almost every active bishop in the church was indebted to him for significant help in solving the problems of educational institutions to which the bishop was related.

HISTORY OF THE COUNCIL OF BISHOPS

Mrs. J. D. Bragg, Mrs. Frank G. Brooks, and Mrs. J. Fount Tillman were leaders of women's work who conferred often with the bishops, and the bishops with them. Mrs. Bragg had the task of bringing together the six women's organizations in the three uniting churches into one organization in 1939. She did it to perfection. Her quiet, plain personality created confidence, and she was a master strategist.

Dr. George L. Morelock was another connectional person with whom the bishops had much contact in the early years. He was elected general secretary of the Board of Lay Activities in the new church. He had been the secretary of Lay Activities in the Church, South since 1922. His concept of lay activities was that of assisting the pastor and playing a strong supportive role. He was always ready to be of assistance to the bishops. Following Dr. Morelock's day the concept of lay activities shifted to that of a more participatory role. Doctor Robert Mayfield who followed him likewise sought to work closely with the bishops.

Still another connectional man closely connected with the bishops was Dr. Harry Denman of the Board of Evangelism. He tried conscientiously and tirelessly to do everything the bishops wanted him and his board to do. He traveled their areas at their request and had his staff do the same thing. He lived out of a suitcase and for years did not have a room anywhere in the world. He wrote letters constantly to each bishop, many of them in longhand. Sometimes the letters would carry a word of thanksgiving or encouragement. Again, they would carry one of the suggestions that were forever emanating from his fertile mind. He loved the bishops sincerely and made it a habit to pray for each one of them every day by name.

The connectional persons who have been mentioned have either retired or died. It is for some future writer to mention others who are currently proving helpful to the bishops as they attempt to serve the church.

For a considerable part of the first forty years of the life of the council, the secretary of the General Conference was Dr. Lud H. Estes of the Memphis Conference. He had

COUNCIL SIDELIGHTS

previously been secretary of the General Conference of the Church, South. As secretary he had frequent contact with the bishops, and they depended upon his help. He was a master of detail, and did a near-perfect job. He was a stocky man with a husky voice. He was quick and had a tendency to get offside, and at time almost to preempt the chair. A few of the bishops sometimes resented his activity and impulsiveness. Nevertheless, he truly sought to be their servant and the servant of the church. He signed all his letters to the bishops and to everyone else, "Your buddy."

Dr. Estes was succeeded by Dr. Leon Moore of Philadelphia, Dr. J. Wesley Hole of California, Dr. Charles White of North Carolina, and Dr. J. B. Holt of Texas. To all of these the bishops found themselves also indebted.

Central Conference "Term" Bishops

Mention should be made at this point of some of the Central Conference bishops who for a period were members of the council, but—where term episcopacy prevailed—were not reelected and have therefore become former bishops.

Arthur Wesley was elected by the Latin America Central Conference in 1944, following the retirement of Bishop Gattinoni, and he served the Buenos Aires area for four years. Bishop Wesley originally joined the Detroit Conference. He taught in succession at the Chicago Evangelistic Institute, a holiness school; at Northern Baptist Theological Seminary, a fundamentalist institution; and at the Chicago Training School. At the invitation of Bishop Oldham he went to South America as a missionary in 1918 and served for the twenty-six years prior to his election to the episcopacy.

Bishop Wesley had been strongly committed to the election of national bishops, and he refused to be considered for reelection in 1948. He then returned to missionary service in Chile until his retirement in 1956. His last days were spent in Lakeland, Florida.

HISTORY OF THE COUNCIL OF BISHOPS

Harry P. Andreassen was elected by the Africa Central Conference in 1964 and again in 1968. He was not reelected in 1972. His area assignment was Angola. Bishop Andreassen was a native of Norway, and after serving in the pastorate there for eight years, he went to Angola as a missionary in 1952. He served effectively as conference evangelist and district superintendent prior to his election. Following his episcopal service, he returned to Norway to work in a home for handicapped children.

Robert F. Lundy was elected by the Southeast Asia Central Conference in 1964 and served the Singapore area until 1968. He had been a missionary in Malaya for some years. It was his strong conviction that the episcopal leader should be a national, and he, therefore, did not wish to be reelected. He had taken the same position in 1964, but the Central Conference at that time chose to elect him, actually against his desire. After 1968 he served for a brief period on the staff of the Board of Global Ministries and was then elected executive secretary of the Southeastern Jurisdictional Council. He is presently pastor of Broad Street Church, Cleveland, Tennessee.

John Wesley Shungu was elected by the Africa Central Conference in 1964 and was reelected in 1968. He served the work in Zaire. He joined the Central Congo Conference in 1942 and served as pastor, district superintendent, and Bible School teacher prior to his election. After not being reelected in 1972, he located in Kananga, Zaire, where he went into business and became active in a local church.

John Victor Samuel was elected in 1968 by the Pakistan Central Conference. Although only thirty-eight years of age at the time, he had already had a notable career, both in his own conference and in ecumenical circles. Bishop Samuel's membership in the Council of Bishops was short, however, as the Pakistan Methodist Church went into the United Church of Pakistan shortly after his election.

Frederico J. Pegura was elected by the Central Conference of Latin America at its last session in 1969. At that session the Central Conference dissolved, and most of it went into

COUNCIL SIDELIGHTS

autonomous churches. A fragment remained, represented by the work in Costa Rica and Panama. Bishop Pegura was assigned to this work until shortly thereafter it went into united churches. His membership in the council, like that of Bishop Samuel, was therefore brief. Following his service as a bishop, he returned to his chosen field of seminary teaching in Buenos Aires, and was later elected bishop of the Methodist Church of Argentina.

Bishops Valencia, Barbieri, Dodge, Zottele, and Zunguze were all elected under term episcopacy but were in office at the time of reaching retirement age. Therefore, they continue as members of the Council of Bishops under a law adopted by the General Conference of 1968.

Bishops Balloch and Amstutz retired, lost their membership in the Council of Bishops for a time under the Alejandro decision of the Judicial Council, but recovered it through remedial legislation adopted by the 1976 General Conference.

The status of the membership of Bishop Ferrer, retired, was unclear for a time since the question was unresolved of exactly what retirement age should prevail in his case. The Judicial Council reviewed the matter and confirmed his membership in the council as a retired bishop.

With certain term bishops not being reelected, the bishops as a company are therefore to be classified as active bishops, retired bishops, and former bishops.

XII

After Forty Years

The Council of Bishops today is quite different from the council of the earlier years.

First of all it is much larger. Its roll includes forty-five active bishops in the United States and sixteen active bishops overseas from the United States.

There are thirty-two retired bishops in the United States and thirteen retired Central Conference bishops, making a total episcopal body of 106 in the year 1979.

Even with the elimination of the Central Jurisdiction, there are still fifteen more episcopal areas in the United States now than there were at the time of union. Overseas from the United States there are seven more episcopal areas than there were at the time of Methodist union.

This large increase in size means that the council faces quite different operational problems and is necessarily a less intimate body than it was in the beginning. At a recent meeting of the council, the Committee on Administration alone had present as many bishops as the total number of active bishops of the large Methodist Episcopal Church at the time of union.

A notable change in the operation of the council, largely growing out of its increased size, is the fact that now only to a limited extent does it sit as a committee of the whole. Earlier every bishop was party to the discussion of every agenda item. Today most agenda items are referred to one of the four committees. A bishop is not party to the initial and full discussion of a particular item unless it happens to be before his committee. Of course there are final recommendations from each committee to the entire body, but there is a tendency to approve or reject most of these without too much discussion.

Likewise, there is more of a tendency today to have a larger number of matters handled by the executive committee than before. Once the executive committee consisted of only five members, and it handled nothing except references to it or genuine emergencies. The council was for years very guarded in the use of the executive committee. Today the executive committee is much larger and more representative and meets with regularity. At times it takes initiatives upon its own motion. The privilege of serving on the executive committee at some time, which now is more of a decision-making body than formerly, is one that every bishop covets.

Another change in the council from the earlier day is the larger involvement of the Central Conference bishops. Today they attend each meeting if they so desire with their expenses paid. Some of them attend only every other meeting. In cases where there is more than one bishop in a Central Conference, they observe a rotation system to save expense for the church. The Central Conference bishops form themselves into a college, similar to the colleges of the jurisdictions, and bring necessary concerns to the full council at each meeting.

In the earlier years there was a tendency to make as little use of the different Colleges of Bishops as possible. A considerable part of The Methodist Church for some years was afraid of the jurisdictional system and inclined to make little use of it. The first rules adopted by the council provided that no College of Bishops should issue any statement without the consent of the entire council. In those years most of the colleges did little more than make necessary nominations. The passing years have seen an expanding function of the colleges, and adequate time at each council meeting is set apart for them to meet. Most of the colleges have called meetings at other times during the year.

The years have also witnessed a lessening emphasis upon the interpretation of church law. The early Minutes show a preponderance of agenda items of this character. Almost every bishop in those days seemed to put on the agenda, with fair frequency, requests for legal interpretations. Today there are far fewer such requests.

For many years the Board of Bishops of the Methodist Episcopal Church and the College of Bishops of the Methodist Episcopal Church, South often spent time discussing specific pastoral appointments, particularly in the stronger churches. At this point they functioned truly as a general superintendency. This procedure was abandoned when union came. Even in the colleges there has been little or no discussion of particular appointments for some years. However, the council itself has often had upon its agenda consideration of the general subject of appointment-making, with position papers, panel discussions, and studies of various kinds.

The council in these forty years has become less of a general superintendency, except in a collective sense. It has become increasingly a body of area administrators meeting to plan together for the entire church.

Originally in both the Methodist Episcopal Church and the Methodist Episcopal Church, South there was strong adherence to the concept of the episcopacy as a general superintendency. For this reason each bishop was assigned responsibility for holding different conferences each year, thus serving the entire church. When the area system was adopted by the Methodist Episcopal Church, effort was made to preserve the general superintendency idea by providing that at least once each quadrennium a conference session would be held by some bishop other than the bishop of the area. In the Church, South, in order to preserve the idea of a general superintendency, the assignment of conferences to a bishop was generally changed each quadrennium.

In the early years of union, the occasional holding of conference sessions by a bishop other than the area bishop was strongly encouraged. This has largely been abandoned, however. Whatever values this earlier practice had have been compensated for, to some extent, by the habit of most present bishops of inviting other bishops to have a part on the conference program. The time has come when there are bishops who have never held conference sessions other than those of their own area. Some of them for their entire episcopacy have had only one area, and that oftentimes is an area composed of a single conference. This would probably occasion surprise to the bishops who were members of the council in its beginning days.

Throughout the forty years of its life, there has always been strong pressure upon the Council of Bishops to lend itself to promotion. This pressure comes from boards and agencies of our own church, from ecumenical bodies, from caucus groups, from individuals, and even from some agencies outside the church. All these know that the support of the bishops can mean much in a system like Methodism, which has so strong a channel of communication. The council has great concern for many of the causes for which its support is solicited, and over the years it has responded favorably in many cases. Nevertheless, it has steadily resisted the temptation to become only a promotional body and has cherished the right of originating its own agenda.

As the years have passed, the council has been marked by a continuing effort to deepen the fellowship of the episcopal body; to play more of a teaching role in the life of the church; to increase the involvement of United Methodists with other Christians; to respond more effectively to the need of the world; and to take primarily the pastoral approach in administration.

When the Council of Bishops was organized in 1939, the age of the giants in the episcopacy was still present. Not all the bishops of that day belonged in this category, but there were in the council certain towering figures like Bishops Welch, McConnell, Hughes, Baker, Oxnam, Arthur Moore, John M. Moore, Kern, and Frank Smith. There are fewer figures dominating the council today by the sheer weight of their personality and gifts than there were in the beginning. It is only fair, however, to observe that there is now a healthy distribution of leadership, a high average of talent, and a strong commitment to the episcopal task. No more needs to be said of the present council and its members. In time history will make its own evaluation.

Appendix A

Regular and Called Meetings of the Council of Bishops

Place	Date	Bishop Presiding
Kansas City	April 25-May 11, 1939	John M. Moore & Hughes
Chicago	Dec. 6-9, 1939	Hughes & Darlington
Atlantic City	April 18–May 6, 1940	Hughes & Darlington
Chicago	July 22-26, 1940	A. Frank Smith
Philadelphia	Nov. 27, 1940	A. Frank Smith
Atlantic City	Dec. 3-5, 1940	A. Frank Smith
Chicago	March 5, 1941	A. Frank Smith
Nashville	May 7-9, 1941	A. Frank Smith
New York City	Dec. 5, 1941	A. Frank Smith
Sea Island, Georgia	Dec. 9-12, 1941	A. Frank Smith
Nashville	May 22-25, 1942	Richardson
Chicago	July 9, 1942	Richardson
Cleveland	Dec. 7-9, 1942	Richardson
Nashville	Feb. 18, 1943	Peele
Washington	Feb. 22-25, 1943	Peele
Chicago	July 13, 1943	Peele

HISTORY OF THE COUNCIL OF BISHOPS

Buck Hill Falls, Pa.	Dec. 8-9, 1943	Peele
Princeton	Dec. 15-17, 1943	Peele
Chicago	Feb. 18, 1944	H. Lester Smith
Kansas City	April 20–May 6, 1944	H. Lester Smith
Chicago	July 24-27, 1944	H. Lester Smith
Buck Hill Falls	Dec. 6, 1944	H. Lester Smith
Chicago	April 23-27, 1945	H. Lester Smith
Buck Hill Falls	Dec. 3-6, 1945	Selecman
Atlantic City	Feb. 20-25, 1946	Selecman
Grand Rapids	Sept. 11-13, 1946	Lowe
Buck Hill Falls	Dec. 10, 1046	Lowe
Nashville	Feb. 25, 1947	Lowe
Riverside, Cal.	May 1-6, 1947	Lowe
Springfield, Mass.	Sept. 26, 1947	Kern
Atlantic City	Dec. 2-6, 1947	Kern
Atlantic City	April 15-21, 1948	Kern
Boston	April 26–May 8, 1948	Kern
Columbus	Oct. 3, 1948	Baker
Cincinnati	Nov. 30–Dec. 2, 1948	Baker
Buck Hill Falls	Dec. 6-8, 1948	Baker
Atlantic City	April 26-30, 1949	Baker
New York City	Nov. 30–Dec. 3, 1949	Holt
Cleveland	April 17-21, 1950	Holt
Indianapolis	Oct. 3, 1950	Magee

APPENDIX A

New York City	Dec. 4-7, 1950	Magee
Grand Canyon	April 23-27, 1951	Magee
Atlantic City	Jan. 10-14, 1952	A. J. Moore
San Francisco	April 23–May 6, 1952	A. J. Moore
Atlantic City	Nov. 17-21, 1952	Corson
Omaha	April 28–May 1, 1953	Corson
Epworth-by-the-Sea	Dec. 8-11, 1953	W. C. Martin
New York City	April 26-30, 1954	W. C. Martin
Chicago	Dec. 18-21, 1954	Brashares
Seattle	April 19-21, 1955	Brashares
Atlantic City	Dec. 6-9, 1955	Purcell
Buck Hill Falls	Jan. 22, 1956	Purcell
Minneapolis	April 25–May 7, 1956	Purcell
Pasadena	Dec. 10-13, 1956	Ledden
Cincinnati	April 23-26, 1957	Ledden
Gatlinburg, Tenn.	Nov. 12-14, 1957	W. Angie Smith
Ocean City, N. J.	Jan. 7-8, 1958	W. Angie Smith
Miami Beach	April 8-10, 1958	W. Angie Smith
Cincinnati	Nov. 11-13, 1958	Oxnam
Washington	April 14-17, 1959	Oxnam

HISTORY OF THE COUNCIL OF BISHOPS

Phoenix	Nov. 17-20, 1959	Franklin
Denver	April 19–May 6, 1960	Franklin & Kennedy
Chicago	Nov. 15-17, 1960	Kennedy
Boston	April 4-6, 1961	Kennedy
Gatlinburg	Nov. 14-16, 1961	Paul Martin
Mexico City	April 24-26, 1962	Paul Martin
St. Louis	Nov. 13-15, 1962	Reed
San Francisco	April 16-18, 1963	Reed
Detroit	Nov. 12-14, 1963	Garber
Pittsburgh	April 17–May 8, 1964	Garber & Wicke
Chicago	Nov. 15-17, 1964	Wicke
Houston	April 18-20, 1965	Wicke
Seattle	Nov. 16-19, 1965	Taylor
Louisville	April 11-14, 1966	Taylor
Chicago	Nov. 5-12, 1966	Raines
Buffalo	March 27-30, 1967	Raines & Mueller
Miami Beach	Nov. 13-16, 1967	Tippett
Dallas	April 15–May 4, 1968	Tippett & Frank
Chicago	Nov. 11-14, 1968	Frank
Charleston, W. Va.	April 8-11, 1969	Frank

APPENDIX A

Columbus, Ohio	Nov. 11-13, 1969	Mueller
St. Louis	April 16-24, 1970	Mueller
Portland, Ore.	Nov. 17-19, 1970	Lord
New York City	March 1-4, 1971	Lord
San Antonio	April 13-15, 1971	Lord
Des Moines	Nov. 15-18, 1971	Hardin
Epworth-by-the-Sea & Atlanta	April 10-28, 1972	Hardin & Slater
Cleveland	Sept. 22-25, 1972	Slater
Washington	April 24-27, 1973	Slater
Nashville	Nov. 12-15, 1973	Golden
Los Angeles	April 15-18, 1974	Golden
Lake Junaluska	Nov. 10-14, 1975	Loder
Minneapolis	March 31–April 4, 1975	Loder
New Orleans	Nov. 10-14, 1975	W. Ralph Ward
Lincoln City, Ore. & Portland	April 20–May 7, 1976	W. Ralph Ward
Philadelphia	Nov. 16-19, 1976	Goodson
Williamsburg, Va.	April 12-15, 1977	Goodson
Milwaukee	Nov. 15-18, 1977	Milhouse

HISTORY OF THE COUNCIL OF BISHOPS

Oklahoma City	March 28-31, 1978	Milhouse
Colorado Springs	Nov. 14-17, 1978	Stuart
Boston	April 17-20, 1979	Stuart

Appendix B
Officers of the Council of Bishops

Presidents

1939—Joint presidents—Bishops Edwin H. Hughes and U. V. W. Darlington
1940—Bishop A. Frank Smith
1941—Bishop Ernest G. Richardson
1942—Bishop W. W. Peele
1943–45—Bishop H. Lester Smith
1945—Bishop Charles C. Selecman
1946—Bishop Titus Lowe
1947—Bishop Paul B. Kern
1948—Bishop James C. Baker
1949—Bishop Ivan Lee Holt
1950—Bishop J. Ralph Magee
1951—Bishop Arthur J. Moore
1952—Bishop Fred P. Corson
1953—Bishop William C. Martin
1954—Bishop Charles W. Brashares
1955—Bishop Clare Purcell
1956—Bishop W. Earl Ledden
1957—Bishop W. Angie Smith
1958—Bishop G. Bromley Oxnam
1959—Bishop Marvin A. Franklin
1960—Bishop Gerald Kennedy

HISTORY OF THE COUNCIL OF BISHOPS

1961—Bishop Paul E. Martin
1962—Bishop Marshall R. Reed
1963—Bishop Paul N. Garber
1964—Bishop Lloyd C. Wicke
1965—Bishop Prince Albert Taylor
1966—Bishop Richard C. Raines
1967—Bishop Donald H. Tippett
1968—Bishop Eugene M. Frank
1969—Bishop Reuben H. Mueller
1970—Bishop John Wesley Lord
1971—Bishop Paul Hardin, Jr.
1972—Bishop Oliver Eugene Slater
1973—Bishop Charles W. Golden
1974—Bishop Dwight H. Loder
1975—Bishop W. Ralph Ward
1976—Bishop W. Kenneth Goodson
1977—Bishop Paul W. Milhouse
1978—Bishop R. Marvin Stuart

Secretaries

1939—Bishop H. Lester Smith
1940–1956—Bishop G. Bromley Oxnam
1956–1972—Bishop Roy H. Short
1972–1976—Bishop Ralph T. Alton
1976—Bishop James K. Mathews

Appendix C
A Listing of Some Major Actions of the Council of Bishops

1939–1944

1—Organization of the council.
2—Forward Movement with rallies across the church to celebrate union.
3—Appointment of Committee on War Emergency and Overseas Relief.
4—Appeal for work in army camps, British missions, and relief.
5—Establishment of Commission on Chaplains, securing and training of chaplains.
6—Establishment of Camp Activities program.
7—Establishment of Methodist Committee on Overseas Relief.
8—Wartime message to the church.
9—Crusade for a New World Order.
10—Consideration of the rural church.
11—Consideration of responsibility for newly developing urban areas.
12—Emphasis upon evangelism.
13—Development of plan of overseas visitation.

HISTORY OF THE COUNCIL OF BISHOPS
1944–1948

1—Promotion of the Crusade for Christ.
2—Establishment of Commission on Relation of Races in The Methodist Church.
3—Establishment of Commission on Central Conferences.
4—Concern for recruitment, leading to establishment of Commission on Christian Vocations.
5—Opposition to peacetime military training.
6—Convocation on Veterans' Affairs.
7—Efforts leading to establishment of a Department of Research.
8—Appointment of Committee on Roman Catholic Relations.
9—Proposal for an Advance for Christ and His Church.

1948–1952

1—Orientation for newly elected bishops.
2—Promotion of Advance for Christ and His Church.
3—Response to the charge of Communist infiltration in the church.
4—Opposition to appointment of an ambassador to the Vatican.
5—Proposal of a manual for district superintendents.
6—Proposal of the establishment of a Methodist Foundation.
7—Proposal that the church establish an official unit on social action.
8—Visitation program of all Methodist college campuses.
9—Proposal for a Methodist Bookshelf.

1952–1956

1—Promotion of Youth Emphasis.
2—Plans for ministry to the Chinese in dispersion.

APPENDIX C

3—Plans to relate American University more closely to the church and to establish a School of International Service.
4—Support of the leadership of the church, particularly Bishop Oxnam in the case of his appearance before the Committee on Un-American Activities in the McCarthy era.
5—Support of the Supreme Court 1954 decision on public school desegregation.
6—Emphasis on higher education.
7—Aid in establishing Alaska University.
8—Endorsement of a church school emphasis.
9—Appeal for support of the United nations and the World Council of Churches.

1956–1960

1—Promotion of Emphasis Upon Higher Education.
2—Promotion of Emphasis Upon the Development of the Local Church.
3—Creation of a standing Message Committee.
4—Consideration of Methodist ecumenical relations, leading to the establishment of the Commission on Ecumenical Relations.
5—Study of appointment procedures.
6—Position on the elimination of segregation in The Methodist Church.
7—Study of the jurisdictional system.
8—Support of Soochow University in Taiwan.
9—Exploration of the possibility of union with the Evangelical United Brethren Church.
10—Cooperation in raising funds for the purchase of the Epworth rectory.
11—Endorsement of Race Relations Day goal of $1,000,000 for Negro colleges.
12—Publication of *History of Methodism*.

HISTORY OF THE COUNCIL OF BISHOPS
1960–1964

1—Promotion of "Jesus Christ Is Lord" emphasis.
2—Plans for training district superintendents.
3—Participation in Study of the Episcopacy.
4—Establishment of Committee on Legislation.
5—Provision for regular conferring with heads of seminaries.
6—Study of the Christian Faith and War in a Nuclear Age.
7—Consideration of divorce in clergy families.
8—Reaction to Second Vatican Council.
9—Development of a Crusade on the Ministry.
10—Consideration of churches in racially changing neighborhoods.
11—Conference with presidents of universities related to The Methodist Church.
12—Efforts toward a truly interracial church.
13—Development of guidelines for conference mergers across racial lines.
14—Development of new system for making nominations to boards and agencies.

1964–1968

1—Establishment of Bishops' Committee on Race and planning for elimination of the Central Jurisdiction.
2—Participation in consultations of the Commission on Structure of Methodism Overseas.
3—Leadership in looking toward union with the Evangelical United Brethren Church.
4—Arrangements for continuing conversations with the Roman Catholic Church.
5—Leadership in development of a concordat with British Methodism.
6—Consideration of participation in the Consultation on Church Union.

APPENDIX C

7—Statement on the war in Vietnam.
8—Consideration of the urban crisis.

1968–1972

1—Suggestion of and promotion of Fund for Reconciliation.
2—Meeting with selected youth at Kansas City.
3—Opposition to use of state funds for private and parochial schools.
4—Study of the parish system.
5—Response to "The Black Manifesto."
6—Consideration of proposed restructure of boards and agencies.
7—Proposal for Bishops' Call for Peace and the Self-Development of Peoples.
8—Consideration of ways and means to meet the needs of minorities in the church, and arrangement for meeting with minority representatives prior to General Conference.
9—Consideration of the relationship of church and state.
10—Plans for restructuring the operation of the council.

1972–1976

1—Acceptance of the policy of open meetings.
2—Promotion of the Bishops' Call for Peace and the Self-Development of Peoples.
3—Extension of program of visitation to include Central Conference bishops and the entire church as a field for visitation.
4—Efforts to be helpful in strike at the Methodist Hospital in Pikeville, Ky.
5—Production of books on "The Holy Spirit" and on "Christian Experiences."
6—Consideration of study of the episcopacy.

7—Consideration of study of the ministry.
8—Promotion of Grain Belt Consultation.
9—Urban study.
10—Emphasis upon evangelism.

1976-1979

1—Support of the three mission priorities—hunger, the ethnic minority local church, and evangelism.
2—Support of majority rule in Southern Africa.
3—Further consideration of the Consultation on Church Union.
4—Participation in world evangelism program of the World Methodist Council.
5—Acceptance of the reports on the Pacific Homes situation.
6—Consideration of the episcopal role in crisis intervention.
7—Consideration of ministry and management.
8—Seminar on divorce in ministerial families.
9—Arrangements for joint meeting with bishops of the African Methodist Episcopal Church; African Methodist Episcopal Church, Zion; and Christian Methodist Episcopal Church.
10—Study of power in the church.
11—Consultation for retired bishops and bishops scheduled to retire in 1980.

I

Index of Names

(Bold face numbers refer to the biographies of the deceased bishops.)

Ainsworth, William N., 14, 31, **36-37,** 102, 240
Alejandro, D. D., 52, 135, 162, 166, 167, 168, 196, 203, **229-30,** 277
Allen, L. Scott, 163, 192, 196, 220, 224, 228, 229, 249, 252, 259
Alton, Ralph T., 132, 135, 137, 141, 164, 172, 201, 220, 221, 222, 228, 249, 256, 268, 290
Ames, Edward R., 57
Ammons, Edsel A., 250
Amstutz, Hobart B., 17, 110, 137, 161, 162, 168, 244, 277
Anderson, William F., 52, 56, **57-58**
Anderson, William K., 58
Andreassen, Harry P., 162, 244, 276
Anthony, Mack, 120
Archer, Raymond L., 109, **202-3**

Armstrong, A. James, 192, 196, 198, 200
Arvidson, Theodor, 52, 107, **143-44**
Asbury, Francis, 117, 185
Ault, James M., 221, 251, 271
Ault, Mrs. James, 271
Auman, O. W., 273

Badley, Brenton T., 15, 51, 70, 79, **80**
Badley, Mrs. Brenton, 80
Baker, Eric, 221
Baker, James C., 15, 16, 22, 29, 35, 51, 70, 71, 72, 74, 89, 90, 91, 169, 202, **203-4,** 271, 282, 284, 289
Baker, Mrs. James C., 266, 271
Balaram, P. C. B., 163, **173-74**
Balloch, Enrique C., 25, 31, 51, 70, 107, 161, 277
Barbieri, Sante U., 72, 137, 161, 169, 192, 228, 242, 277

297

HISTORY OF THE COUNCIL OF BISHOPS

Bast, Anton, 217
Batdorf, G. B., 186, 189
Baughman, L. L., 189
Baxter, Bruce R., 25, 26, 51, 56, **58**
Baxter, Mrs. Bruce, 265
Bennett, John C., 75
Benson, F. Murray, 135
Birney, Lauress, J., 23, 148
Blackburn, Robert M., 221
Blackmum, Harry A., 228
Blake, Edgar, 15, 16, 24, 31, **36-37**
Boaz, Hiram A., 143, **145-46**
Booth, Newell S., 52, 107, 130, 161, 164, 169, 202, **205-6**
Booth, Mrs. Newell, 265
Borgen, Ole E., 193, 220, 224, 227, 249
Bowen, J. W. E., Sr., 146
Bowen, John W. E., Jr., 71, 79, 89, 107, 110, 133, 143, **146**
Bragg, Mrs. J. D., 274
Branscomb, John W., 90, 91, 107, 110, 114, **119-20,** 241, 271
Branscomb, Mrs. John, 271
Brashares, Charles W., 17, 52, 54, 70, 77, 89, 94, 95, 113, 127, 130, 136, 141, 162, 220, 271, 285, 289
Brashares, Mrs. Charles, 271
Brawner, Bryan, 273
Bromley, G., 14
Brooks, Mrs. Frank G., 274
Brooks, Robert N., 71, 93, **96-97,** 183
Broomfield, John C., 14, 15, 16, 19, 50, 51, 79, **80-81,** 231, 271

Broomfield, Mrs. John, 271
Brown, Wallace E., 15, 16, 21, 23, 25, 49
Bryan, A. Monk, 250
Bucke, Emory Stevens, 116
Bunche, Ralph, 94
Burgoyne, Mrs. Samuel (Mary Esther), 80
Burns, Charles W., 24
Burns, Francis, 158, 218

Camphor, Alexander P., 242
Candler, Asa G., 39
Candler, Warren A., 14, 36, **38-39,** 102, 239
Cannon, James, Jr., 28, 31, 38, 56, **58-60,** 166, 198, 211, 227, 249, 251, 252
Cannon, James, III, 61
Cannon, William R., 192, 227
Carleton, Alsie H., 192, 252
Carroll, Edward C., 221, 253, 255, 256, 271
Carroll, Mrs. Edward, 271
Carter, Jimmy, 221, 250, 255
Carter, Randall A., 42
Chen, W. Y., 25, 31, 32, 50, 70, 78, 107, 161, 202, **206**
Chih Ping, Wang, 40, 148
Chitambar, Jashwant R., 16, 22, 31, 36, **39-40,** 68
Choy, W. Y., 204, 222, 229, 249, 252
Church, Frank, 229
Clair, Matthew W., Sr., 20, 36, **40-41,** 150, 242
Clair, Matthew W., Jr., 90, 91, 107, 114, 135, 138, 139, 162-63, 202, **206-7,** 242, 271
Clair, Mrs. Matthew, Jr., 139, 271

298

INDEX OF NAMES

Clement, Frank, 137
Clippenger, A. R., 186, 187
Clymer, Wayne K., 222, 224, 227, 271
Clymer, Mrs. Wayne, 271
Cohen, Benjamin, 94
Colwell, Ernest, 115
Connally, John, 165
Cooke, Don, 273
Coors, Stanley D., 91, 119, **120-21**
Coors, Mrs. Stanley, 271
Copeland, Kenneth, 132, 136, 163, 186, 220, 229, **231,** 247
Cordier, Andres, 94
Corson, Fred P., 51, 54, 70, 74, 89, 90, 92, 107, 112, 114, 115, 130, 133, 137, 138, 139, 140, 141, 161, 166, 167, 169, 170, 186, 191, 271, 285, 289
Corson, Mrs. Fred, 265, 271
Cranston, Earl, 17
Crutchfield, Finis A., 222, 228, 271
Crutchfield, Mrs. Finis, 271
Cushman, Ralph S., 15, 22, 51, 89, 90, 143, **146-47**
Cushman, Robert L., 111
Cushman, Mrs. Robert, 266

Dabney, Virginius, 61
Darlington, Urban V. W., 14, 16, 19, 20, 22, 34, 51, 70, 96, **97-98,** 102, 124, 239, 283, 289
Dawson, Dana, 71, 107, 133, 161, 173, **174-75**
deCarvalho, Emilio, 222, 250
DeMille, Cecil B., 111
Decell, John L., 14, 16, 22, 35, 51, 56, **62-63**

Denman, Harry, 127, 274
Dennis, Fred L., 186, 187
Denny, Collins, 13, 36, **41-42**
Deschner, John, 171
DeWitt, Jesse R., 222, 253, 271
DeWitt, Mrs. Jesse, 271
Diffendorfer, Ralph E., 272
Dixon, Ernest T., 222
Dobbs, Hoyt M., 14, 22, 51, 70, 96, **99,** 124
Dodge, Ralph E., 110, 130, 161, 166, 226, 244, 250, 277
DuBose, Horace M., 14, 36, **42-43**, 61
Dunn, Winfield, 225

Eddy, Sherwood, 75
Eisenhower, Dwight, 117
Elphick, Roberto V., 32, 70, 107, 143, **147-48**
Ensley, Gerald F., 91, 96, 106, 107, 110, 111, 114, 115, 116, 130, 133, 137, 138, 139, 140, 141, 161, 163, 164, 166, 169, 170, 171, 186, 194, 196, 197, 200, 220, 250, **256-58,** 271
Ensley, Mrs. Gerald, 256, 271
Epp, George, 115, 170, 187, 191, 202, **207-8**
Estes, Lud H., 274, 275

Fama, Onema, 222
Fannin, Paul, 118
Ferrell, Francis D., 35
Ferrer, Cornelio M., 192, 277
Finger, H. Ellis, Jr., 162, 165, 200, 225, 249, 269, 271
Finger, Mrs. Ellis, 271
Fischer, Louis, 75

299

Fleming, Arthur, 117
Flint, Charles W., 14, 16, 28, 31, 34, 51, 56, 90, 112, 161, 173, **175-77**
Flint, Mrs. Charles, 266
Flynn, John T., 77
Ford, Gerald, 226
Foreman, James, 194
Fout, H. H., 186, 189
Frank, Eugene M., 110, 130, 137, 139, 163, 164, 172, 186, 193, 194, 196, 249, 250, 269, 271, 286, 290
Frank, Mrs. Eugene, 271
Franklin, Marvin A., 71, 89, 107, 118, 130, 137, 162, 229, **231-32**, 286, 289
Frederick, Pauline, 224
Fowler, Charles, 84

Galloway, Paul, 132, 138, 141, 167, 186, 221, 231
Gant, D. R., 200
Garber, Paul N., 52, 65, 70, 79, 89, 109, 116, 130, 132, 133, 135, 140, 141, 161, 164, 166, 191, 229, **233-35**, 286, 290
Garrison, Edwin R., 132, 140, 161, 186, 191, 194, 195, 200, 226
Garth, Schuyler E., 52, 54, 55, 56, **63,** 68
Gattinoni, Carlos, 208
Gattinoni, Juan E., 13, 70, 107, 151, 161, 202, **208,** 275
Glasse, James D., 253
Godwin, Mills E., Jr., 252
Golden, Charles F., 132, 134, 137, 139, 164, 171, 186, 192, 199, 220, 225, 226, 249, 271, 287, 290
Golden, Mrs. Charles, 271
Goodrich, Robert E., Jr., 222, 224
Goodson, W. Kenneth, 162, 171, 196, 199, 220, 224, 249, 250, 251, 252, 271, 287, 290
Goodson, Mrs. Kenneth, 271
Gowdy, John, 24, 27, 28, 31, 32, 107, 143, **148,** 206
Granadosin, Paul L. A., 192, 252
Grant, Raymond A., 91, 95, 138, 141, 173, **177-78,** 204, 216
Grant, Mrs. Raymond, 271
Gregory, D. T., 189, 190
Gross, John O., 78, 86, 273
Guansing, Benjamin I., 163, 202, **208-9**
Guerra, Eleazar, 138
Gum, Walter C., 132, 141, 161, 191, 202, **209**

Hagen, Odd A., 91, 161, 186, 202, **210**
Hall, Harris Franklin, 263
Hammaker, Wilbur E., 15, 16, 22, 51, 71, 161, 202, **210-12**
Hammaker, Mrs. Wilbur, 266
Hammarskjold, Dag, 94, 137
Hardin, Paul, Jr., 120, 132, 137, 141, 149, 164, 186, 199, 200, 221, 287, 290
Harmon, Nolan B., 17, 110, 114, 115, 118, 130, 138, 140, 149, 161, 162, 163, 170, 186, 269

INDEX OF NAMES

Harrell, Costen J., 33, 52, 71, 73, 74, 89, 92, 93, 95, 107, 109, 141, 202, **212-13**
Harris, Lafayette, 132, 138, 140, 164, 168, 173, 178
Hartel, Armin, 193, 198
Hartman, Lewis O., 51, 70, 71, 77, 96, **99-101,** 269
Hartzell, Joseph C., 158, 242
Hatfield, Mark, 198
Hay, Samuel Ross, 16, 36, **44-45**
Hayes, Woody, 195
Heininger, Harold R., 185, 189, 191
Hendrix, Eugene R., 17, 179
Henley, James W., 132, 140, 167, 172, 186, 221, 271
Henley, Mrs. James, 271
Herrick, Paul M., 189, 198, 229, **235-36**
Hicks, Kenneth W., 250
High, Stanley, 76
Hodapp, Leroy D., 250
Hodge, Bachman G., 110, 130, 143, **149**
Holderman, Ralph, 223
Hole, J. Wesley, 275
Holloway, Fred G., 17, 132, 138, 139, 161, 163, 171, 191, 194, 231
Holt, Ivan Lee, 14, 15, 16, 22, 27, 71, 75, 89, 107, 124, 169, 173, **179-80,** 284, 289
Holt, J. B., 275
Holter, Don W., 222, 224, 249, 250
Horton, Paul R., 217
Houston, Ralph, 228
Howard, J. Gordon, 139, 170, 171, 185, 186, 189, 191, 195, 196, 221, 230, **236-37**
Hughes, Edwin H., 14, 16, 18, 19, 20, 22, 24, 28, 33, 50, 57, 70, 79, **81-82,** 282, 283, 289
Hughes, Harold, 200
Hughes, William A. C., 25, 26, 36, **45**
Humphrey, Hubert, 117
Humphrey, John P., 94
Hunt, Earl G., 162, 171, 196, 224, 226, 227, 249, 271
Hunt, Mrs. Earl, 271
Hunter, George, 253
Hurst, John Fletcher, 92
Huston, Robert W., 252

Jackson, Henry M., 166
John, XXIII, 139
Johnson, Eban S., 13, 20, 23
Johnson, Lyndon, 117, 171
Jones, E. Stanley, 144
Jones, Robert E., 15, 16, 22, 31, 40, 51, 132, 143, **150**
Joshi, Ram Dutt, 192, 256, **258**

Kaebnick, Herman W., 189, 191, 220, 221
Kai-shek, Chiang, 121
Kai-shek, Madame Chaing, 121
Kaplan, Joseph, 118
Kaung, Z. T., 25, 74, 78, 107, 119, **121**
Kearns, Francis E., 162, 165, 186, 226, 249, 250, 271
Kearns, Mrs. Francis, 271
Keeney, Frederick Thomas, 96, **101-2**
Kellaway, John, 221
Kelly, Edward W., 51, 70, 89, 90, 161, 173, **181**

Kennedy, Gerald M., 71, 79, 89, 107, 110, 111, 118, 130, 131, 133, 135, 136, 161, 169, 172, 186, 196, 204, 221, 271, 286, 289
Kennedy, Mrs. Gerald, 265, 271
Kennedy, John F., 117, 134, 136
Kern, John A., 102
Kern, Paul B., 14, 16, 19, 21, 22, 30, 35, 43, 54, 56, 70, 77, 88, 89, 90, 96, **102-4,** 124, 156, 239, 271, 282, 284, 289
Kern, Mrs. Paul, 267, 271
Kilgo, John C., 59
Kimball, John C., 197
King, Lorenzo, 25, 26, 51, 57, **63-64**
King, Martin Luther, 172
King, Willis, 93, 107, 114, 115, 130, 133, 192, 193, 242, 256, **258-59**
Knudson, Christine, 268

Lacy, Carlton, 25, 50, 51, 70, 74, 79, **82-83**
Lance, Joseph R., 192
Laney, James, 225
Ledden, Earl W., 52, 70, 77, 107, 110, 111, 132, 161, 224, 227, 231, 285, 289
Lee, Edwin F., 15, 22, 29, 30, 31, 51, 71, 79, **83**
Lee, Mrs. Edwin, 83
Lee, Robert E., 155
Leete, Frederick D., 70, 119, **122-23**
Leete, William, 122
Leonard, Adna W., 14, 17, 19, 20, 21, 23, 24, 28, 33, 36, **45-46,** 63, 108, 271

Leonard, Mrs. Adna, 271
Lewis, Thomas Hamilton, 17
Lieffer, Murray, 35
Lincoln, Abraham, 155
Lindstrom, David, 35
Little, Ernest Freemont, 263
Locke, Charles E., 13, 23, 47
Loder, Dwight E., 162, 169, 170, 186, 196, 199, 220, 224, 226, 227, 249, 287
Lord, John Wesley, 71, 79, 89, 95, 107, 108, 130, 133, 134, 137, 138, 139, 161, 163, 164, 169, 186, 196, 197, 198, 200, 221, 223, 226, 287, 290
Lord, Mrs. John Wesley, 267
Love, Edgar A., 77, 90, 91, 112, 138, 141, 161, 162, 168, 192, 193, 230, **237,** 271
Love, Mrs. Edgar, 271
Lovern, J. Chess, 250
Lowe, Titus, 15, 16, 17, 19, 21, 35, 51, 56, 71, 96, 108, 119, **123-24,** 284, 289
Lugg, Thomas B., 273
Lundy, Robert F., 163, 186, 244, 276

Magee, Dorothy, 134
Magee, J. Ralph, 15, 16, 19, 35, 51, 53, 56, 73, 74, 77, 78, 89, 90, 123, 147, 161, 202, **213-14,** 271, 284, 285, 289
Magee, Mrs. J. Ralph, 271
Mann, Martha, 269
Mardian, Sam, 118
Martin, Paul, 70, 89, 95, 99, 107, 112, 130, 133, 136, 137, 161, 163, 164, 165, 166, 169, 171, 191, 286, 290

INDEX OF NAMES

Martin, Mrs. Paul, 265
Martin, William C., 14, 15, 16, 17, 24, 31, 51, 52, 54, 71, 72, 79, 89, 93, 94, 110, 111, 113, 114, 116, 118, 130, 133, 137, 138, 139, 140, 161, 162, 171, 230, **238-39,** 246, 271, 285, 289
Martin, Mrs. William C., 265, 271
Mathews, James K., 132, 136, 137, 139, 141, 161, 163, 166, 167, 170, 171, 174, 186, 194, 196, 198, 220, 223, 224, 226, 229, 249, 253, 254, 268, 271, 290
Mathews, Mrs. James, 271
Mayfield, Robert, 274
McCallie, Mrs. Barbara Niswonger, 268
McCarthy, Joseph, 93
McConnell, Dorothy, 105, 166, 194
McConnell, Francis J., 14, 16, 19, 21, 22, 30, 37, 51, 70, 82, 91, 96, **104-6,** 257, 271, 282
McConnell, Mrs. Francis, 106, 267, 271
McDavid, Joel D., 222, 249
McDowell, William F., 17, 24
McElroy, Neil H., 117
McMahon, Brien, 77
McMurray, William F., 44, 49
McTyeire, Holland N., 41, 43
Mead, Charles L., 15, 16, 17, 22, 24, 36, **46,** 108, 271
Mead, Mrs. Charles, 271
Meeker, Frances, 268
Melle, T. H. Otto, 29, 52, 54, 55, 57, **64-65**

Mencken, H. L., 60
Mercado, LaVerne D., 250, 252
Middleton, W. Vernon, 132, 140, 141, 161, 164, 165, 166, 173, **182,** 271
Middleton, Mrs. W. Vernon, 271
Milhouse, Paul W., 170, 171, 189, 190, 199, 220, 249, 252, 253, 254, 271, 287, 288, 290
Milhouse, Mrs. Paul, 271
Miller, George, 27, 70, 107, 143, **151**
Mitchell, Charles B., 13, 36, **47,** 196
Mitchell, Eric A., 192
Moede, Gerald F., 252
Mondol, Shot K., 25, 31, 70, 130, 162, 166
Mondol, Mrs. Shot, 265
Moody, Ida M., **100-101**
Moore, Arthur J., 15, 16, 19, 20, 21, 22, 24, 28, 50, 51, 70, 79, 89, 90, 93, 102, 107, 112, 113, 115, 124, 130, 133, 156, 201, 230, **239-41,** 245, 271, 282, 285, 289
Moore, Mrs. Arthur, 267, 271
Moore, John M., 16, 18, 54, 59, 79, 83, **86,** 102, 157, 179, 282, 283
Moore, Leon, 275
Moore, Noah W., 132, 140, 169, 173, 186, 192, 221
Morelock, George L., 274
Mott, John R., 159
Mouzon, Edwin D., 17, 61, 102
Muelder, Walter, 193, 225

Mueller, Reuben R., 168, 170, 172, 185, 186, 189, 191, 194, 195, 196, 221, 286, 287, 290
Muzorewa, Abel T., 192, 253

Nagbe, Stephen T., 163, 186, 230, **241-42**
Nall, Otto T., 90, 132, 138, 139, 141, 163, 171, 186, 191, 227, 269
Newell, Frederick B., 90, 91, 96, 115, 130, 132, 141, 164, 166, 169, 170, 271
Newell, Mrs. Frederick, 265, 271
Nichols, Roy C., 192, 194, 196, 199, 220, 224, 249, 251, 256
Nicholson, Thomas, 13, 20, 36, **47-48**
Nicholson, Mrs. Thomas, 267
Niebuhr, Reinhold, 75
Nixon, Richard M., 117, 223
Northcott, H. Clifford, 71, 107, 130, 133, 256, **259-60**
Northcott, Mrs. Clifford, 267
Nuelson, John L., 15, 22, 24, 57, **65-67,** 183

O'Neil, C. William, 112
Oehler, Carolyn R., 255
Oldham, William F., 24, 151, 275
Otterbein, Philip, 185
Outler, Albert, 166, 186, 225, 255
Oxnam, G. Bromley, 16, 19, 21, 23, 28, 31, 34, 52, 55, 56, 70, 71, 73, 77, 89, 92, 93, 95, 107, 109, 110, 116, 117, 127, 130, 132, 136, 143, **151-53,** 193, 207, 268, 269, 271, 282, 285, 289, 290, 293
Oxnam, Mrs. G. Bromley, 266, 271

Palmer, Everett W., 132, 137, 161, 166, 171, 186, 198, 199, 202, 204, **214-15,** 271
Palmer, Mrs. Everett, 271
Parker, Edwin W., 69
Parker, Franklin N., 59
Parlin, Charles, 166, 194
Peele, William W., 14, 16, 20, 22, 23, 33, 34, 50, 51, 56, 71, 107, 119, **124-25,** 233, 283, 284, 289
Pegura, Frederico, J., 192, 276, 277
Pendergrass, Edward J., 120, 162, 220, 221
Penicela, Almeida, 250, 252
Pennington, Chester, 166
Peters, Elia, 222
Phillips, Glenn R., 71, 89, 92, 112, 130, 138, 140, 161, 162, 202, 204, **215-16,** 226, 271
Phillips, Mrs. Glenn, 271
Phillips, Randall, 226
Pickett, J. Waskom, 17, 22, 107, 108, 109, 174, 244
Pickett, Mrs. J. Waskom, 68, 265
Pickett, Jean, 268
Pope, W. Kenneth, 132, 161, 164, 170, 173, 220, 221, 271
Pope, Mrs. Kenneth, 271
Potts, J. Manning, 19, 53
Praetorius, E. W., 187, **188,** 223

INDEX OF NAMES

Pryor, Thomas M., 162, 220, 221, 228, 255, 271
Pryor, Mrs. Thomas, 271
Purcell, Clare, 14, 16, 22, 51, 56, 89, 107, 109, 143, **153-55,** 285, 289

Raines, Richard C., 17, 71, 89, 90, 110, 115, 130, 131, 133, 137, 161, 163, 164, 165, 168, 169, 170, 186, 191, 195, 196, 271, 286, 290
Raines, Mrs. Richard, 265, 271
Reed, Marshall R., 71, 77, 79, 89, 112, 120, 130, 133, 138, 139, 140, 161, 162, 163, 220, 230, **242-43,** 271, 286, 290
Reed, Mrs. Marshall, 265, 271
Reeves, Floyd W., 35
Rice, Merton, 126
Richards, David E., 200
Richardson, Ernest G., 14, 16, 18, 20, 22, 31, 32, 51, 57, **67-68,** 271, 283, 289
Richardson, Mrs. Ernest, 271
Richardson, Mrs. Faith, 268
Roberts, John W., 242
Robertson, Frank L., 222, 224
Robinson, J. W., 20, 27, 57, **68-69**
Rockey, Clement D., 25, 109, 110, 162, 230, **243-44**
Rockey, Mrs. Clement, 265
Roosevelt, Franklin D., 30, 31, 54
Rosenberger, S. W., 16

Sabanes, Julio M., 91, 143, **155**

Samuel, John Victor, 110, 192, 276, 277
Sanders, Carl J., 222
Schaefer, Franz W., 163
Schaller, Lyle, 194
Schisler, John Q., 272
Scott, I. B., 242
Selecman, Charles C., 14, 15, 16, 19, 29, 51, 54, 70, 71, 90, 119, **125-27,** 246, 284, 289
Sexsmith, E. A., 16
Shaeffer, Franz, 194
Shamblin, J. Kenneth, 250
Shannon, Paul E. V., 189, 190
Shaw, Alexander P., 15, 22, 51, 70, 89, 90, 93, 167, 173, **182-83**
Shaw, Alfred J., 163
Short, Roy H., 17, 71, 89, 95, 107, 109, 110, 118, 130, 132, 134, 135, 137, 138, 139, 141, 161, 163, 164, 165, 166, 167, 168, 169, 170, 172, 185, 191, 193, 194, 195, 196, 197, 198, 201, 207, 218, 220, 221, 223, 228, 235, 242, 255, 268, 271, 290
Short, Mrs. Roy, 265, 271
Showers, J. B., 186, 187
Shuler, Bob, 76
Shungu, John Wesley, 162, 186, 205, 276
Sigg, Ferdinand, 91, 166, 173, **183-84**
Simpson, Matthew, 57
Singh, Mangal, 110, 130, 161, 192
Slater, O. Eugene, 132, 141, 163, 167, 169, 171, 196,

Slater, O. Eugene (cont.)
199, 200, 220, 222, 249,
250, 271, 286, 290
Slater, Mrs. Eugene, 271
Smith, A. Frank, 15, 16, 22,
26, 28, 29, 30, 51, 71, 75, 76,
89, 107, 110, 112, 124, 130,
133, 143, **156-57,** 282, 283,
289
Smith, Mrs. A. Frank, 267
Smith, Al, 60
Smith, Eugene, 166
Smith, H. Lester, 15, 16, 18,
19, 22, 50, 51, 52, 53, 71, 79,
86-87, 108, 271, 284, 289,
290
Smith, Mrs. Lester, 271
Smith, Horace G., 263
Smith, John Owen, 132, 141,
186, 201, 221, 256, **260-61,**
271
Smith, Mrs. John, 271
Smith, M. C., 35
Smith, Roy L., 273
Smith, W. Angie, 27, 52, 55,
70, 89, 90, 107, 112, 113,
114, 115, 130, 164, 169,
186, 191, 220, 230, 238,
245-47, 285, 289
Smith, Mrs. Angie, 265
Sommer, C. Ernst, 106, 207,
250
Sommer, J. W. Ernst, 52, 96,
106
Sorokin, Pitirim, 75
Sparks, W. Maynard, 189,
191, 199, 221
Spellmann, Norman W., 157
Spring, John M., 15, 22, 26,
51, 143, **158-59,** 242
Stamm, John S., 187, **188**

Stauffacher, C. H., 187, **188**
Stewart, George R., 149
Sticher, Hermann L., 250,
251
Stockwell, B. Foster, 132, 143,
159
Stokes, Mack B., 222, 224
Stoody, Ralph, 268
Stone, Fred, 273
Stowe, W. McFerrin, 162, 169,
171, 186, 196, 220, 249,
252, 253
Straughn, James H., 14, 15,
16, 21, 22, 24, 51, 70, 220,
230, **247-48,** 231
Stuart, R. Marvin, 162, 164,
204, 254, 255, 288
Subhan, John A., 52, 89, 107,
162, 167, 256, **261-62**
Sunderam, Gabriel, 110, 192

Taft, Charles P., 112
Taylor, William, 158, 161,
163, 164, 165, 167, 242, 249
Taylor, Prince A., 110, 130,
132, 192, 197, 242, 249,
250, 269, 286, 290
Thirkield, Wilbur F., 24
Thoburn, James M., 158
Thomas, George, 256
Thomas, James S., 162, 186,
192, 196, 200, 224, 228,
249, 251, 252, 271
Thomas, Mrs. James, 271
Thomas, Norman, 75
Tigert, John J., 68
Tillman, Mrs. J. Fount, 166,
274
Tippett, Donald H., 71, 89,
110, 114, 115, 130, 132,
139, 141, 161, 163, 167,

INDEX OF NAMES

170, 172, 173, 185, 186, 191, 204, 216, 254, 271, 286, 290
Tippett, Mrs. Donald, 265, 271
Truman, Harry S., 54
Tuell, Jack M., 222, 229, 249, 271
Tuell, Mrs. Jack, 271
Tullis, Edward L., 222, 229
Twining, Nathan, 117

Valencia, José A., 72, 130, 137, 138, 192, 277
Van Dyke, Henry, 57
Visser't Hooft, W. A., 136
Voight, Edwin E., 89, 91, 140, 162, 256, **262-64**

Wade, Raymond J., 15, 24, 50, 51, 55, 71, 202, **216-18,** 271
Wade, Mrs. Raymond, 266, 267, 271
Wakadilo, N. K., 250
Waldorf, Ernest L., 14, 16, 21, 22, 26, 28, 36, **48-49**
Waldorf, Lynn, 49
Walton, Aubrey G., 27, 132, 140, 163, 221, 256, **264**
Ward, Ralph A., 22, 29, 90, 115, 119, **128**
Ward, W. Ralph, 132, 141, 161, 170, 171, 172, 186, 228, 249, 252, 271, 287, 290
Ward, Mrs. W. Ralph, 271
Ward, William Norman, 17, 76, 220, 226, 227, 228
Warman, John B., 222, 231
Warner, Bennie, 222, 252
Warner, Ira D., 186, 188, 250, 252

Warren, Earl, 117
Washburn, Paul, 185, 189, 190, 191, 196, 197, 220, 249, 254
Washington, George, 117
Watkins, William T., 14, 16, 22, 30, 32, 107, 133, 143, **159-60,** 232
Watson, Richard L., 61
Watts, Bascom, 44, 92, 119, **128-29,** 271
Watts, Mrs. Bascom, 271
Watts, Henry B., 91
Weatherhead, Leslie, 144
Webb, Lance, 162, 186, 220, 228, 251
Webb, Pauline, 221
Weidler, V. O., 186, **188**
Welch, Herbert, 16, 51, 70, 77, 88, 91, 92, 107, 110, 115, 117, 124, 133, 169, 193, 202, **218-19,** 282
Warner, Hazen G., 71, 90, 107, 112, 130, 132, 161, 220
Werner, Mrs. Hazen, 271
Wertz, D. Frederick, 192, 194, 199, 220, 271
Wertz, Mrs. Frederick, 271
Wesley, Arthur E., 52, 54, 275
Wesley, Charles, 136, 176
Wesley, John, 93, 102
West, Arthur, 268, 269
Wheatley, Melvin E., Jr., 204, 222, 254, 271
Wheatley, Mrs. Melvin, 271
White, C. Dale, 250, 253
White, Charles, 275
Wicke, Lloyd C., 71, 89, 107, 113, 130, 132, 137, 161, 163, 164, 165, 167, 168, 170, 172, 186, 195, 198,

200, 220, 221, 224, 286, 290
Wicke, Mrs. Lloyd C., 265
Williams, Jane, 268
Woolridge, Norman, 221
Wunderlich, Friedrich, 91, 130, 137, 161, 170, 186, 192

Yeakel, Joseph H., 222, 249

Zottele, Pedro R., 148, 192, 277
Zunguze, Escrivao A., 162, 205, 252, 277

I

General Index

Advance for Christ and His Church, 56, 73, 75, 292
Advance Program, 213
Advance Special, 73, 95
African Methodist Episcopal Church, 254, 296
African Methodist Episcopal Church, Zion, 254, 296
African Task Force, 255
Aldersgate celebration (1938), 126
Anti-Saloon League, 60, 211

Bishops' Call for Peace and the Self-Development of Peoples, 223, 226, 295
Bishops' Committee on Race, 164, 166, 294
Bishops' Crusade on the Ministry, 138, 140, 294
bishops' hymn, 17, 108, 118-19
bishops' seal, 32-33, 171, 223
Black College Fund, 116
"Black Manifesto," 194-95, 296

Board of Church Extension, 145
Board of Church Extension, South, 145
Board of Discipleship, 253
Board of Education, 57, 92, 95, 103, 238, 271, 272
Board of Evangelism, 29, 127, 134, 147, 274
Board of Foreign Missions, 83
Board of Global Ministries, 231, 276
Board of Higher Education, 103
Board of Lay Activities, 274
Board of Missions, 25, 45, 95, 128, 159, 182, 195, 202, 237, 240, 271, 272
Board of Publications, 134
Board of Social Concerns, 78
Board of Temperance, 211, 238
Book Concern (Sweden), 144
Book of Hymns, 213

Centenary Campaign, 67

Centenary Movement, 150, 217
Central Christian Advocate, 97, 146, 182
Chinese Methodism, 75-76, 90, 121, 128
Circuit Riders, 76
Christian Basis for a World Order Conference, 32
Christian Methodist Episcopal Church, 240, 254, 296
Christian Advocate, 273
Colored Methodist Episcopal Church, 42
Commission on Camp Activities, 28, 291
Commission on Central Conferences, 53, 292
Commission on Chaplains, 31, 46, 56, 83, 291
Commission on Christian Vocations, 54, 292
Commission on Church Union (EUB), 141, 170
Commission on Interdenominational Relations and Church Union, 150
Commission on the Relation of Races in The Methodist Church, 52, 292
Commission on Social Action and Industrial Relations, 78
Commission on the Status and Role of Women, 225, 255
Commission on the Study of the Episcopacy and District Superintendency, 225, 249
Commission on Worship, 263
Committee on Administration, 278
Committee on Christian Faith and War in a Nuclear Age, 138, 294
Committee on Ecumenical Consultation, 114
Committee on Episcopacy (Church, South), 38, 60
Committee on Jurisdictional System, 113
Committee on Law and Administration, 21, 30, 92
Committee on Legislation, 137, 294
Committee on a Methodist Bookshelf, 79, 292
Committee on a Methodist Foundation, 77, 292
Committee on the Ministry (1975), 227
Committee on Overseas Relief, 28, 124, 218, 291
Committee on Pastoral Concerns, 73, 74, 229
Committee for the Preservation of Methodism, 76
Committee on Recruitment for the Ministry, 54
Committee on Reference, 21, 92
Committee on Response to Minorities, 199
Committee on Structure and Functioning of the Council, 197, 200
Committee on the Structure of Methodism Overseas, 165, 167, 294
Committee on the Study of the Episcopacy, 140
Committee on the Study of the Ministry, 167

GENERAL INDEX

Committee on Veterans' Affairs, 55
Committee on War Emergency and Overseas Relief, 28, 30
Communism, 73, 75, 76, 137
Confession of Faith (EUB), 190
Consultation on Church Union, 170, 252, 294, 296
Convocation on Urban Life, 92
Corrupt Practices Act, 60
Council on Finance and Administration, 229
Council on World Service, 33, 74, 171
Council on World Service and Finance, 238, 273
Crusade for Christ and His Church, 53, 56, 181, 214, 292
Crusade for Evangelism, 35
Crusade for a New World Order, 34, 53, 292
Crusade Scholarship Program, 53

Day of Compassion, 29, 34
death-of-God theology, 219
Declaration of Union, 13
Department of Research, 55
Discipline, 11, 68, 71, 95, 125, 131, 143, 158, 167, 172, 188, 213
divorce in ministerial families, 139, 253, 294, 296
"dry cause," 60
Dunbarton oaks proposals, 53

Emphasis upon Development of the Local Church, 109, 111, 112, 293
Emphasis upon Higher Education, 109, 111, 293
Encyclopedia of World Methodism, 227
Episcopal Address, 50, 56, 70, 73, 75, 77, 78, 88, 103, 107, 109, 118, 130, 161, 168, 169, 172, 186, 195, 200, 220, 228, 249, 254
Epworth League Board, 103
Epworth Rectory, 116, 293
Evangelical Church, 207
Evangelical United Brethren Church, 11, 131, 139, 141, 163, 164, 166-71, 185-93, 207, 223, 235, 236

Federal Council of Churches, 34, 188
Forward Movement, 19, 291
Fund for Reconciliation, 193, 295

General Board of Education, 47
General Board of Evangelism, 245
General Commission on Courses of Study, 58
Grain Belt Consultation, 228, 251, 296

History of Methodism (McTyeire), 43, 293
History of Methodism in Europe (Garber), 235
History of the Methodist Episcopal Church, South, (DuBose), 43

House Committee on Un-American Activities, 73, 92, 153
Hymnal, The (1964), 263-64

Indian Mission, 246
Indian Witness, 68
International Missionary Council, 204

Judicial Council, 25-26, 95, 115, 167, 203, 205, 228, 229, 230, 277

Korean Creed, 218

Manual of the Discipline (McTyeire), 41
Message Committee, 110, 133, 293
Methodist Centenary, 101
Methodist Church, The, 11, 13, 21, 24, 27, 30, 41, 46, 51, 55, 94, 99, 131, 134, 139, 140, 143, 153, 163, 164, 185, 186, 189, 193, 200, 213, 219, 242, 248, 279
Methodist Episcopal Church, The, 11, 13, 16, 17, 18, 22, 23, 26, 27, 37, 40, 45, 46, 47, 48, 49, 51, 57, 61, 65, 67, 81, 83, 86, 101, 104, 105, 122, 123, 146, 151, 158, 159, 175, 182, 203, 212, 213, 216, 217, 218, 278, 280
Methodist Episcopal Church, South, The, 11, 13, 16, 17, 18, 19, 23, 26, 27, 36, 37, 38, 39, 41, 42, 43, 44, 49, 51, 59, 61, 62, 83, 84, 97, 98, 99, 102, 124, 125, 134, 144, 153, 156, 159, 160, 179, 239, 240, 246, 280
Methodist Federation for Social Action, 76-77, 100, 104, 218
Methodist Information, 268-69
Methodist Protestant Church, The, 11, 13, 14, 16, 17, 18, 19, 26, 61, 70, 71, 247, 248
Methodist Publishing House, The, 32, 134, 194, 273
Methodist Publishing House (Zurich), 66, 183-84
Million Unit Fellowship, 101
Missionary Society (Evangelical Church), 207

National Council of Churches, 153, 188, 195
Native American Caucus, 199, 227, 253
Nazi government, 54, 55, 64-65, 66-67

Oxford Conference (1937), 64

Pikeville, Ky., Methodist Hospital dispute, 223-24
Plan of Union, 14, 150
Poverty Program, 171

race relations, 78, 94, 136, 138, 141, 150, 164, 194-95, 232
Race Relations Day (1958), 116, 293

School of International Service, 92, 95
"Six Pillars of Peace," 34

GENERAL INDEX

Social Creed, 116, 224
Southwestern Christian Advocate, 150
Supreme Court decision (1954), 108, 116, 293

Temperance Movement, 48, 60, 211-12
Together, 109

Union with Evangelical United Brethren, 163, 164, 166-71, 185-87, 247
United Brethren Church, 186-90
United Brethren Publishing House, 187
United Methodist Church, The, 27, 138, 166, 185-86, 190, 193, 199, 207, 219
United Nations, 95, 198, 293
Uniting Conference (1939), 13, 14, 15-17, 18, 20, 23, 24, 40, 67, 72, 80, 81, 86, 160, 211
Uniting Conference (1968), 185-86, 191-92, 195

Vatican, relationship with, 74

Vatican II, 55, 139, 294
Vietnam War, 170, 296
Vocational Guidance Conferences, 54

Wesley Foundation Movement, 203
Women's Foreign Missionary Society, 48, 106
Women's Society of Christian Service, 141
World Council of Churches, 73, 95, 111, 136, 137, 153, 258, 293
World Outlook, 106
World War I, 57, 64-65, 66-67, 237
World War II, 83, 106, 128, 144
World Methodist Council, 116, 180, 210, 235, 247, 252, 258, 296
Worldwide Evangelistic emphasis, 258

Youth emphasis, 56, 89, 108, 292

Zion's Herald, 54, 100

Autographs

Autographs

Autographs

Autographs

Autographs

Autographs

Autographs